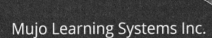

Mujo Learning Systems Inc.

SOCIAL MEDIA MARKETING STRATEGIES

COURSE THREE

Teacher's Manual

Mujo Learning Systems Inc.
804 Pacific Street, 3rd Floor, Vancouver, British Columbia V6Z 1C2
Telephone/Fax: 1-888-536-6856
Copyright, 2017, by Mujo Learning Systems Inc.

ISBN-13: 978-1523399086

ISBN-10: 1523399082

TM-SMMS-02060017

SOCIAL MEDIA MARKETING STRATEGIES

Course Three

By Shawn Moore and Adam Wilkins

Edited by Rebecca Saloustros

MUJO
LEAD · EDUCATE · INSPIRE

FOREWORD

Why did I commission and co-author this series of books?

When I started my company in 1997, it was a year before Google even came on to the scene. We were one of four companies hired to build, market, and sell online advertising for the Yellow Pages.

I learned about 'Digital Darwinism' fast in that you have to adapt quickly or die in the field of Internet marketing. This means that you have to stay up to date and current with the ever-changing ways of using digital marketing to help build a business and remain on top.

Owning and running a digital marketing agency for more than two decades has made me realize that my mission in life is to help educate others about the power of digital marketing. What better way to do that than to share my Agency's hands-on knowledge in this series of books? Students and businesses around the globe can now experience the Mujo difference.

Understanding digital marketing technology, and creating a practical and easy-to-understand process, and implementing that process, is what my Agency does for our clients every day; it's why we get hired.

My goal is simply to provide you, the reader, with a real-world understanding of digital marketing and help you gain employment in your chosen field. Whether your vision is to lead or be part of a team, start your own company or even your own agency, I am confident this series of books will provide you with the intellectual capital to help you realize your dreams.

Having worked directly with over 1600 educators, manufacturers, retailers, hoteliers, and service providers during my tenure, I feel our publications will give you an edge in your search across virtually any industry sector that you choose to pursue.

The learning outcomes in these books are based on my Agency's proven experience and my team's daily real-life interactions with clients. These texts will provide you with more than just theoretical concepts, often the focus in educational publications. You will discover actual, hands-on practical skills and techniques that are essential in the running of our Agency today. 'Keeping it real' is a saying that I firmly believe in. Talk is cheap, doing means everything. So roll your sleeves up and let's get busy doing in this exciting domain of digital marketing!

To your digital marketing success,

Shawn Moore, co-author
https://ca.linkedin.com/in/thinkprofits

This is an amazing time to be entering a career in marketing. Never before have marketers been able to communicate with their audience with such precision. When I started my career in technology 30 years ago, we reached our customers through radio, TV, conferences, and brochures. However, we were never quite sure who received our message. Over time, I have witnessed marketing tools evolve to where each customer can now expect marketers to deliver a message unique to their needs and we in turn know much more about our audience. While the tools have evolved, understanding how to weave them together into a coherent marketing strategy is more confusing than ever. Our aim in these books is to provide students with a good grasp of all the elements they need to be successful. We also continue to monitor trends and best practices to keep our resources current.

These books would not have been possible without the expertise and assistance of the team at Think Profits.com Inc. Our collective hope is that our experience and observations benefit you wherever you are on your digital marketing journey.

Regards,

Adam Wilkins, co-author

COURSE DESCRIPTION

Social Media Marketing Strategies

Course Three: Social Media Marketing Strategies

By the end of this course students will:

1. Become familiar with how various social media channels are utilized for personal and business purposes

2. Be able to analyze social media marketing case studies

3. Be able to gather the required information to initiate and maintain a social media campaign

4. Discover how social media analytics function and enable marketers to make informed, data-driven decisions

COURSE CONTENT

Chapter One:
Social Media **20**
Governing Strategy

The Social Media Campaign Goals 22
The Target Consumer's Persona. 23
The Competitors' Social Media Strategies 27
The Selection of Social Media Channels 30
Utilizing Social Media Channels 33

Chapter Two:
Facebook **40**
Marketing Strategies

Facebook: History 41
Facebook: Personal. 42
Facebook: Business 47
Facebook: Advertising 55
Facebook: Running a Targeted Campaign 61
Facebook: Analytics 64

Chapter Three:
Twitter **74**
Marketing Strategies

Twitter: History 75
Twitter: Personal. 76
Twitter: Business. 82
Twitter: Advertising 86
Twitter: Running a Targeted Campaign 90
Twitter: Analytics 99

Chapter Four:
Instagram **106**
Marketing Strategies

Instagram: History 107
Instagram: Personal 108
Instagram: Business 113
Instagram: Advertising 120
Instagram: Running a Targeted Campaign. 123
Instagram: Analytics 128

Chapter Five:
LinkedIn **140**
Marketing Strategies

LinkedIn: History. 141
LinkedIn: Personal 142
LinkedIn: Business 149
LinkedIn: Advertising 154
LinkedIn: Running a Targeted Campaign 156
LinkedIn: Analytics 160

Chapter Six:
YouTube **169**
Marketing Strategies

YouTube: History. 170
YouTube: Personal 171
YouTube: Business 174
YouTube: Advertising 177
YouTube: Running a Targeted Campaign 181
YouTube: Analytics 184

Chapter Seven:
Yelp **187**
Marketing Strategies

Yelp: History. 188
Yelp: Personal 189
Yelp: Business 193
Yelp: Advertising 198
Yelp: Running a Targeted Campaign 201
Yelp: Analytics 205

Chapter Eight:
Pinterest **210**
Marketing Strategies

Pinterest: History 212
Pinterest: Personal 213
Pinterest: Business 217
Pinterest: Advertising. 222
Pinterest: Running a Targeted Campaign. 224
Pinterest: Analytics 227

Postscript **232**

Social Media Marketing Analysis 234
Social Media Fatigue and Fickleness 236

Note: Students will be expected to utilize online and multimedia resources in addition to this text.

ASSESSMENT

Participation and Attendance	10%
Midterm Exam	25%
Social Media Strategy Project	35%
Assignments	30%

Participation and Attendance:

You are expected to attend class regularly. Be prepared to participate in group and pair activities. Also, make contributions to class discussion. Your instructor will go over your institution's specific attendance policy with you.

Midterm Exam:

The midterm exam will cover all the material in Chapters One through Four. Questions will be multiple choice, fill in the blanks, and short answer.

Legend

 **Activity**    **Discussion**    **Case Study**

Note for Teachers

Online articles, videos, and images have been incorporated into this text to enhance the learning experience. Every effort will be made to update the course material regularly. However, links can change or become inactive at any time. Therefore, it is important that teachers preview all online material before showing it to students and/or giving them a web link to it. In some cases, it may be necessary for teachers to find replacements for links in the text and to make modifications to exercises. A simple search for the topic keyword should yield current results.

Social Media Strategy Project Description

PART ONE: INTERVIEW A SMALL BUSINESS OWNER

1. Find a small business that maintains an active social media presence.

2. Write a one- to two-paragraph description of what the business does/sells, where it's located, who its clientele is, how long it has been in operation, etc.

3. Contact the business owner and ask if you can conduct a five- to ten-minute video interview with him or her about the social media marketing the company engages in. Give the owner your assurance that the video interview will only be utilized for in-class purposes.

Create a permission form for students to give the business owner. Both parties should sign the document and each person should keep a digital and hard copy for their records.

4. Interview the small business owner and find out:
   a. Which social media platform(s) he or she uses
   b. Which platform(s) he or she uses most often
   c. What social media strategies he or she has in place
   d. What kind of success he or she has had with those social media strategies
   e. Which social media platform(s) he or she does not use and why, OR Which social media platform(s)he or she has, but underutilizes and why

*Feel free to ask any follow-up questions that you feel are necessary during the course of the interview.

PART TWO: DEVELOP A SOCIAL MEDIA STRATEGY

1. Choose **one** of the social media channels that the small business owner does **not** utilize or underutilizes.

2. Develop a social media campaign for the business based around that social media channel. Ensure that that social media channel makes sense for the type of business you choose (e.g. Pinterest would be a great choice for a design company, but not a great one for a plumbing business).

3. Do **not** launch the campaign. Instead, create a description of it and some examples of what it might look like.

PART THREE: PRESENT YOUR CAMPAIGN

1. Rather than present your campaign to the class, you are going to present it to the small business owner you interviewed. Pitch it as if you were a marketer for the company, and your objective was to convince the owner that the campaign would be successful and generate increased brand awareness, and perhaps additional business.

2. Ask the small business owner to provide you with either video recorded feedback on your campaign or written feedback.

Upon completion of this project, you will be giving your instructor:
- The one- to two-paragraph description of the small business
- A copy of the video interview with an accompanying transcript
- A description and examples of your social media campaign
- Either video-recorded or written feedback about the campaign from the small business owner

Show students the sample social media campaign (Appendix), including the sample video interview: "Farzad's Barber Shop" (07:32) (Available from Mujo Learning Systems).

ASSIGNMENTS:

You will be asked to hand in a series of assignments throughout this course. Your instructor will select some of these assignments and assign specific grades to them. He or she will provide you with more details as you progress through the text.

Hourly Running Orders

Chapter One, Social Media Governing Strategy

Hours	Timing Estimate	Tasks
Hour One	15 minutes	Orientation, Course Objectives, Assessment, The Elements of Digital Marketing, Preface, Glossary* *Explain to students that words in green are in the glossary
	10 minutes	Introduction The Social Media Campaign Goals • Discussion Questions
	15 minutes	The S.M.A.R.T. Goals Formula The Target Consumer's Persona
	20 minutes	Activity: Creating Buyer Personas (Part One)* *Assign Remaining work on Part One and all of Part Two
Hour Two	30 minutes	Presentations: Creating Buyer Personas
	30 minutes	How to Research Buyer Personas Activity: Sizing Up the Competition* *Ask students to complete the remainder of activity at home
Hour Three	30 minutes	How's the Profile? Activity: Images* Activity: Content* *Individual online research, followed by whole-class discussion *Extension Activity available
	15 minutes	Activity: Social Media Alphabetics The Selection of Social Media Channels
	15 minutes	Activity: Reading "How to Choose the Best Social Media Site for Your Business"* *Ask students to complete the remainder of activity at home
Hour Four	10 minutes	The Best Practices for Utilizing Social Media Channels
	30 minutes	Activity: Creating Top Ten Lists
	20 minutes	Case Study: TransLink* *Ask students to complete the remainder of activity at home
	Optional	Chapter Review

Chapter Two, Facebook Marketing Strategies

Hours	Timing Estimate	Tasks
Hour One	10 minutes	Facebook: History* *All reading of history infographics should be followed by a whole-class discussion regarding recent developments within each social network (Students can search online for recent news to fuel such discussion if necessary).
	10 minutes	Facebook: Personal • Discussion Questions
	10 minutes	Developing Your Personal Brand on Facebook Activity: Taking Stock of Your 'Digital Dirt'* *Assign this activity for homework
	10 minutes	Facebook: Business • Introduction • Facebook for Business is Different *Extension Activity/Video available
	20 minutes	Activity: What is Facebook Insights?
Hour Two	10 minutes	Discussion Questions
	20 minutes	Activity: Making a Small Business Page Better
	20 minutes	Facebook: Advertising • Three Kinds of Facebook Advertising *Extension Activity/Article available
	10 minutes	Facebook Fails and Wins Case Study: Smucker's Gets in a Jam
Hour Three	15 minutes	Case Study: Smucker's Gets in a Jam (Discussion Question)
	10 minutes	Case Study: C&A Rethinks Buying Off the Rack
	15 minutes	Facebook: Running a Targeted Campaign • Facebook and the Big Picture • Tips for Writing a Facebook Ad
	20 minutes	Activity: Finding a Fabulous Facebook Ad The Budgetary Pie Activity: Budgeting for a Facebook Campaign* *Can be completed for homework
Hour Four	10 minutes	Facebook: Analytics • Introduction • Analytics Tools
	20 minutes	Activity: Facebook Analytics
	30 minutes	Activity: Google Analytics Timing is Everything *Two Extension Activities available
	Optional	Chapter Review

Chapter Three, Twitter Marketing Strategies

Hours	Timing Estimate	Tasks
Hour One	10 minutes	Twitter: History* *See history infographics note in Chapter Two Running Order
	15 minutes	Twitter: Personal • Twitter Personal Profile Page Notes • Twitter Changes The Way It Counts Characters • Discussion Questions
	25 minutes	How Consumers Interact With Brands on Twitter Activity: Responding to Consumer Complaints on Twitter *Extension Activity available
	10 minutes	Twitter: Business • The Business of Twitter • More About Hashtags
Hour Two	10 minutes	Activity: Responding to Consumer Complaints on Twitter (Presentations)
	30 minutes	The Essence of an Effective Tweet Activity: Creating a Great Tweet *Extension Activity available
	10 minutes	Twitter: Advertising • Twitter Wins and Fails: Celebrity Edition
	10 minutes	Activity: Finding Twitter Wins and Fails* *Explain examples in class, and assign the activity for homework. This activity can be done in-class, if time permits.
Hour Three	20 minutes	Twitter: Running a Targeted Campaign • Getting Started • Twitter Cards *Extension Activity/Article available
	40 minutes	Activity: Making a Twitter Ads Campaign
Hour Four	10 minutes	Twitter: Analytics • Introduction • Home • Tweets (Tweet Activity) • Audiences
	30 minutes	Activity: Check the Pulse of Your Twitter Account Analytics for Twitter Cards
	20 minutes	Social Media Strategy Project (Explanation, Example, and Preparation Time)
	Optional	Chapter Review

Chapter Four, Instagram Marketing Strategies

Hours	Timing Estimate	Tasks
Hour One	10 minutes	Instagram: History* *See history infographics note in Chapter Two Running Order
	15 minutes	Instagram: Personal • Navigating Instagram • Instagram Personal Profile Page Notes (Mobile View)
	35 minutes	Activity: Points of Comparison *Extension Activity/Article available
Hour Two	10 minutes	Instagram: Business • Before Paid Ads • The Nature of Instagram • Instagram Photos
	15 minutes	Activity: Instagram Video
	20 minutes	Instagram: Advertising • Instagram Fails and Wins • Case Study: Not Much McLovin' on Instagram
	10 minutes	Case Study: Starbucks' White Cup Challenge
	5 minutes	Activity: Get the Picture?* Loop Giveaway* *Assign for homework
Hour Three	20 minutes	Activity: Get the Picture (whole-class discussion) Loop Giveaway (whole-class discussion)
	15 minutes	Instagram: Running a Targeted Campaign • Campaign Strategy for Branded Posts
	5 minutes	Effective Use of Hashtags on Instagram Activity: Using Hashtags on Instagram* *Assign for homework
	20 minutes	Activity: The Evolution of and Campaign Strategy for Paid Ads • The Carousel Ad • Call-To-Action Buttons
Hour Four	20 minutes	Instagram: Analytics • Digital Marketers Get the Inside Track on Their Ad Performance • Account Insights • Ad Insights
	30 minutes	Activity: Underperfoming Instagram Ads Ad Staging Activity: Improving an Instagram Ad
	10 minutes	Time Management* *Ask students to complete the remainder of activity at home *Extension Activity/Article available
	Optional	Chapter Review

Chapter Five, LinkedIn Marketing Strategies

Hours	Timing Estimate	Tasks
Hour One	30 – 45 minutes	Midterm Exam
	10 minutes	LinkedIn: History* *See history infographics note in Chapter Two Running Order
	10 minutes	LinkedIn: Personal • Discussion Questions
Hour Two	10 minutes	LinkedIn Personal Profile Page Notes
	20 minutes	Activity: Improving the Profile
	10 minutes	LinkedIn: Business • Setting Up a LinkedIn Company Page *Extension Activity available
	20 minutes	Updates and Posts on a Brand's Company Page Activity: Expanding on Updates* *To be continued next class
Hour Three	15 minutes	Activity: Expanding on Updates
	25 minutes	Follow-up
	20 minutes	LinkedIn: Advertising • Case Study: Cushy Jobs, Courtesy of Fruit of the Loom
Hour Four	30 minutes	LinkedIn: Running a Targeted Campaign • Goals Before Strategy Activity: Lead Generation
	30 minutes	Activity: A Range of LinkedIn Ads
*Additional Time Needed Due to Midterm	45 minutes	LinkedIn: Analytics • Company Page Analytics • Case Study: ABC Digital Agency Analytics *Extension Activity/Articles available
	Optional	Chapter Review

Chapter Six, YouTube Marketing Strategies

Hours	Timing Estimate	Tasks
Hour One	10 minutes	YouTube: History* *See history infographics note in Chapter Two Running Order
	10 minutes	YouTube: Personal • Discussion Questions • Introduction
	10 minutes	Video Tutorial: YouTube for Viewers and Uploaders
	30 minutes	Activity: Viral Videos *Extension Activity available
Hour Two	40 minutes	YouTube: Business • Video Tutorial: The Components of a Business' YouTube Channel Activity: Evaluating a Business' YouTube Channel
	20 minutes	Optimizing a YouTube Channel Activity: Tagging
Hour Three	20 minutes	YouTube: Advertising • YouTube Fails and Wins • Case Study: Hyundai's Pipe Job
	20 minutes	Case Study: Metro Trains
	20 minutes	YouTube: Running a Targeted Campaign • Discussion Questions • Different Kinds of YouTube Ads* *Ask students to complete the remainder of activity at home
Hour Four	15 minutes	YouTube Cards Types of Cards Activity: Selecting YouTube Cards* *Ask students to complete the remainder of activity at home
	45 minutes	YouTube: Analytics • Activity: YouTube Analytics and Cards Analytics
	Optional	Chapter Review

Chapter Seven, Yelp Marketing Strategies

Hours	Timing Estimate	Tasks
Hour One	10 minutes	Yelp: History* *See history infographics note in Chapter Two Running Order
	15 minutes	Yelp: Personal • Discussion Questions
	15 minutes	Personal Profile Page Notes
	20 minutes	Yelp: Business • Introduction • Business Page Layout and Components
Hour Two	30 minutes	Activity: Critique a Business Page
	30 minutes	Yelp: Advertising • Discussion Questions *Extension Activity/Video available Case Study: Botto Bistro: A Big Pizza Pie in Yelp's Eye
Hour Three	30 minutes	Yelp: Running a Targeted Campaign • Advertising on Yelp • Activity: Linking Ads with Goals
	30 minutes	Marketing on Yelp Without Paid Ads Activity: A Five-Star Contest Idea
Hour Four	30 minutes	Yelp: Analytics • Analytics for the Yelp Business Page • Yelp Knowledge • Activity: An Analytics Utopia
	30 minutes	Social Media Strategy Project Consultations
	Optional	Chapter Review

Chapter Eight, Pinterest Marketing Strategies

Hours	Timing Estimate	Tasks
Hour One	10 minutes	Pinterest: History* *See history infographics note in Chapter Two Running Order
	15 minutes	Pinterest: Personal • Discussion Questions
	15 minutes	Personal Profile Page Notes :How Consumers Interact With Brands on Pinterest
	20 minutes	Pinterest: Business • Introduction • Pinterest Busines Profile • Promoted Pins
Hour Two	20 minutes	Activity: Buyable Pins and Rich Pins *Extension Activity/Article available
	40 minutes	Pinterest: Advertising • Case Study: Jetsetter's Cure for Wanderlust
Hour Three	30 minutes	Pinterest: Running a Targeted Campaign • Pin Optimization Activity: Creating an SEO-Friendly Pin
	30 minutes	Pin Image Prime Pinning Time Activity: Tying It All Together
Hour Four	15 minutes	Pinterest: Analytics • Analytics for the Pinterest Business Page: Profile, Audience, Website
	45 minutes	Activity: Analyze This
	Optional	Chapter Review
Hour Five	30 minutes	Social Media Strategy Project Debriefing
	15 minutes	Postscript • Social Media Marketing Analysis
	15 minutes	• Social Media Fatigue and Fickleness

Total Timing for Course 3:

Regular Content = 33.75 hours

Final Exam/Student Survey = 1 hour

Optional Chapter Reviews = 2 hours

Optional Extensions = 4 hours, 45 minutes

Total Course Time: 41 hours, 30 minutes
(Homework assignments can be completed in class also)

The Elements of Digital Marketing

#1 DIGITAL MARKETING FUNDAMENTALS

Brand	Audience	Goals	Domain Names	Keyword Research	Online Marketing	Email Marketing	Budget

#2 STRATEGIC WEB DESIGN

Getting Started	The Creative Effort	Security & Analytics	Integration & Maintenance	Blogging	Multimedia

#3 SOCIAL MEDIA MARKETING STRATEGIES

Facebook	Twitter	Instagram	LinkedIn	YouTube	Yelp	Pinterest

Preface: Social Media Today

Social media is really a phenomenon of the new millennium. In the 20th century, no one 'liked', 'tweeted', or 'pinned' anything. With the arrival of Facebook, Twitter, Pinterest, and other social media sites, people began to communicate and relate to one another differently. Social media has also directly affected media (TV, radio, newspapers, magazines, etc.) and the speed at which news is reported. The expression 'old news' is now more prevalent than ever, and nowhere more evident than in the political realm.

Right now, people around the world are sending their thoughts, questions, images, and videos in real time through a myriad of social media channels. Turn on your computer, fire up your tablet, or tap on an app on your smart phone and you'll see what people you know, and don't know, have been up to. Your best friend just posted a selfie of himself on Instagram posing in front of the Eiffel Tower. Your coworker spent her lunch hour endorsing colleagues on LinkedIn. And, even your mom uploaded a video to YouTube of her new grandson taking his first steps.

As well as all these individuals, you'll find businesses on social media too. The electronics store you shopped at for your friend's birthday just put up photos on Flickr from its latest midnight madness sale. The bakery where you bought cupcakes for Valentine's Day posted a recipe tutorial for those very same cupcakes on Google+. Oh, and that fashion boutique that sold you two pairs of pants and three shirts, has just put up some ideas on Tumblr for how to create a stylish outfit.

It's important to recognize that social media is now regarded as an effective advertising tool by many companies. Yet, business owners often don't know how to use all these social media channels to their best advantage. That's why it's important for digital marketing professionals to be well-versed in how each online platform works and can be used to reach their clients' target audience.

In this text, we will examine the following social media sites:

- Facebook

- Twitter

- Instagram

- LinkedIn

- YouTube

- Yelp

- Pinterest

Each chapter will examine a particular social network in detail, but for a brief description of the purpose, use, and key features of each platform, please refer to 'Social Media in Brief" in the Appendix.

Note: All trademarked brands referenced in this text are the property of their respective owners.

SOCIAL MEDIA
GOVERNING STRATEGIES

Social Media Campaign Goals	The Target Consumer's Persona	Competitors' Social Media Strategies	Social Media Channels	Utilizing Social Media Channels
22	**23**	**27**	**30**	**33**

Introduction

Before a marketer launches a social media campaign, he or she needs to formulate an effective strategy. To create such a strategy, the digital marketing specialist must research and consult with the business' stakeholders. The result of such research and consultation should be:

- A well-defined social media campaign goal(s)
- An understanding of the target consumer's persona
- A thorough knowledge of the competitors' social media strategies
- The selection of social media channels
- The best practices for utilizing those social media channels[1]

These are covered in detail elsewhere in this textbook series, but a brief refresher is provided in the following pages.

Note for Teachers

Doubling the number of Facebook likes is not a social media campaign goal, rather it is a step towards achieving one, such as increasing a business' brand awareness. It is important to point out to students that there may be multiple strategies to achieve the goal of increasing brand awareness going on at the same time. Some of them may be focused on online activity, whereas others may be concentrated on offline actions. It is possible to regard doubling Facebook likes as a short-term goal that brings a business one step closer to achieving a long-term aim like increasing brand awareness.

The Social Media Campaign Goals

Discussion Questions

What is and is **not** a social media campaign goal?

• Doubling the number of Facebook likes on a business' page

or

• Increasing a business' brand awareness

Discuss this question with your classmate(s). Select your answer and be prepared to defend your choice with several reasons.

THE S.M.A.R.T. GOALS FORMULA

What are S.M.A.R.T. goals?

Change the campaign goal you identified in the previous activity, so that it is S.M.A.R.T.

Note for Teachers

Ask students who have taken Course 1, **Digital Marketing Fundamentals** to recall this content. Note down anything they remember and then include all of the following information that was not mentioned:

S.M.A.R.T. stands for: Specific, Measurable, Attainable, Relevant, and Time-based.

A specific goal is a detailed aim. It is based on what the business owner wants to achieve.

A measurable goal is quantifiable. In other words, a company needs to specify how many or how much of something.

An attainable goal is one that has a realistic chance of coming to fruition.

A relevant goal needs to make sense for its audience at a particular moment in time.

A time-based goal identifies a deadline. This is when the goal should be realized.[1]

So, while "increasing a business' brand awareness" is a social media campaign goal, it needs refining in order to incorporate all of the S.M.A.R.T. elements, which are discussed in detail in **Digital Marketing Fundamentals**.

Answers will vary, but should include all facets of the S.M.A.R.T. formula.

The Target Consumer's Persona

Once a company has established what it wants to achieve, it is important for the **digital marketing** professional to create a target consumer persona or **target market** profile. A **target consumer persona** is another term for identifying the ideal potential customer a business wants to attract with its marketing efforts.

It's key that everyone marketing a company's products and/or services knows the characteristics of this target consumer or buyer persona to ensure that the right demographic is targeted at the right times, in the right places with the right messages.[2]

In terms of social media, it is clear that by establishing an accurate, specific target consumer persona, a business will be able to determine which social media channels to utilize to achieve its goals. Furthermore, a company is likely to get more **engagement** through those channels. Conversely, a business that creates an inaccurate target consumer persona will get low engagement on social media.[3]

⏰ ACTIVITY: CREATING BUYER PERSONAS

PART ONE	1. Brainstorm some ideas as to what information a marketer and a company need in order to establish a target consumer persona. Generally, a business wants "to know who the person is, what they value, and how best to speak them."[4] 2. Organize those ideas into a template.
PART TWO	1. Select a business that you have purchased from in the past. Conduct some research on it (e.g. its products and/or services, history, etc.). 2. Depending on the business, a company should have anywhere from one to five buyer personas to represent its target **audience**. "This number is big enough to cover the majority of [its] customers yet small enough to still carry the value of specificity."[5] However, for the purpose of this activity, you are just going to create one using the template you made in part one. Ensure that you include a picture as part of your persona. 3. Present a brief overview of the company you selected and the persona you created.

Students can complete some of this activity for homework. In the hourly breakdown, 20 minutes of class time is allotted. It is recommended that students complete this activity in pairs. See sample buyer persona template.

An FAQ about Buyer Personas:

Why does a buyer persona include a picture and a name?

Attaching a name or a face to a buyer persona makes it more real and helps the marketer to put himself or herself in the potential customer's shoes.

BUYER PERSONA TEMPLATE: TEACHER'S SAMPLE [2,3]

Name: _____

Photo

Demographics

Gender: _____

Age: _____   Income: _____

Cultural/Ethnic Background: _____

Geographic Region: _____

Education: _____

Other

Hobbies: _____

Online Habits: _____

Needs and Wants

-
-
-

Concerns

-
-
-

Solutions We Can Offer

-
-
-

HOW TO RESEARCH BUYER PERSONAS

In the previous activity, you created a buyer persona for a company. You used your own knowledge of that company and conducted some additional online research to build that persona. However, if you were a digital marketer, you would do a variety of other things as well, because a buyer persona needs to be as accurate as possible:

1. **Questionnaires:** When meeting with a customer, you might get him or her to fill out a questionnaire. That customer would answer questions related to the categories in the template you designed (e.g. target customer demographics, preferences, where the potential client looks for information, etc.).[6]

2. **Analytics:** By using website analytics, a business is able to "see where [its] visitors came from, what keywords they used to find [the business], and how long they spent [on the site] once they arrived. **This data is key for personas** as it can reveal the desires that led [a business' target] audience to [its] site as well as the tools they used to get there."[7]

   There are many analytics tools that can be employed. However, Google Analytics is often the first choice for many businesses because it is:

   » Quite universal
   » Fairly comprehensive
   » Free

3. **Social Media Listening:** Social media listening is all about paying attention. It involves reading through what people are saying and taking note of what they are doing on the company's social media channels. For example:

   » What are they 'liking' on Facebook?
   » What are they complaining about on Twitter?
   » What are they 'pinning' on Pinterest?

   The kind of information a marketer gathers through social media listening is a sense of what people are interested in, not interested in, and annoyed by. It also becomes very clear which social media channels are getting the most traffic, and what can be gleaned from that traffic. In other words, if a company's Instagram posts are getting a lot of views that same company might want to get on Pinterest too, as opposed to a more content-heavy channel.

In the next section, sizing up the competition will be discussed. However, it is appropriate at this point to mention that social media listening also involves paying attention to what is being said, 'liked', 'retweeted', etc. on competitors' social media channels. This practice is an integral part of not repeating competitors' mistakes, and learning from their successes.

The Competitors' Social Media Strategies

"And while the law of competition may be sometimes hard for the individual, it is best for the race, because it ensures the survival of the fittest in every department." —Andrew Carnegie[8]

Competition, good or bad, has always been a part of society, and the driving force behind capitalism. Therefore, it is crucial that businesses are aware of who the competition is and what kind of marketing activities they are engaged in.

Note for Teachers

It is recommended that students complete this activity in groups or pairs. Students can be asked to present and/or hand in their information as part of their assignment mark.

⏰ ACTIVITY: SIZING UP THE COMPETITION

1. Recall the business you researched for "Activity: Creating Buyer Personas".
2. Find out who the company's top three to five competitors are.
3. Note down the following for each competitor:
   a. Which social media channels the competitor uses (check its websites, most companies list them; type the company name into a search engine and check which social networks are listed along with the company name[9])
   b. The number of followers the competitor has on three major channels: Facebook, Twitter, and one other (e.g. Instagram)
   c. The competitor's posting frequency (e.g. every day, every few days, once a week, etc.)
   d. What the competitor posts (e.g. type of content, images, videos, etc.)
   e. How the competitor interacts with its consumer base (e.g. Does the competitor 'like' comments and/or respond to them? Does the competitor 'retweet' and/or respond to tweets directly? Etc.)[10]
4. Pretend you are a marketer employed by the business you researched for "Activity: Creating Buyer Personas". What recommendations would you make to the owner regarding social media strategy, based on the information you gathered throughout this activity?

Note: There are social media competitor analytics that can be used by businesses and marketers to monitor their competitors' social media activity and how well they are engaging their audience. These tools will be discussed in subsequent chapters as they apply to other social media channels.

HOW'S THE PROFILE?

How a business' competitors lay out their social media profiles is also important when it comes to analyzing their social media strategies. A social media profile is part of a business' brand and it is usually preferable that a business present the same image of its brand across its social media channels, but at the same time it could choose to present different aspects of its image on each social media network.[11] The reasoning behind this has to do with the buyer persona(s) the business is trying to reach, as different individuals will respond to different things.

IMAGES

On sites like Facebook and Twitter, account holders have a profile. That profile consists of images and text. The two central images are the profile picture and cover photo.

 ACTIVITY: IMAGES

Take a look at some of the businesses you follow on Facebook and Twitter. What are they using for their profile picture and cover photo? Are they using the same images on both social networks? If not, why do you think that is?

Students will probably find that most businesses use their logo as their profile picture. Cover pictures will vary more widely. They could be pictures of:

- *A business' products*
- *The interior or exterior of the business' retail location (if applicable)*
- *A celebrity wearing the products or utilizing the service*
- *Their packaging*
- *A quotation*
- *Etc.*

CONTENT

Another key component of any business' profile page, and consequently its brand, is the description or 'about us' part of the profile. "Why are bios, short descriptions and About information so important? It's simple; your . . . bio could be the first impression a potential customer gets of your business. You'll want to make that count."[12]

ACTIVITY: CONTENT

Take another look at the businesses you follow on Facebook and Twitter. Which one has the best bio? Why? How do you think that bio helps to improve the brand presence of that business and make it stand out in the sea of businesses on social media?

Extension Activity: Ask students to get into pairs and select the worst 'about us' on a business' Facebook page. Students should edit and/or rewrite the 'about us', so it better represents the brand and makes it stand out among its competitors.

ACTIVITY: SOCIAL MEDIA ALPHABETICS

1. Using the letters A through Z, try to list one social media channel per letter. Avoid checking online until you have exhausted your own knowledge and that of your classmates'.

2. Then, rank the channels in terms of how frequently you use them (where one is the most and 26 is not at all).

3. It's already been established that Facebook and Twitter are excellent channels to use for marketing purposes. Of all the channels you've listed, which three would you rank along with Facebook and Twitter to round out the top five and why?

Note for Teachers

The purpose of this activity is to demonstrate the vast range of social networks that are available worldwide. It is important that students recognize that, as future digital marketers, they will need to pick and choose the best social channels for each particular client. It is also important that they consistently monitor channels. New features are regularly added, old ones taken away, and modifications made. Channels can also become inactive very quickly.

This list is not exhaustive, but some suggested responses are provided for each letter:

A: ask.fm
B: Bebo
C: Classmates.com
D: Delicious, Digg
E: English baby!, eToro
F: Facebook, Flickr, Foursquare
G: Google+, Goodreads
H: hi5

I: Instagram
J: Jiepang
K: Kiwibox
L: LinkedIn
M: MyHeritage, Meetup
N: NING
O: Ozmosis
P: Pinterest
Q: Quora

R: Reddit
S: Snapchat
T: Twitter, TripAdvisor, Tumblr
U: Unmetric
V: Vimeo, VK
W: Whisper
X: XING
Y: YouTube, Yelp
Z: Zorpia

The Selection of Social Media Channels

How does a digital marketer select the best social media channels? He or she must consider many factors:

• Who the business is marketing to

• Where its potential clientele is geographically

• What the business is selling (i.e. the type of product and/or service) and what industry it's part of

• Which social media channels its competitors are using

It is crucial that a business or marketer doesn't select too many channels because it will be difficult to utilize so many to their full potential.

⏰ ACTIVITY: READING "HOW TO CHOOSE THE BEST SOCIAL MEDIA SITE FOR YOUR BUSINESS"

Note for Teachers

Provide students with the link to the article, "How to Choose the Best Social Media Site for Your Business": http://www.inc.com/michelle-manafy/how-to-choose-the-best-social-media-sites-to-market-your-business.html.[13] *The following activity can be started in class and completed for homework. Students may respond in point form. The assignment can be collected for marks, if so desired.*

1. Using your own knowledge, identify whether you think **Business-to-Business (B2B)** or **Business-to-Consumer (B2C)** is the primary user of each of the following social media channels when it comes to marketing.

2. Read the article from **Inc. Magazine**: "How to Choose the Best Social Media Site for Your Business". Your instructor will provide you with the link.
   According to author Michelle Manafy, what kinds of businesses should use each of the following social media marketing channels?

Facebook	LinkedIn	Pinterest
Twitter	Other	• Tumblr • Google +

3. Recall the businesses you looked at in "Activity: Sizing up the Competition." Are there any social media channels you think those businesses aren't utilizing, but should be? Justify your response by referencing points made by the **Inc. Magazine** article.

   Answers will vary.

Answers

Facebook

1. B2C is the primary user, but the B2B numbers are increasing.
2. Businesses that want to:
   - Build a community presence
   - Reach the broadest possible audience

LinkedIn

1. B2B is the primary user.
2.
   - Businesses that can help people with career questions/decisions, and/or industry-specific information
   - Small proprietors/freelancers looking for networking opportunities/contracts
   - Businesses that are looking to reach educated, higher-income individuals

Pinterest

1. B2C is the primary user.
2.
   - Businesses in a very visual industry that have customers and potential customers who express themselves visually and/or use images to assist them with buying decisions
   - Women; this social network really appeals to the female demographic

Twitter

1. B2C and B2B are the primary users.
2. Customers and potential customers:
   - Of both genders, particularly in a younger demographic
   - Who are 'information junkies'; so, good for businesses that provide topic-based news or commentary on current events

Instagram

1. B2C is the primary user.
2. Businesses that want to attract:
   - A similar audience to Pinterest's in terms of visual appeal
   - A similar audience to Twitter
   - People in urban areas
   - Certain ethnic groups (Hispanics and African-Americans[4])

Other:

- Tumblr

  1. B2C is the primary user.
  2. Customers and potential customers in a younger, poorer demographic tend to use Tumblr.

- Google+

  1. B2C is the primary user.
  2. Male customers and potential customers[5]

The Best Practices for Utilizing Social Media Channels

🕐 ACTIVITY: THE TOP FIVE DOS OF SOCIAL MEDIA MARKETING PRACTICES

Listen to the social media marketing specialist. He will describe the top five dos for business owners when it comes to social media marketing practices. Take notes.

Note for Teachers

Show students "Social Media Dos and Donts" (02:09), available on Mujo's YouTube playlist.

Do:

1. *Develop a strategy that is unique for your business needs and appropriate for your budgets.*
2. *Assign a realistic budget.*
3. *Acquire the appropriate human resources for ongoing maintenance, be it internally, externally, or as is often the case, a combination of both.*
4. *Integrate a proactive reputation strategy and review process.*
5. *Develop a social marketing advertising campaign strategy.*

⏱ ACTIVITY: THE TOP FIVE DON'TS OF SOCIAL MEDIA MARKETING PRACTICES

Listen to the social media marketing specialist. He will describe the top five don'ts for business owners when it comes to social media marketing practices. Take notes.

Note for Teachers

Don't:

1. Assume social media is irrelevant and doesn't affect your business.

2. Allow your junior staff to run your online social business for you. You can leverage their enthusiasm and knowledge base, but make sure they have a competent leader who has the corporate experience to manage and keep them on track with your bigger picture.

3. Hire multiple companies to manage your social media. Do the due diligence, choose one, and then give them the keys to do the job.

4. Employ a company that doesn't have a solution for reporting. You need to see if your social media campaigns are successful.

5. Clog your followers' feeds with too many postings per day. This will irritate them and, most often will result in unfollows, rather than conversions.

⏰ ACTIVITY: CREATING TOP TEN LISTS

Do some research about social media marketing practices. You can look online, and/or interview marketing professionals and business owners. Add five more 'dos' and five more 'don'ts' to the lists you heard the speaker share. Be prepared to discuss your findings.

Note for Teachers

This activity can be done in pairs or groups. It can also be started in class and finished for homework. The points that follow can be mentioned to the students, if they are not already brought up in discussion.

An adaptation of the activity could involve asking a guest speaker(s) from a digital marketing agency to come in and expand on the points mentioned in the recording. He or she could add more dos and don'ts that the students could note down. **Additional dos and don'ts:**

Dos:

1. Create clear and achievable goals for each social media channel whether they be likes, follows, leads, sales, etc. to promote your brand or deliver a specific message.
2. Spend the time to understand the mechanics of each social media outlet.
3. Identify your audience and listeners or watchers on every channel you engage. You'll be surprised at how different they are from channel to channel.
4. Speak the language that your audience on each channel will understand. Your message's tone may take a more formal or professional form on LinkedIn compared to all other channels.
5. Measure and analyze your progress on achieving the first 'do' above on a regular basis! Use analytical tools available online like downloadable spreadsheets to more sophisticated proprietary tools.
6. Contribute something useful and relevant that your target audience can use or learn from.

Don'ts:

7. Assume all social media channels are created equal. Each one offers a specific level of engagement and more importantly has a different audience from channel to channel.
8. Use only your desktop or laptop to distribute your messages. Social media apps on mobile devices are more widely used now than ever.
9. Leave your social media channels unattended or unmonitored for any significant amount of time. As Warren Buffet once said, "It takes 20 years to build a reputation and five minutes to ruin it. If you think about that, you'll do things differently."[6]
10. Use just text to distribute your messages. Use powerful images like infographics, videos, animated gifs, etc. to make your message more interesting and shareable.
11. Forget about your specific target audience. Focus your energy on them, not everyone. You'll be wasting a lot of time and money if you do.

👓 CASE STUDY: Translink

Some companies and organizations use social media very effectively. One particular standout on one of the most widely used social media channels, Twitter, is British Columbia's transit organization, TransLink. Transit systems often get many complaints from their ridership about everything from delays to overcrowded buses. However, a study conducted by the University of Southern California found that agencies like transit systems "which actively use Twitter for public relations messaging and responding to user complaints get better positivity rankings among social media users."[14]

TransLink and the customer information officers who interact with the B.C. ridership are utilizing Twitter especially well when compared to other North American transit systems. The same Southern California study "used computer algorithms to rank 64,000 comments on Twitter . . . about various city agencies . . . But of the 10 major North American [transit] agencies studied, Translink was the most popular."[15] What is TransLink doing right, and what can businesses learn from the agency?

First, TransLink 'tweets' much more frequently than its counterparts. In fact, according to the Southern California study, "Translink is by far the most active Twitter user among the transit agencies studied. They tweet often, on average about 90 times per day, while most other agencies tweet between 10 and 30 times a day."[16] It is critical that businesses find the sweet spot in terms of how many tweets they put out daily. Not so many that followers get annoyed by a flood of tweets, but frequently enough that the company's message stays at the forefront of their minds.

Next, the B.C. transit agency has developed a personal connection with its followers. In an interview with News 1130, Robert Willis, TransLink's senior communications advisor said, "'our tweets have initials on them, to represent a team member. Some people wait for certain initials to come online, so that person can have conversations with them.'"[17] The key message that businesses can learn from this is that people make connections with individuals **not** companies. The same is true for blogs; someone is more likely to relate to an author's style or voice, rather than a business'.

It's also important to note that TransLink communicates with its followers in real time or very close to real time. Willis claims that if an individual 'tweets' Translink between 6:30 a.m. and 11:30 p.m., he or she will receive a response in approximately three minutes.[18] Any real-time interaction a business can have with its followers is truly valuable. It helps to grow the connection between people and the organization. TransLink fosters that connection to an even greater degree by following more of its followers in return than the other transit agencies examined in the study.[19] Again, if businesses understand the reciprocal nature of social channels like Twitter, they will embrace opportunities like this to connect with their potential and existing customers.

Note for Teachers

Students are given 20 minutes to complete this activity in class, but it is possible that they may need to finish it for homework.

QUESTIONS

Respond to the following questions in point form, with reference to the case study.

1. Summarize the finding of the University of Southern California study.

2. Why is the posting **frequency** of a business or organization on social media so important?

3. What evidence is there in the case study that TransLink has developed a personal connection with its Twitter followers?

4. Do you think a company or organization should make it standard digital marketing practice to refollow its followers? Why or why not?

Answers

1. • Transit systems that use Twitter for PR and correspondence purposes have a higher ranking among social media users.

   • TransLink was the most popular transit agency out of the ten looked at in the study.

   • TransLink 'tweets' about 90 times a day compared to the 10 – 30 times a day that other transit systems do.

   • TransLink follows more of its followers back than other agencies in the study do.

2. Answers will vary, but basically if the business finds the right balance between posting too frequently and not frequently enough, it will gain more followers and a higher online profile.

3. Some followers are waiting for certain initials to come up in the tweets, so that they can communicate with a particular customer information officer.

4. Answers will vary.

CHAPTER REVIEW

1. What does S.M.A.R.T. stand for?

2. What kind of information appears in a buyer persona?

3. How can a company gather information to create an accurate persona?

4. How does a digital marketer choose which social media channels to utilize?

5. Note two dos and two don'ts related to social media practices.

Chapter Review (Optional)

The following questions can be utilized in a variety of ways (e.g. Students can complete them for homework, in class with a partner, orally in a whole-class format, etc.).

1. Specific, Measurable, Attainable, Relevant, and Time-Based

2. A photo, demographics, hobbies/online habits, needs and wants, and concerns

3. Through questionnaires, analytics, and social media listening

4. • Who the business is marketing to

   • Where its potential clientele is geographically

   • What the business is selling and what industry it is part of

   • Which social media channels its competitors are using

5. Answers will vary. Suggested responses could be:

   Do:

   1. Take the time to develop a strategy that is unique for your business needs and appropriate for your budgets.

   2. Assign a realistic budget.

   Don't:

   1. Assume social media is irrelevant and doesn't affect your business.

   2. Allow your junior staff to run your online social business for you. You can leverage their enthusiasm and knowledge base, but make sure they have a competent leader who has the corporate experience to manage and keep them on track with your bigger picture.

FOOTNOTES: CHAPTER 1

1 Daoud, Houssem. "8 Essential Elements of a Social Media Marketing Strategy." Social Media Examiner. 16 Jul. 2014. Web. 26 May 2015. http://www.socialmediaexaminer.com/essential-elements-social-media-marketing-strategy/.
2 Ibid.
3 Ibid.
4 Lee, Kevan. "Marketing Personas: The Complete Beginner's Guide." Buffersocial. 27 Mar. 2014. Web. 03 Jun. 2015. https://blog.bufferapp.com/marketing-personas-beginners-guide.
5 Ibid.
6 Ibid.
7 Ibid.
8 "Andrew Carnegie Quotes." BrainyQuote. 2015. Web. 27 Oct. 2015. http://www.brainyquote.com/quotes/quotes/a/andrewcarn100917.html.
9 Hines, Kristi. "How to Create a Social Media Strategy By Spying Your Competitors." Social Media Examiner. 10 Dec. 2013. Web. 06 Jun. 2015. http://www.socialmediaexaminer.com/social-strategy-competitor-research/.
10 Daoud, Houssem. "8 Essential Elements of a Social Media Marketing Strategy." Social Media Examiner. 16 Jul. 2014. Web. 26 May 2015. http://www.socialmediaexaminer.com/essential-elements-social-media-marketing-strategy/.
11 Ibid.
12 Ibid.
13 Manafy, Michelle. "How to Choose the Best Social Media Site for your Business." *Inc. Magazine*. 09 Jul. 2014. Web. 06 Jun. 2015. http://www.inc.com/michelle-manafy/how-to-choose-the-best-social-media-sites-to-market-your-business.html.
14 Cooper, Sam. "TransLink is the most popular transit system in North America, says new study." *The Province*. 15 Feb. 2015. Web. 08 Jun. 2015. http://www.theprovince.com/technology/TransLink+most+popular+transit+system+North+America+says+study/10815443/story.html.
15 Ibid.
16 News Staff. "Translink's Twitter team gives transit a human touch." News1130. 27 Feb. 2015. Web. 08 Jun. 2015. http://www.news1130.com/2015/02/27/translinks-twitter-team-gives-transit-a-human-touch/.
17 Ibid.
18 News Staff. "Translink's Twitter team gives transit a human touch." News1130. 27 Feb. 2015. Web. 08 Jun. 2015. http://www.news1130.com/2015/02/27/translinks-twitter-team-gives-transit-a-human-touch/.
19 Ibid.

FOOTNOTES: CHAPTER 1

1 Moore, Shawn and Adam Wilkins. *Digital Marketing Fundamentals*. Vancouver: Mujo Learning Systems Inc., 2016.
2 Lee, Kevan. "Marketing Personas: The Complete Beginner's Guide." Buffersocial. 27 Mar. 2014. Web. 16 Oct. 2015. https://blog.bufferapp.com/marketing-personas-beginners-guide.
3 Moore, Shawn and Adam Wilkins. *Digital Marketing Fundamentals*. Vancouver: Mujo Learning Systems Inc., 2016.
4 Duggan, Maeve, Nicole B. Ellison, Cliffe Lampe, Amanda Lenhart, and Mary Madden. "Demographics of Key Social Networking Platforms." Pew Research Centre. 09 Jan. 2015. Web. 06 Jun. 2015. http://www.pewinternet.org/2015/01/09/demographics-of-key-social-networking-platforms-2/.
5 Manafy, Michelle. "How to Choose the Best Social Media Site for your Business." *Inc. Magazine*. 9 Jul. 2014. Web. 6 Jun. 2015. http://www.inc.com/michelle-manafy/how-to-choose-the-best-social-media-sites-to-market-your-business.html.
6 "Warren Buffet Quotes." BrainyQuote. 2015. Web. 29 Jun. 2015. www.brainyquote.com/quotes/w/warrenbuff108887.html.

#2 FACEBOOK
MARKETING STRATEGIES

Facebook: History	Facebook: Personal	Facebook: Business	Facebook: Advertising	Facebook: Targeted Campaign	Facebook: Analytics
41	42	47	55	61	64

FACEBOOK: HISTORY

More than ten years ago, Facebook was founded by Harvard student Mark Zuckerberg and several of his classmates. The site is now the most popular social networking channel in the world. Back in 2004, 'the Facebook', as it was originally called, was just for Harvard students. However, it was expanded to other North American colleges and universities and quickly grew in popularity. By December 1st, 2004, the site had 1 million users. In the course of more than a decade, Facebook has had many significant milestones and launches.

Launches

Oct. 3, 2016	Facebook Marketplace
Jun. 30, 2013	Video on Instagram
Oct. 11, 2011	Facebook for iPad
Sept. 22, 2011	Facebook Timeline
Aug. 18, 2010	Facebook Places
Feb. 9, 2009	'Like' Button
Jun. 22, 2007	Facebook Video
Apr. 4, 2006	Facebook for Mobile
Oct. 1, 2005	Facebook Photos
Sept. 1, 2004	Facebook Wall
Feb. 4, 2004	Facebook Launches

Milestones

June 2016
1.13 Billion Users (on average)

March 2015
936 Million Users (on average)

Feb. 4, 2014
Facebook's 10th Anniversary

Dec. 4, 2012
1 Billion-Plus Users

May 18, 2012
Presented IPO

Apr. 9, 2012
Bought Instagram for 1 Billion Dollars

Dec. 1, 2009
360 Million Users

Dec. 6, 2006
12 Million Users

1, 2, 3, 4

Facebook: Personal

The following questions could be discussed in a whole-class format or in groups.

 Discussion Questions

Pretend you are giving a seminar in a foreign country to people who have never seen Facebook. Discuss the following questions with your classmates and note down the responses you come up with.

1. How would you describe a Facebook profile?

2. How would you explain the purpose of Facebook for individuals?

3. How would you describe how businesses use Facebook to reach followers?

Answers

1. *Students can utilize the sample Facebook profile page for this activity.*

   A profile contains:
   - *Personal information (e.g. name, age, contact information, hometown, current city, place of employment)*
   - *Photos (e.g. profile photo, cover photo, albums, timeline photos)*
   - *Status updates and links (e.g. updates on daily activities, links to a personal blog, links to external content of interest)*
   - *Places (e.g. a restaurant he/she is eating at, an airport he/she is flying out of, etc.)*

2. *An individual can connect with other individuals who have Facebook profiles. Friend requests can be sent. People will typically 'friend' anyone, from an acquaintance to a personal friend to a professional connection to a family member.*

   Facebook also allows account holders to connect with businesses and organizations that they like. They can 'like' their pages, become fans, or even friends with these companies or groups.

   Once individuals are connected, they can 'like' and/or share status updates and/or links, depending on the privacy settings established by the individuals.

3. **The purpose of this question is just to gauge students' pre-knowledge of this topic. Explain to them that this subject area will be explored in this chapter of the text.*

FACEBOOK PERSONAL PROFILE

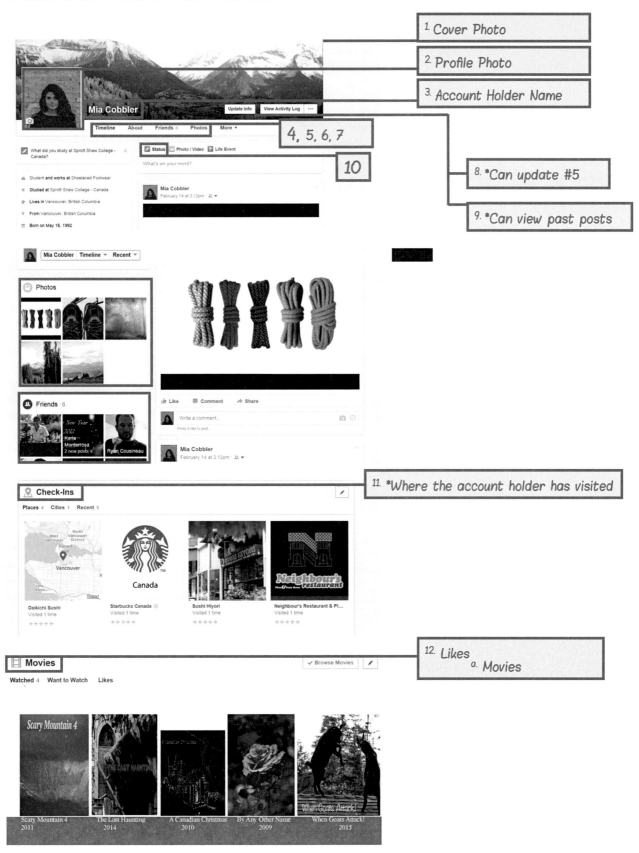

1. Cover Photo
2. Profile Photo
3. Account Holder Name

4, 5, 6, 7

10

8. *Can update #5

9. *Can view past posts

11. *Where the account holder has visited

12. Likes
  a. Movies

MUJO
LEAD • EDUCATE • INSPIRE

12. Likes
   b. TV Shows

12. Likes
   c. Businesses, Organizations, etc.

DEVELOPING YOUR PERSONAL BRAND ON FACEBOOK

Facebook is a very personal platform, especially when compared to other social media channels like LinkedIn. There must be a high level of trust between the individual and his or her 'friends'. However, that being said, people need to change their thinking about how they represent themselves on Facebook. It should be considered a representation of their personal brand and how they may be regarded by the business community, as that's how it gets used.

Even with privacy setting adjustments, there is the possibility that information and images could become more public than intended and harm individuals' online reputations. Thus, the following things should be avoided:

- Photos that are sexually suggestive or include nudity (e.g. If they wouldn't be appropriate to show a future employer, they aren't appropriate for Facebook)

- Links to material that is sexist, racist, homophobic, or could be considered offensive or threatening to a particular group

- 'Liking' controversial groups' pages (e.g. violent extremist organizations)

- Making controversial statements without appropriate forethought

Note: Because Facebook allows its account holders to be spontaneous and post at every available opportunity, people sometimes do so without thinking and offend others in the process.

At the same time, there are certainly things individuals can do to improve their personal brand on Facebook and promote their business:

1. Connecting and engaging with family members online. This demonstrates positive connections and personal integrity. For business owners in particular, family ethic is important because it shows loyalty and responsibility.

2. Establishing personal integrity on Facebook, so that that integrity can extend to any recommended page, including the company page; the company blog, events, and more.

3. Encouraging people to 'like' their place of employment or related industry pages.

4. Creating multiple profiles. This way, groups can be established and content tailored so that each group receives knowledge that would be of interest to them. At the same time, this is a good way to separate the personal from the professional.

Note: People will judge you on your social media behavior. They will check various channels to see if you can be trusted and what kind of reputation you have. People buy people, and if they buy you, they'll be more likely to buy from you.[5]

🕐 ACTIVITY: TAKING STOCK OF YOUR 'DIGITAL DIRT'

Note for Teachers

Provide students with the following links:

Klout: Klout.com

Google News Alert: https://www.google.com/alerts

It's time to take stock of what is online about you. Utilize the following (Your instructor will provide you with the relevant links):

1. Google yourself.
2. Use Klout to see how influential you are online (Facebook, Twitter, Instagram).
3. Set up Google News Alert to monitor what's being said about you and how frequently you are being talked about online.

Then, respond to the following questions:

1. What does your Facebook, and other online information, tell people about you (i.e. If you had to describe your brand perception in three sentences or less based on what's online, what would you say?)?
2. What is the most positive element of your Facebook profile in terms of promoting your personal brand?
3. What would you remove, edit, or add to your Facebook profile to improve how others perceive you online (e.g. unflattering photos, rude status updates, etc.)?

Finally, take a look at a friend's or classmate's profile. Select someone who has interests similar to yours.

1. How does that individual present himself or herself?
2. What can you take away from his or her profile to improve your own?

A final maxim to remember: "Aim to have content on the web be 'professional' not 'confessional'."[6] Also, the longer an individual maintains professional, active social media accounts, the more valuable those accounts will become for his or her career.

Facebook: Business

INTRODUCTION

Facebook for business is a no-brainer. The social network:

1. Is the most widely used across the globe

2. Knows more about its account holders than any other competing channel

3. Allows business owners and advertisers to refine their target market with absolute precision based on the users' likes and dislikes and the information that each user has shared with Facebook

It's important for digital marketers to have these facts at their fingertips. Some smaller businesses will be resistant to incorporating social media into their overall marketing strategy. They may feel that traditional advertising methods are sufficient to reach their target audience. Yet, it's clear that Facebook is essential if a business wants to be where its customers are interacting. The concept is the same as having a billboard displayed in a central downtown location, for example.

Facebook has the additional advantage of having very specific groups of people that are easily identifiable within its large number of subscribers. Thus, advertisers can more easily target ads so they can build on their marketing strategy.

FACEBOOK FOR BUSINESS IS DIFFERENT

In the previous section, it was discussed how Facebook works for individuals, and how a Facebook profile can be leveraged to improve an individual's business and professional image. Facebook also offers its business subscribers more than personal account holders.

Refer to the sample business page while going through this section. And, if time permits, ask students to visit "Getting Started with Pages": https://www. facebook.com/business/ learn/facebook-page-basics

Facebook for business has many advantages:

1. It puts a business on the map in the virtual world.

2. It gives a business an unlimited friend count (instead of being restricted to 5000 friends, as is the case for a personal profile).[7]

3. It allows a company to include its hours of operation, note promotions (e.g. happy hour), and consequently attract more customers.

4. A company can advertise its page, which it couldn't do with a personal profile page.[8]

5. A company can also access important information through Facebook Insights.[9]

FACEBOOK BUSINESS PAGE NOTES

Refer to the sample Facebook business page and read through the following notes.

#1: Insights:
* Refers to Facebook Insights, the platform's internal analytics. More details will be provided in an upcoming section.

#2: Publishing Tools:
* Includes lists of published posts and each post's **reach**, clicks/actions on the post, and time stamp, as well as, videos, lead ad forms, and canvas ads. Read: "6 Publishing Tools From Facebook for Marketers" for more details about these tools. Your instructor will provide you with the link.

#7: Shop Section:
* This is a new feature being tested in 2016. Read "Shop Section on Pages" for more details. Your instructor will provide you with the link.

Note for Teachers

Provide students with links to:

"6 Publishing Tools From Facebook for Marketers": http://www.socialmediaexaminer.com/6-publishing-tools-from-facebook-for-marketers/

"Shop Section on Pages": https://www.facebook.com/business/help/846547442125798

FACEBOOK BUSINESS PAGE

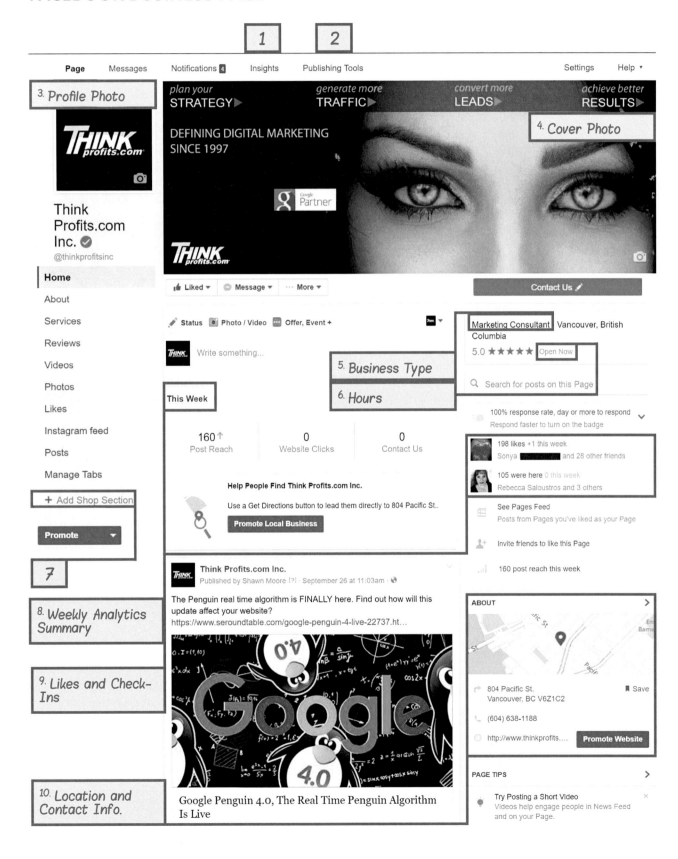

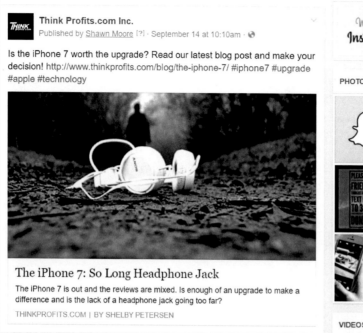

Extension Activity: In 2012, Facebook launched Facebook Premium. To promote this advertising service, Facebook has included videos featuring major companies like Sport Chek and Ben & Jerry's that have used it and found success. Groups of students could be assigned a video to watch and asked to find the answer to the following question:

How has Facebook Premium helped the company to advertise more effectively and/or change its advertising?

Give students the link to the Facebook for Business playlist on YouTube:

https://www.youtube.com/playlist?list=PLE6673621EA00DF45

Follow up group discussions with a whole-class discussion of the question and case studies featured.

Think Profits.com Inc.
Published by Shawn Moore [?] · August 22 · 🌐

The Social Media Olympics http://www.thinkprofits.com/blog/social-media-olympics/ #newblog #rio #rio2016 #olympics #socialmedia #thinkprofits #vancouver

The Social Media Olympics | Think Profits
The 2016 Rio Olympics are truly the social media Olympics. With more and more people tuning in via social media this has been a year for the records.

THINKPROFITS.COM | BY HANNA PETERSEN

114 people reached | **Boost Post**

👍 Like   💬 Comment   ➤ Share

🔵 Bong Serrano, Rebecca Saloustros and 3 others

REVIEWS ⟩

5.0 ★   **5.0 of 5 stars**
7 reviews

 Joselle ▇▇▇▇
5★ Think Profits has been a true pleasure to work with and we look forward to continuing our relationship to achieve great ... See More
February 26, 2016 · 🌐

👍 Like   💬 Comment   ▾

 Rhonda ▇▇▇▇
5★ I've gotten to know Shawn and his team over the last year. He has always been professional. With over 20 years experienc... See More
April 19, 2016 · 🌐

👍 Like   💬 Comment   ▾

 Tell people what you think
★ ★ ★ ★ ★

15. *Average Star Rating and Number of Reviews*

PEOPLE ALSO LIKE

16. *Other Similar Businesses*

egg   **egg**
Advertising Agency

straydog   **Straydog Branding**
Graphic Designer

OS   **Organic Sulfur,OS**
ORGANIC SULFUR   Health/Beauty

Marketing Consultants in Vancouver, British Columbia

LIKED BY THIS PAGE ⟩

Canada Intercambio

🕐 ACTIVITY: WHAT IS FACEBOOK INSIGHTS?

Do some online research and respond to the following questions:

1. What does Facebook Insights allow business subscribers to do?

2. What information can Facebook Insights give a business subscriber about likes?

3. What could a business subscriber do with the information you noted in question two?

4. Find one more useful feature that is offered by Facebook Insights. Describe it and how this feature can best be utilized by a business subscriber.

Answers

1. • Track user interaction
   • Discover which time of day and day of the week to post
   • Find out which content is most popular[1]

2. Demographic information about fans:
   a. Their locations
   b. Languages they read
   c. Age groups
   d. Gender[2]

3. The subscriber could tailor his or her postings to better attract the attention of fans. For example, if the majority of the fans are between the ages of 18 - 24, there could be posts with links to sites popular with that age range.

4. Answers will vary. Refer to: "A Beginner's Guide to Facebook Insights":

   https://blog.kissmetrics.com/guide-to-facebook-insights/

   ### Example response:
   A business subscriber with a physical location can see how many check-ins his or her company has had, and the demographic data on those individuals. This data allows a business subscriber "to monitor the social media impact on sales [and monitor his or her] busiest days."[3]

Discussion Questions

Anyone who has a Facebook account has seen pages associated with the biggest of businesses, Walmart, Microsoft, Chevron, and more. Although these companies do benefit from having a Facebook presence, "contrary to what many believe, online-business marketing on Facebook benefits small, traditional retailers the most."[10]

Why do you think this is the case?

Facebook account holders like to show their support for small, local businesses, often more so than larger corporations. Why?

Note for Teachers

These questions should be discussed in a whole-class format. Note students' responses on the whiteboard, and add the following points if they are not mentioned:

- "Small businesses offer unique products or services to a smaller range of customers and Facebook provides an excellent opportunity to reach the exact target audience with a personal approach."[4]
- Facebook levels the playing field and enables smaller businesses to compete with larger corporations.[5]
- A company that offers a niche product or service may have a competitive advantage because a large business won't be able to focus in depth on a single niche.[6]
- Small, local businesses have a community appeal. People see them as they walk around their neighborhood. If they do well, money stays in the community, rather than going elsewhere. Thus, they tend to benefit the community. This can be in contrast to some big businesses. They are visible, but not necessarily directly connected to a particular local area. They can be perceived by many as profit-driven. Some regard them as entities that primarily take money out of the community, rather than contribute to it. This is why some big businesses try to forge connections with the local community by engaging in activities that benefit it (e.g. Ronald McDonald House).

🕐 ACTIVITY: MAKING A SMALL BUSINESS PAGE BETTER

Note for Teachers

Ask students to work individually, and then either discuss their findings in a whole-class format or hand them in for participation marks.

1. Select a small business page that you 'like' on Facebook.

2. Take a look at the following:

   » The business' hours, location, and contact information: Are they up-to-date?

   » The content posted: Is there "content that gives people some kind of extra value? For instance, [a company] can highlight other great businesses nearby, or share interesting content that relates to its business."[11]

   » Are photos and videos of the products and/or services included?

   » Are there special offers?

3. Note this information down and be prepared to share it, along with some recommendations as to how this small business could improve its Facebook business page.

Example:

Business: Spool of Thread

https://www.facebook.com/SpoolofThread?ref=profile

>>The contact information is up-to-date, and it's a great idea that the business included transit directions to the location on its 'about' page.

>>This is an area for improvement. The vast majority of the company's posts relate to its products or the items that clients have sewn. There is the occasional reference to local event happenings (e.g. Dine Out Vancouver), but it would be better if there were more craft-related posts (e.g. links to cool sites about sewing, details about local craft shows, etc.).

>>The page has lots of colorful, appealing photos, but no videos. This is also an area for improvement. A short tutorial on how to make a quick sewing project would be engaging. The business could also show clips of a teacher instructing a class or students being interviewed before and after a class.

>>There is a mention about an upcoming sale, but nothing specific (e.g. mention this Facebook post and get 10% off fabric). Again, this could help improve the page and get more people to 'like' it.

Facebook: Advertising

THREE KINDS OF FACEBOOK ADVERTISING

As was noted earlier, one of the advantages of advertising on Facebook is that a business is able to target the audience for its advertising with great precision based on the personal information that people have shared with the social network. The focus can go beyond demographic information, though. It can extend to what a particular audience is talking about at a particular time. This highly targeted advertising is very advantageous for any company, and a variety of options are available when it comes to how a business wants to advertise on Facebook. Three of the methods include:

1. Setting Up Promoted or Suggested Posts

   - A company can pay Facebook to display its posts on people's news feeds. These posts are labeled 'suggested post' to differentiate them from friends' status updates and other content.
   - View the slideshow, "Facebook Promoted Posts: A Step-By-Step Guide" to see how a business owner can create a promoted post. Your instructor will provide you with the link.

Note for Teachers

Provide students with the following link:

"Facebook Promoted Posts: A Step-By-Step Guide": http://mashable.com/2012/05/31/facebook-promoted-posts-tips/#gallery/facebooks-promoted-posts-for-brand-pages/521294c95198406611000eed

2. Creating Right-Hand Column Ads

   - A company can also pay Facebook to place its ads in the right-hand column of a person's home page. Above the ads, account holders will see the word 'sponsored'.
   - Facebook used to put a larger number of ads in the right-hand column, but in April 2014 the social network made some changes. Your instructor will provide you with a link to "A New Look for Ads in the Right-Hand Column".

   Note: The cost of advertising on Facebook ranges widely. It can be as cheap as $1/day or as high as thousands of dollars/day. Although it could be considered expensive, the precision targeting of advertising means the advertisement will reach fewer people that are more likely to buy.

3. Utilizing Contest Apps

   - So many different contests are launched by companies around the world on Facebook. However, as with all marketing efforts, both the contest and its promotion must be linked to a company's overall marketing goals.
   - The **Social Media Examiner** focuses on six types of contests and notes the pros and cons of implementing each kind in "How to Choose the Right Type of Facebook Contest". Your instructor will provide you with the link.

Note for Teachers

Provide students with the following links:

"A New Look for Ads in the Right-Hand Column": https://www.facebook.com/business/news/A-New-Look-for-Ads-in-the-Right-Hand-Column

"How to Choose the Right Type of Facebook Contest": http://www.socialmediaexaminer.com/how-to-choose-the-right-type-of-facebook-contest/

Extension Activity: *Facebook and its clients have been known to fall victim to click fraud (i.e. it is possible for computers to automatically generate clicks that are not associated with real people). Ask students to look online for articles detailing this issue and ask them to present a brief summary of the information in class.*

Example article: *"This Man's $600,000 Facebook Disaster Is A Warning For All Small Businesses":*

http://www.businessinsider.com/mans-600000-facebook-ad-disaster-2014-2#ixzz3em3X5YNd

OLD STYLE, RIGHT-HAND COLUMN FACEBOOK AD:

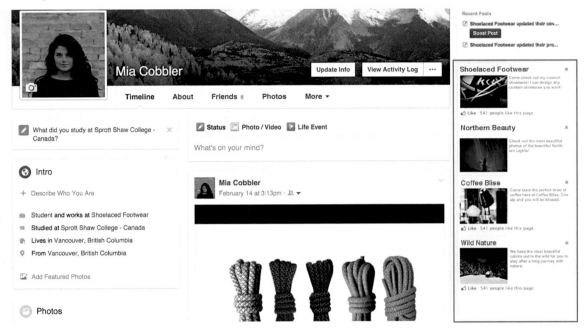

NEW RIGHT-HAND COLUMN FACEBOOK AD:

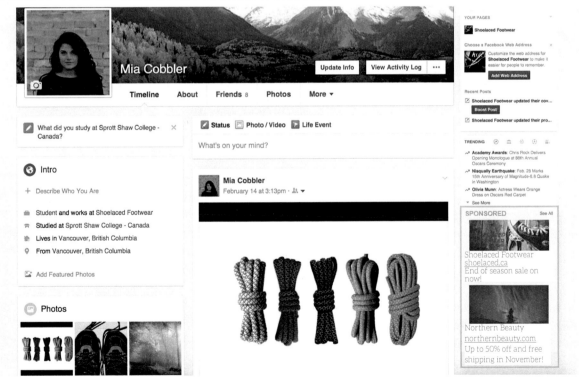

FACEBOOK FAILS AND WINS

Some companies are better at utilizing Facebook as a marketing tool than others. Effective Facebook marketing comes with the understanding that a wide range of people will see a message instantly. This doesn't just apply to advertising messages, but to more personal and casual interactions with the public.

Good Facebook profile managers understand that with this greater level of access comes a higher potential to enhance or damage a business' image. Thus, all Facebook strategies must be carefully considered before they hit this very public of social network stages.

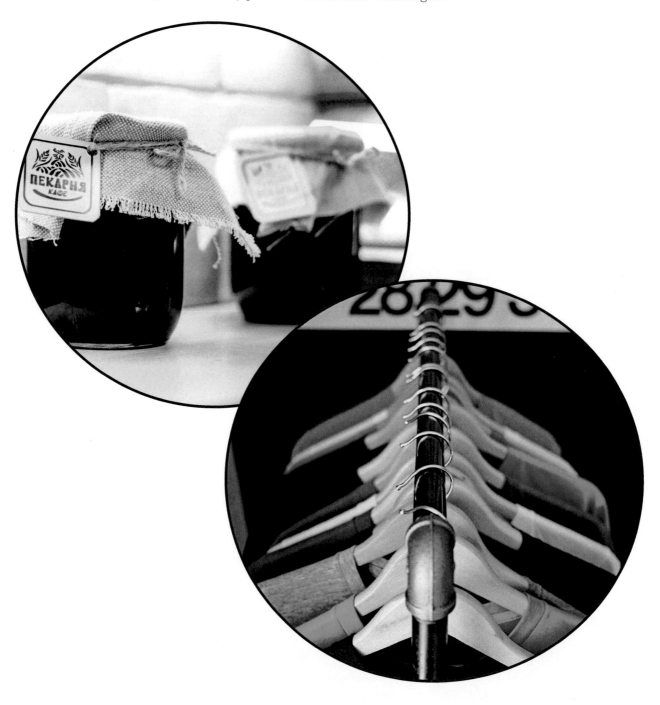

FACEBOOK FAIL

☺ CASE STUDY: Smucker's Gets in a Jam

About Smucker's

Smucker's is an iconic brand that can chart its origins back to late-19th century America. The company emphasizes that it makes traditional, quality products for discerning consumers. Initially, the company was just associated with jams and jellied spreads, but The J.M. Smucker Company's scope has grown to include: "retail packaged coffee, peanut butter, shortening and oils, ice cream toppings, sweetened condensed milk and natural food products in North America."[12]

Smucker's and Genetically Modified Organisms (GMO)

In 2014, a controversy erupted on Smucker's Facebook page. The blow up occurred when "a report from the Cornucopia Institute allege[d] that Smucker's was a major financial contributor to interests opposing legislation in the states of Oregon and Colorado - legislation that would compel food manufacturers to label foods containing ingredients that were genetically engineered."[13]

Fans of Smucker's Facebook page began to critique the company's funding of special interest groups who opposed GMO labeling ballot initiatives, and question what exactly goes into Smucker's products.[14]

Smucker's Response to the Facebook Controversy

On its website, Smucker's posted a statement in response to the controversy. Your instructor will provide you with a link to that statement. Read it carefully.

Back on Facebook, Smucker's allowed critical posts, but deleted those associated with GMOs and its position on them.[15] "The company even posted a comment explaining the deleted posts fell under its definition of spam. This only served to further anger some users, who called for a boycott of the brand."[16]

It is clear that Smucker's response to the controversy damaged its brand image. Deleting the GMO-related comments was certainly not the company's only option when it came to dealing with negativity and criticism on Facebook.

How would you have advised Smucker's to proceed? Discuss your ideas.

Note for Teachers

Provide students with the link to "Smucker's Jelly Company Hides Behind a Traditional Image While Saying This About GMOs": http://althealthworks.com/1714/the-smuckers-jelly-company-traditional-brand-comes-out-in-support-of-gmos-will-boycotts-result/
Answers will vary, but the following points are worth noting, if students do not bring them up:

- *It's bad practice for a company to delete Facebook comments "unless the comments are violations of terms of service, illegal, or threatening. If a company is at the point of having to delete comments, they have already missed the opportunity to get ahead of the issue."[7]*

- *The company should have an online reputation management program in place to defuse any negative online publicity that may occur. This is a proactive, rather than reactive strategy which would continue to serve the company in the long-term.[8]*

- *Smucker's certainly had the option of responding to each comment publicly and showing that it cared about consumers and respected their opinions.*

FACEBOOK WIN

👓 CASE STUDY: C&A Rethinks Buying Off the Rack

About C&A

A Dutch fashion retailer with a long history, C&A sells various clothing lines out of its retail locations in Europe and Latin America. It offers ready-to-wear apparel for men, women, children, and babies. The company's focus is summed up well on its website, "Fashion is always changing, but what doesn't change is C&A's commitment to providing fresh, modern style for the entire family at the best quality and a fair price."[17]

C&A's Off-the-Hook Strategy

Walking into a clothing store and being confronted with lots of items to choose from can be daunting. It's difficult to know what to select and what's considered truly fashionable. Many shoppers will seek opinions from salespeople, friends, family, or even random strangers when it comes to buying that must-have item.

In 2012, C&A decided to utilize Facebook and some high-tech coat hangers to assist its Brazilian customers with this process. The strategy was called 'FashionLike'. The company put pictures on its Facebook page of outfits for sale in store. If customers thought they were stylish and attractive, they 'liked' them. The likes "were then counted in real time on the physical hangers of the actual clothing in the store, thus revealing the popularity of each item."[18]

Why This Strategy is a Win

C&A has done something that few advertisers have yet to capitalize on; the ability to take Facebook beyond the computer screen. 'FashionLike' effectively does what Mashable calls "marry[ing] online groupthink with real-world decision making."[19] Also, as more and more companies and advertisers initiate the same kind of campaigns, creativity stands out and a greater number of people take notice of companies that position themselves as innovators.

C&A Brazil has continued to connect social media behavior with real-world actions in its marketing campaigns. In 2014, C&A launched another campaign that did just that, in a somewhat different style. Your instructor will provide you a link to images and information about the campaign.

Write a summary about the campaign. Then, describe what you think C&A's next move should be when it comes to launching another Facebook and real-world advertising effort.

Note for Teachers

Provide students with the link to "C & A Fashion Magazine Ad With Like Buttons By DM9DDB": http://www.theinspiration.com/2014/09/c-fashion-magazin-add-like-buttons-dm9ddb/

Facebook: Running a Targeted Campaign

FACEBOOK AND THE BIG PICTURE

When campaigns are initiated, they are focused on achieving a big picture goal. For many, that goal will often be to grow its brand awareness. One way to measure how close a campaign is to achieving that goal is to see how quickly its number of followers and likes is increasing. A startup will generally work on achieving this goal in-house, especially given the limited **budget** most startups have.

A larger or more established company might hire a digital marketing agency or specific in-house talent to help achieve its big picture goal. An agency will have more resources and experience than the company however, and can utilize them to make the big picture goal a reality. It is important that the digital marketer assigned to the project meets with the company executives to look at the budget, determine whether Facebook is part of a larger campaign or strategy, and then move forward.

Note: As mentioned earlier, it is advantageous for virtually all companies to incorporate Facebook into campaign strategies simply by the sheer number of people that are on that particular social network. Also, Facebook overlays demographic information that is particularly useful for pay-per-click (PPC) campaigns.

Example:
> » A digital marketer's client is Fifth Gear Automotive Supplies.
> » The campaign goal is to sell snow tires in late fall, before winter arrives.

It has been established that a portion of the client's budget will go towards launching the campaign on Facebook. Yet, to ensure that the campaign is successful, the digital marketer will also tap into offline marketing channels, as well as other social media channels to reach the company's existing and potential clientele.

However, modifications will be made to reach Fifth Gear Automotive Supplies' Facebook fans and a portion of the campaign budget will be allotted to marketing specifically on Facebook.

Note for Teachers

Provide students with the link to "Guidelines and Specs for Creating Ads": https://www. facebook.com/business/help/www/458369380926902

TIPS FOR WRITING A FACEBOOK AD

Copywriters compose text for many different online mediums. Each medium requires a different kind of voice or style, and Facebook is no exception. On Facebook, several choices are at an advertiser's disposal. He or she can write a short headline that entices a reader to check out a link to a blog or landing page. A digital marketer should also write an ad that includes a **call to action (CTA)**.

How does that digital marketer write an effective Facebook ad?

1. **Create a short, attention-grabbing headline.**

   Facebook headlines have to be short, many types of ads are limited to 25 characters. Others have an overall text restriction of 90 characters. Go to the "Guidelines and Specs for Creating Ads" on Facebook for more details. Your instructor will provide you with the link.

   Whatever the character limit, it's important to write a compelling headline. Try a question or imperative statement.

   Got your snow tires yet? – 20 characters (no spaces)

   Snow is coming! – 13 characters (no spaces)

   What happens if someone looks at your question-style headline and thinks, "Well, yes, I do have snow tires" and doesn't click on the ad? That's not a bad thing. "That's exactly what I was hoping you'd do. If you don't have the problem that my business helps people solve, then I don't want you to click on my ad because I don't want you to bring down the **conversion** rate on my landing page."[20] Your headline is another way to target your ad at the right people.

2. **Include a visual or video.**

   Copywriters aren't exactly fans of the old saying, "A picture is worth a thousand words." However, images can complement text. And, like many social media channels, Facebook is highly visual. So, along with a good headline, it's a good idea to incorporate an amazing image or video.

   For Fifth Gear Automotive Supplies, that could be of cars skidding around in an unexpected snowfall, while the car with snow tires drives through the storm smoothly.

3. **Be clear**

   It's important to get to the point in a Facebook ad. Too many flowery adjectives or too long a lead up is counterproductive. "Make sure your ad tells me what I'm going to get if I click, what problem you're going to solve, or how I'm going to end up feeling as a result of what you're offering. No more, no less."[21]

   Click here to stay safe on the roads this winter.

4. **Include a CTA**

   This concept relates back to the previous statement. There needs to be something for the potential consumer to click on. Two points to keep in mind here:

   a. Generate a sense of urgency: "Give people a reason to click your advert there and then. Don't allow them to think they'll just click it next time it appears. Limited offers and anything else that gives the reader a deadline are safe bets."[22]

   Save 20% off snow tires at Fifth Gear Automotive Supplies this weekend only!

   b. Be obvious: "Don't be afraid to include copy that may seem over-the-top obvious like 'Click here to sign up' or 'Grab your free guide here.' Lots of people need step-by-step instructions – give 'em what they need!"[23]

   Click here to get your snow tires coupon.

ACTIVITY: FINDING A FABULOUS FACEBOOK AD

Take a look at the ads on your Facebook home page or search for Facebook ad examples online. Select one that you think is fabulous. Refer to the four writing tips just outlined and note how your fabulous Facebook ad incorporates those elements. Share your example and discuss your findings.

THE BUDGETARY PIE

How much a company spends on Facebook as part of a larger campaign is very much industry- and business-dependent. In a B2C scenario, more money will tend to be spent on Facebook than in a B2B scenario. In the latter case, LinkedIn would be more likely to receive a larger slice of the budgetary pie when it comes to social media marketing.

ACTIVITY: BUDGETING FOR A FACEBOOK CAMPAIGN

For the sake of argument, let's assume that Facebook is a part of the social media marketing campaign. How much should be spent on Facebook ads?

Play the podcast and/ or give students the opportunity to read the accompanying text from Jon Loomer's "How Much Should You Budget for Facebook Ads?" http://www.jonloomer. com/2014/07/08/facebook-ads-budget-2/

QUESTIONS

Respond to the following questions based on the information your instructor provides.

1. What kinds of questions should you ask before presenting a Facebook budget?
2. What advantage do companies in the entertainment industry have over non-social industries?
3. Why is it important for a business to have a well-designed website if it is advertising on Facebook?
4. How much should be spent per Facebook fan, and what factors could affect the amount spent?
5. How should the overall Facebook campaign budget be broken up?

Answers

1. • *What are your goals?*
   • *What is your current Facebook presence?*
   • *What is your niche?*
   • *What is your product?*
   • *What is your website?*
   • *What is your customer list?*
   • *What is your time window?*[9]

2. *They can expect cost per conversion to be lower.*[10]

3. *The business will be linking from the Facebook ad to its website. If the site isn't mobile-friendly, gives incorrect information, or isn't user-friendly in anyway, it is not a good place to be sending potential clients to.*[11]

4. *$0.50 – $1; "niche, brand recognition, established presence and country"*[12]

5. *"Monthly depending on length of engagement"*[13]

Facebook: Analytics

INTRODUCTION

Once a Facebook campaign has been up and running for a reasonable period of time, the digital marketer should check and see how well it's doing. This kind of checking in shouldn't only occur once. It should happen at regular intervals during the campaign and a more comprehensive analysis should be performed once the campaign has concluded. This final analysis will enable both the marketer and client to determine what was and wasn't successful. Ideally, this information will help them both to create better, more effective campaigns in the future.

For example, let's assume a company is running a single Facebook ad (it may be a better plan to run more than one, but this assumption is made so that the analytics process can be simplified). What must be determined is how many impressions and clicks there were and what the cost per action (CPA), more commonly known as **cost per conversion**, was.

In order to understand the final section of this chapter, it is crucial that several definitions are established first:

Impression: the number of times a particular ad appears on a page (e.g. The ad appears on Facebook's sidebar, but nothing happens, it's just displayed for viewing purposes.)

Click: what happens when someone actually clicks on the ad
*What a digital marketer and/or business owner wants to happen after the 'click' is conversion.

Cost per Action (CPA): measures how much it costs in advertising to convert one person from a visitor to a client for the company. The company may pay for ten clicks for each new customer (the other nine failed to buy or take action).

ANALYTICS TOOLS

The level of sophistication required from analytics tools will vary according to the big picture goal, the complexity of the campaign, and the level of detail required by the client.

If the company is a startup, the big picture goal may simply be to increase brand awareness. The Facebook aspect of the campaign may involve merely recording the number of likes the company page received during the campaign on a downloadable spreadsheet.

However, if an ad was run for a company looking to increase sales of a particular product during a specific time period, it would be better to employ more sophisticated social media dashboard tools. That's why many companies combine Facebook Insights with tools like Google Analytics to monitor clicks and conversions.

🕐 ACTIVITY: FACEBOOK INSIGHTS FOR ANALYTICS

Earlier in this chapter, Facebook Insights was discussed in terms of how it could help digital marketers to more accurately target their ads at the right audiences. At this point, it is now appropriate to explore another way in which Facebook Insights can be a valuable tool: analyzing the success of campaigns.

Watch the video, "Facebook Insights" to discover how to utilize this social media analytics tool. Respond to the following questions in point form after the video has concluded.

1. In this video, Facebook Insights is allowing the digital marketer to see: _____.
2. How does the digital marketer limit how much information and the kind of information he sees at a particular time?
3. What is the different between organic and paid reach?
4. What is Edgerank?
5. Why is it important to get to know your fans?

Note for Teachers

Show students the video, "Facebook Insights for Analytics" (05:35), available upon request, from Mujo.

Answers

1. *Page likes, post reach, and engagement*
2. *He changes the date range of the report by toggling on the slider from left to right on both ends of the timeline*
3. • *Organic reach is the number of people the company is attracting without spending any money.*
   • *Paid reach is the number of people the company is attracting through its paid ads.*
4. *The formula used by Facebook to determine how many of your fans get to see your posts in their newsfeed (wall).*
5. *By finding out more about your fans, you'll be able to improve your targeting.*

Script: Facebook Insights for Analytics (Links are not clickable)

Slide 1: https://www.facebook.com/prlvancouver/insights/

On this Facebook page, I'm browsing to 'Insights' at the top of the page.

Slide 2: Navigating Page Insights from Left to Right

'Page Insights' roll up from left to right at the top of the page: 'Page Likes', 'Post Reach', and 'Engagement' during the last seven days.

Page Likes: https://www.facebook.com/prlvancouver/insights/?section=navLikes

'Page Likes' is pretty self-explanatory. It represents the number of people who have 'liked' or followed your page. When someone 'likes' your Facebook business page, they become a 'fan'.

Slide 3: You can change the date range of the report by toggling on the slider from left to right on both ends of the timeline.

Slides 4 and 5: Post Reach: https://www.facebook.com/prlvancouver/insights/?section=navReach

'Post Reach' refers to the number of people who have seen your post. Your post counts as 'reaching' someone when it's shown in the 'News Feed'. Figures are for the first 28 days after a post was created and include people viewing your post on desktop and mobile devices

Slide 6: Engagement:
https://www.facebook.com/prlvancouver/insights/?section=navReach&target=engagement

'Engagement' represents the unique number of people who 'liked', commented, shared, or clicked on your posts. It is highly regarded as the most important metric of the three when it comes to measuring the performance of the page.

Slides 7 and 8

Slide 9: Reach & Impressions: https://www.facebook.com/prlvancouver/insights/?section=navPosts

You can use Page Insights to learn how your audience is engaging with your posts. For example, in the 'Posts' section of your Page Insights, you can go to 'Types' to see the kinds of posts, such as, link or photo, that have the highest average reach and engagement.

'Impressions' are the number of times a post from your page is displayed, whether the post is clicked or not. People may see multiple impressions of the same post. For example, someone might see a page update in news feed once, and then a second time if a friend shares it.

'Reach' refers to the number of people who received impressions of a page post. Reach might be less than impressions because one person can see multiple impressions.

'Organic reach' is the total number of unique people who were shown your post through unpaid distribution. On the other hand, 'paid reach' is the total number of unique people who were shown your post as a result of ads.

Therefore, 'organic impressions' is the total number of times your page is displayed organically, not paid with ads.

Slide 10

Edgerank is the formula used by Facebook to determine how many of your fans get to see your posts in their newsfeed or wall. The most important factor used to determine Edgerank is user engagement. It is based on three variables: Affinity Score or Closeness, Edge Weight or Media, and Time Decay (Recency).

To put it simply, if your fans regularly engage with your content, your Edgerank will improve and more of your fans will start to see your posts in their newsfeeds. In other words, your 'reach' will increase.

And the reverse is true as well. If your fans don't engage with your page, your Edgerank will go down and fewer fans will see your future posts. In other words, your 'reach' will decrease.

Slide 11: Navigating Page Insights from Top to Bottom

'Page Insights' roll down from top to bottom from the left side navigation: 'Overview', 'Likes', 'Reach', 'Page Views', 'Posts', 'Videos', and 'People' during the last seven days.

You can change the date range of the report by toggling on the slider from left to right on both ends of the timeline.

Find the Information You Need

https://www.facebook.com/prlvancouver/insights/?section=navOverview

Slide 12: You can move between the different tabs to learn more about what's happening with your page. The overview tab gives you a seven-day snapshot of the most important activity on your page. Navigate through the other tabs to see a more detailed picture of what's going on.

Slide 13: Watch Your Audience Grow:

https://www.facebook.com/prlvancouver/insights/?section=navLikes

See how many likes your Page has gained and lost each day, and learn where on Facebook your likes are coming from.

Slide 14: Understand Your Reach:

https://www.facebook.com/prlvancouver/insights/?section=navReach

Posts that get more likes, comments, and shares show up more in news feed and are seen by more people. Posts that are hidden, reported as spam, or cause people to 'unlike' your page reach fewer people.

If you notice a sharp rise or decline, look at what you posted that day to learn more about how you might have influenced your reach.

Slide 15: See Where Your Fans Are Coming From:

https://www.facebook.com/prlvancouver/insights/?section=navVisits

See where on the Internet people are coming from to get to your page, and where on your page they're going once they arrive.

Slide 16: Compare Post Performance:

https://www.facebook.com/prlvancouver/insights/?section=navPosts

Understand how people are responding to your posts to help you create content that your audience cares about.

See how specific posts and types of posts perform so you can focus your efforts on what works.

Slide 17: Get To Know Your Fans:

https://www.facebook.com/prlvancouver/insights/?section=navPeople

Find out more about who 'likes' your page and who 'likes', comments, and shares your posts to improve your targeting.

See how they're similar or different from other people on Facebook.

ACTIVITY: GOOGLE ANALYTICS

Watch the "How to Track Facebook Ads in Google Analytics" video to discover how to utilize this social media dashboard tool. After your instructor shows you the video, respond to the following questions in point form.

1. What kind of ad is being analyzed in the video?
2. How does the digital marketer make the URL trackable in Google Analytics?
3. What did the digital marketer fill in beside each of the following:

   Campaign Source:

   Campaign Medium:

   Campaign Name:

4. After the digital marketer clicks 'Generate URL' what does he do?
5. Take a look at the final presentation slide, note down at least one thing you can learn about how the campaign performed during the specified time period.

Note for Teachers

Show students the video, "How to Track Facebook Ads in Google Analytics" (04:17), available upon request, from Mujo.

Answers

1. An ad that sends traffic to a landing page for digital marketing textbooks for the post-secondary classroom
2. He uses the URL Builder
3. Campaign Source: Facebook
   Campaign Medium: cpc
   Campaign Name: facebook_course_administrators
4. Copies the URL to his clipboard
5. Answers will vary.

Script: How to Track Facebook Ads in Google Analytics (Links are not clickable)

Slide 1: Google Analytics is a very powerful tool. It is used to collect data and analyze the traffic that comes to your website, as well as browsing activities within your website from various channels, such as organic search, paid search, direct browsing, referrals, e-mail, and social media.

Once Google Analytics tracking code is installed on every page of your website, you can pretty much see all of the browsing activities of users worldwide on your website, including any campaigns you may be running outside the Google network.

Keep in mind that this is not the same as Google AdWords campaign tracking, which does auto-tagging for you.

Facebook ads are a very popular for advertising campaigns due to the sheer number of users on Facebook. In the last quarter of 2015, Facebook passed 1.19 billion monthly active users, 874 million mobile users, and 728 million daily users.

Your Facebook ad will contain a call to action or CTA that you'll want to achieve through your digital marketing efforts. 'Learn More', 'Download Now', and 'Contact Us' buttons that users click on are CTAs. Once your ad is served on the user's timeline, it will take the user to a specific page on your website to achieve a specific goal. This goal could be anything from opting-in email addresses, or contacting the business owner for more information about products or services by submitting a form.

In this video, I'll show you how to track the traffic from your Facebook ad to your website in Google Analytics. Let's get started.

Step One: In this example, I want to boost traffic to our website and get people we care about to visit a specific landing page for course administrators from the Mujo website at the link indicated below:

http://www.mujo.com/digital-marketing-textbooks-for-the-post-secondary-classroom-and-beyond

Slides 2 and 3:

Step Two: I capture the website address or URL of the landing page as the destination page where I want to send traffic to our website. In this case, the URL is the landing page for digital marketing textbooks for the post-secondary classroom and beyond:

http://www.mujo.com/digital-marketing-textbooks-for-the-post-secondary-classroom-and-beyond

So, I copy the URL from the search bar in my browser.

Slide 4:

Step Three: I then need to make my URL trackable in Google Analytics by using the URL Builder. I could never memorize the website for Google Analytics' URL Builder, so I just Google "URL Builder" and click the matching search result.

Slide 5:

Step Four: I fill in the blanks, beginning with pasting the website URL which I have copied from my browser.

The Website URL:

http://www.mujo.com/digital-marketing-textbooks-for-the-post-secondary-classroom-and-beyond

I enter 'Facebook' for the campaign source.

'CPC' for campaign medium

'course_curriculum' for campaign term

'course_administrators_landing_page' for campaign content

And, 'facebook_course_administrators' for campaign name

I typically save this information in a spreadsheet to keep track of my URLs generated from the URL Builder.

Step Five: Click on the 'Generate URL' button and swipe your cursor to highlight the entire generated URL and press 'Ctrl-C' on your keyboard to copy the URL. The website address is then copied to your clipboard.

Slide 6:

Step Six: Paste the URL to the URL field of your 'Boost Website' Facebook campaign and complete the rest of your ad creative.

Slide 7:

Step Seven: Finally, when your ads are running, you can track the performance of your Facebook ads in Google Analytics by selecting the date range of when your ads are running from the top right corner of the page and navigating your way to Acquisition > Campaigns > All Campaigns and navigating to your Facebook 'cpc' Source / Medium campaign report.

Slide 8

TIMING IS EVERYTHING

On Facebook, there are prime posting times. Certain days and times of day will garner more attention than others. According to **Adweek**:

1. "86% of posts are published during the work week with engagement peaking on Thursday and Friday."[24]

2. "Engagement rates fall 3.5% below average for posts published Monday through Wednesday."[25]

3. "Specific Industries vary slightly, but most spike towards the end of the week."[26]

4. The best time to post is between 9 a.m. and 7 p.m., with 1 p.m. being the time when the highest number of shares happen and 3 p.m. when there are the most clicks (all numbers are approximate and variations can occur).[27]

Extension Activity 1: *Ask students to monitor their Facebook posts for a week. They should try to post on different days and at different times, but ensure that they are posting a few times during the peak periods* **Adweek** *refers to. They should see which posts are 'liked' and shared the most, and if their experience on a personal level mirrors what digital marketers might see when posting on behalf of their clients. They can share their findings with the class or submit them for homework.*

Extension Activity 2: *Ask students to look at a small business' posting history (at least three months' worth). They should note which ones got the most likes and shares. Then, they should indicate whether those posts were made during the peak periods that* **Adweek** *refers to. They can share their findings with the class or submit them for homework.*

CHAPTER REVIEW

1. What kind of things should people avoid posting on their Facebook profiles?

2. Why should companies use Facebook for marketing purposes?

3. What are three kinds of Facebook advertising mentioned in the text?

4. It is important in a call to action to generate a _____ and be _____.

5. Define the following terms:

   Impression: _____

   Click: _____

   Cost per Action (CPA): _____

Chapter Review (Optional)
The following questions can be utilized in a variety of ways (e.g. Students can complete them for homework, in class with a partner, orally in a whole-class format, etc.).

1. • Photos that are sexually suggestive or include nudity (e.g. If they wouldn't be appropriate to show a future employer, they aren't appropriate for Facebook)
   • Links to material that is sexist, racist, homophobic, or could be considered offensive or threatening to a particular group
   • 'Liking' controversial groups' pages (e.g. violent extremist organizations)
   • Making controversial statements without appropriate forethought. Because Facebook allows account holders to be spontaneous and post at every available opportunity, people sometimes do so without thinking and offend others in the process.

2. • It is the most widely used social network across the globe.
   • Facebook knows more about its account holders than any other competing channel.
   • It allows business owners and advertisers to refine their target market with absolute precision.

3. • Promoted or suggested posts
   • Right-hand column ads
   • Contest promotions

4. It is important in a call to action to generate a <u>sense of urgency</u> and be <u>obvious</u>.

5. **Impression**: the number of times a particular ad appears on a page (e.g. The ad appears on Facebook's sidebar, but nothing happens, it's just displayed for viewing purposes.)

   Click: what happens when someone actually clicks on the ad

   Cost per Action (CPA): measures how much it costs in advertising to convert one person from a visitor to a client for the company

FOOTNOTES: CHAPTER 2

1   Joss, Elizabeth. "A Beginner's Guide to Facebook Insights." Kissmetrics. 2015. Web. 02 Jul. 2015. https://blog.kissmetrics.com/guide-to-facebook-insights/.
2   Ibid.
3   Ibid.
4   "Facebook for business." Qwaya. 2015. Web. 02 Jul. 2015. http://www.qwaya.com/facebook-for-business.
5   Ibid
6   Ibid
7   Alcala, Lori. "The Smucker's Facebook Fail: How to Protect Your Brand." **CMSWire**. 06 Nov. 2014. Web. 29 Jun. 2015. http://www.cmswire.com/cms/customer-experience/the-smuckers-facebook-fail-how-to-protect-your-brand-027083.php#null.
8   Ibid.
9   Loomer, Jon. "How Much Should You Budget for Facebook Ads?" JonLoomer.com. 08 Jul. 2014. Web. 02 Sept. 2015. http://www.jonloomer.com/2014/07/08/facebook-ads-budget-2/.
10 Ibid.
11 Loomer, Jon. "How Much Should You Budget for Facebook Ads?" JonLoomer.com. 08 Jul. 2014. Web. 02 Sept. 2015. http://www.jonloomer.com/2014/07/08/facebook-ads-budget-2/.
12 Ibid.
13 Ibid.

FOOTNOTES: CHAPTER 2

1   Facebook, Inc. Facebook. 2015. Web. 25 May 2015. http://newsroom.fb.com/company-info/.
2   Zeevi, Daniel. "The Ultimate History of Facebook [INFOGRAPHIC]." Social Media Today. 21 Feb. 2013. Web. 25 May 2015. www.socialmediatoday.com/content/ultimate-history-facebook-infographic.
3   Constine, Josh. "Facebook launches Marketplace, a friendlier Craigslist." TechCrunch. 03 Oct. 2016. Web. 04 Oct. 2016. https://techcrunch.com/2016/10/03/facebook-marketplace-2/.
4   Facebook, Inc. "Stats." Facebook. 2016. Web. 04 Oct. 2016. http://newsroom.fb.com/company-info/.
5   Nanton, Nick and JW Dicks. "4 Big Ideas on How to Manage Your Online Persona." **Fast Company**. 07 Mar. 2014. Web. 06 Jul. 2015. http://www.fastcompany.com/3026514/work-smart/4-big-ideas-on-how-to-manage-your-online-image.
6   Bryan, Chandlee E. "Creating & Maintaining an Online Persona." Best Fit Forward. 2010. Web. 29 Jun. 2015. http://graduate.dartmouth.edu/docs/Creating_an_online_persona_Linked_In_Twitter_Blogging.pdf.
7   Steimle, Josh. "Should I have a Facebook Page for Business or Just Use My Personal Profile?" **Forbes**. 06 Aug. 2013. Web. 02 Jul. 2015. http://www.forbes.com/sites/joshsteimle/2013/08/06/should-i-have-a-facebook-page-for-business-or-just-use-my-personal-profile/.
8   Ibid.
9   Ibid.
10 "Facebook for business." Qwaya. 2015. Web. 02 Jul. 2015. http://www.qwaya.com/facebook-for-business.
11 Facebook, Inc. Facebook for Business. "5 Tips for Using Facebook on Small Business Saturday." Facebook. 22 Nov. 2013. Web. 02 Jul. 2015. https://www.facebook.com/business/news/5-Tips-for-Using-Facebook-on-Small-Business-Saturday.
12 Smucker Foods of Canada Corp. "About Smucker's." Smuckers. n.d. Web. 02 Jul. 2015. http://www.smuckers.ca /About-Smuckers.
13 "Social Media Fail: Smucker's." Social Media Knowledge. 26 Mar. 2015. Web. 02 Jul. 2015. http://smk.co/article/2960.
14 Karimi, Shireen. "GMO Inside: With a Social Media Policy Like Smuckers, a Comment Has to be Good...Or It's Gone." **GMO Inside**. 03 Nov. 2014. Web. 21 Dec. 2015. gmoinside.org/gmo-inside-social-media-policy-like-smuckers-comment-good-gone/.
15 Ibid.
16 "Social Media Fail: Smucker's." Social Media Knowledge. 26 Mar. 2015. Web. 02 Jul. 2015. http://smk.co/article/2960.
17 C&A, Inc. "Labels". C&A Company. n.d. Web. 03 Jul. 2015. http://www.c-and-a.com/uk/en/corporate/company/About-ca/labels/.
18 Sawers, Paul. "10 more Facebook campaigns to inspire your business." The Next Web. 11 Sept. 2013. Web. 03 Jul. 2015. http://thenextweb.com/facebook/2013/09/11/10-more-facebook-campaigns-to-inspire-your-business/.
19 Laird, Sam. "High Tech, High Fashion: Clothes Hangers Show Real-Time Facebook Likes [VIDEO]." **Mashable**. 07 May 2012. Web. 03 Jul. 2015. http://mashable.com/2012/05/08/hangers-update-facebook-likes/.
20 Pelletreau, Claire. "How to Write Facebook Ad Copy that Gets Clicks." Claire Pelletreau. 07 Aug. 2014. Web. 06 Jul. 2015. http://clairepells.com/facebook-ad-copy/.
21 Ibid.
22 Parker, Rob. "Copywriting for Facebook Ads." Voz Media. 23 May 2013. Web. 06 Jul. 2015. http://vozmedia.co.uk/copywriting-for-facebook-ads/.
23 Pelletreau, Claire. "How to Write Facebook Ad Copy that Gets Clicks." Claire Pelletreau. 07 Aug. 2014. Web. 06 Jul. 2015. http://clairepells.com//facebook-ad-copy/.
24 Bennett, Shea. "What are the Best Times to Post on #Facebook, #Twitter and #Instagram? [INFOGRAPHIC]." **Adweek**. 06 Jan. 2015. Web. 06 Jul. 2015. http://www.adweek.com/socialtimes/best-time-to-post-social-media/504222.
25 Ibid.
26 Ibid.
27 Ibid.

#3 TWITTER
MARKETING STRATEGIES

Twitter: History	Twitter: Personal	Twitter: Business	Twitter: Advertising	Twitter: Targeted Campaign	Twitter: Analytics
75	76	82	86	90	99

Twitter: History

Once upon a time, 'twitter' was something only birds did. Now, the word has become synonymous with a social network that has account holders worldwide. Back in 2006, when Jack Dorsey, Evan Williams, and Biz Stone created the social network, they could never have imagined that it would become what it is today: a source of amusing 140-character thoughts one moment, and breaking news the next.

Memorable Moments & Milestones

June 2011
Native Multimedia Sharing Introduced

September 2010
145 Million Registered Users

April 2010
Promoted Tweet Introduced

November 2008
1 Billion+ Tweets Posted

August 2007
First Hashtag Is Used

July 15, 2006
Twitter Publicly Released

January 2012
Ad Revenue in 2011 Estimated at 139 Million+ Dollars

November 6, 2013
IPO Launched

March 2, 2014
Most-Retweeted Tweet: Ellen DeGeneres' Oscar Group Selfie

January 4, 2015
Est. 500 Million Tweets Made Daily

October 6, 2015
Moments Launched

June 2, 2016
310 Million Monthly Active Users

1, 2, 3, 4, 5, 6

Twitter: Personal

TWITTER PERSONAL PROFILE PAGE NOTES

Refer to the sample Twitter page and read through the following notes.

#2: Moments:

- Gives instant access to current popular or relevant subjects on Twitter[7]

#3: Notifications:

- Tells the account holder who has followed him or her, retweeted a tweet or retweet, favorited a tweet, replied to a tweet, and mentioned the account holder in a tweet

#8: Account Holder's Statistics:

- The number of tweets the account holder has posted to date
- The number of people **the account holder is following**
- The number of people who are **followers of the account holder**

#9: Edit Profile:

- Allows the account holder to change his or her: header photo, profile photo, bio, location, website, theme color, and birthday
- Following #12, students can add their birthday and adjust **visibility** settings.

#15: Retweet:

- The account holder cannot view tweet activity when retweeting
- **d. More:** share via direct message, copy link to tweet, embed tweet (Twitter content can be added to an account holder's website or article, mute, block, and report)

#17: Who to Follow:

- This makes recommendations about what other Twitter accounts the account holder might want to follow, also listing which of the account holder's followers are already following these accounts.

#18: Tweet:

- **d. More:** share via direct message, copy link to tweet, embed tweet, pin to your profile page (tweet then appears at the top of the account holder's profile), and delete tweet

#19: Trends:

- Lists popular topics, individuals, hashtags, etc.

TWITTER PERSONAL PROFILE

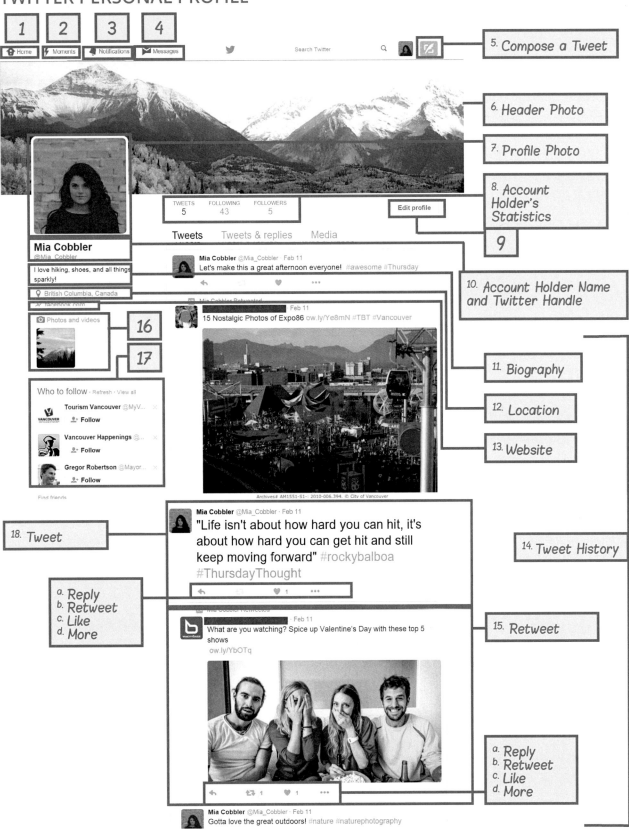

1

2

3

4

🏠 Home   ⚡ Moments   🔔 Notifications   ✉ Messages

5. Compose a Tweet

6. Header Photo

7. Profile Photo

8. Account Holder's Statistics

9

10. Account Holder Name and Twitter Handle

11. Biography

12. Location

13. Website

14. Tweet History

15. Retweet

16

17

18. Tweet

a. Reply
b. Retweet
c. Like
d. More

a. Reply
b. Retweet
c. Like
d. More

TWEETS 5   FOLLOWING 43   FOLLOWERS 5

Edit profile

Tweets   Tweets & replies   Media

Mia Cobbler
@Mia_Cobbler

I love hiking, shoes, and all things sparkly!

📍 British Columbia, Canada

📷 Photos and videos

Who to follow · Refresh · View all

Tourism Vancouver @MyV...   ✕
Follow

Vancouver Happenings @...   ✕
Follow

Gregor Robertson @Mayor...   ✕
Follow

Find friends

Mia Cobbler @Mia_Cobbler · Feb 11
Let's make this a great afternoon everyone! #awesome #Thursday

Feb 11
15 Nostalgic Photos of Expo86 ow.ly/Ye8mN #TBT #Vancouver

Archives# AM1551-S1-: 2010-006.394. © City of Vancouver

Mia Cobbler @Mia_Cobbler · Feb 11
"Life isn't about how hard you can hit, it's about how hard you can get hit and still keep moving forward" #rockybalboa #ThursdayThought
❤ 1

Feb 11
What are you watching? Spice up Valentine's Day with these top 5 shows
ow.ly/YbOTq

↻ 1   ❤ 1

Mia Cobbler @Mia_Cobbler · Feb 11
Gotta love the great outdoors! #nature #naturephotography

> Trends · Change
>
> #CanMNT
>
> #ALDS
> @theScore, @Sportsnet and 4 more are
> Tweeting about this
>
> #RCMP
> 'We failed you' — RCMP head apologizes
> for sexual harassment on the force
>
> #NationalPoetryDay
> @BlueJays and @ROMtoronto are Tweeting
> about this
>
> #thanksforgiving
>
> #ERRE
>
> #HurricaneMatthew
> @JustinTrudeau and @CBCNews are
> Tweeting about this
>
> #KinderMorgan
>
> Welland
>
> Vancouver School Board

19

TWITTER CHANGES THE WAY IT COUNTS CHARACTERS

In 2016, Twitter changed the way it counted characters. Moving forward, Twiter will no longer include the following as part of the 140-characters/tweet restriction:

- Videos

- Pictures

- GIFs

- Polls

- Quoted Tweets[8]

"Each of these items used to take up 23 characters in any given tweet. That's about 16% of each tweet."[9]

Note: In 2015, the 140-character limit on direct messages was lifted. Now, users [can] send messages up to 10,000 characters in private between themselves."[10]

Note for Teachers

Lead a whole-class discussion on the following questions. Note students' responses on the whiteboard. Some ideas that should be discussed are also listed. Later, it will be beneficial to refer back to them and make a comparison between Twitter for personal use versus business. If time permits, ask students what disadvantages Twitter has, and why they may prefer to use other social network channels.

Students can refer to the sample Twitter profile page to assist them in responding to these questions, as well.

💬 Discussion Questions

1. There is no shortage of social media networks, so why do so many people choose to be on Twitter?
2. What makes this particular channel stand out in the crowd?
3. What advantages does it have over other social networks?

Answers (Suggested Responses):

1. • *There is no faster medium for real-time communication.*

• *Hashtags organize content effectively, making it easy for people to locate information quickly. Hashtags also help people track online trends quickly and easily.*

• *Twitter has become a source of breaking news, not just frivolous content.*

2. • *"You can follow anyone and anyone can follow you. There's none of the mutual agreeing to be friends required by Facebook, so if you want to follow 500 complete strangers then that's your right." If none follow you back then it doesn't matter a jot."[1]*

• *"You only have 140 characters to say what you want to say in a tweet (excluding URLs). This means people are forced to get to the point quickly, paring the facts down to their core essence…it's surprising how much information you can consume purely from reading tweets."[2]*

3. • *A huge number of people are on Twitter. This alone makes being on it more beneficial to the account holder (i.e. increased numbers = greater value).*

• *It's a way for Twitterers to connect with celebrities. They can actually have a conversation with someone famous in real-time.*

HOW CONSUMERS INTERACT WITH BRANDS ON TWITTER

Big brands are easy to find on Twitter and many people choose to follow them. Interactions between big brands and their followers are not necessarily passive either. In addition to seeing updates about the company's latest promotion, or end-of-season sales, they can connect with the company in a very personal way.

The simplest interaction is the retweet. Why would someone 'retweet' a company tweet? Simple: the company offers an incentive. One example of this is a Twitter-based contest. A company offers a prize, but it can only be won if a consumer 'retweets' the brand's carefully composed tweet. Thus, the consumer gets a chance to win and the company gets word-of-mouth advertising online.

Another common interaction between a consumer and a brand occurs when a company solicits responses from its followers. It may be as simple as:

1. Egg nog, candy cane, or chocomint? – Pick our featured flavor! Reply to @IceIceBaby #Decembertreat

2. Got a case of the Mondays? How could @SockItToMe make your day a whole lot better? #PopUpPromo #Yourfeetdeserveit

Twitter has also become the medium of choice for some, if they are seeking quick customer service. Instead of phoning in a complaint or filling in an online form, now followers can take to Twitter. They've only got 140 characters to state their beef with a particular company, but it's amazing how succinct people can be if they have no other option. Even celebrities will complain about brands on Twitter:

Ellie Goulding (@Ellie Goulding): "On the subject of Smarties, they don't taste like they used to. In fact now they just taste gross. Genuinely disappointed."[11]

Neil Patrick Harris (@ActuallyNPH): "AT&T wifi is killing me! Had so many problems! How can our Internet be so spotty? How?!? Curses! #shakingmyfist."[12]

Patrick Stewart (@SirPatStew): "All I wanted to do was set up a new account with @TWCable_NYC but 36hrs later I've lost the will to live."[13]

🕐 ACTIVITY: RESPONDING TO CONSUMER COMPLAINTS ON TWITTER

1. Pretend that you have been given the job of responding to customer complaints on Twitter for a major brand.

2. People expect to receive a speedy response from a brand when they 'tweet' a complaint on its Twitter page. You need to create a list of five tips for dealing with these complaints so you can respond swiftly and appropriately.

3. Brainstorm some ideas with your classmates, before doing some online research. Then, create your list and be prepared to present it to the class.

Note for Teachers

Students can prepare the list of tips in class and perhaps finish it for homework (this activity would work well in a pair format). At the start of Hour Two, students can present their lists. It would be a good idea to compare them and see if all of the tips on each list are good ones and note any similarities or differences between them. A sample list of tips follows.

Note for Teachers

List of Tips:

1. *Monitor real-time mentions of the brand with social media tools using hashtags, the user name, and keywords using the company name. Companies can then proactively engage the customer on Twitter.*

2. *Create a separate Twitter account just to deal with complaints, questions, and concerns. That way, the company can reserve its main Twitter account for promotional efforts.*

3. *Acknowledge the complainer. Do not ignore complaints. Also, ensure that the person monitoring the complaints knows how to respond to them appropriately.*

4. *Encourage the complainer to communicate through another means in addition to Twitter (e.g. by phone or email). It is difficult to resolve some complaints within the constraints of a 140-character limit. People can misinterpret text responses and some complaints may be better handled out of public scrutiny.[3]*

5. *Personalize the interaction. It will often make a person feel better if he or she thinks a sympathetic individual, rather than a heartless corporation is dealing with the complaint. "That's why many organizations like TD Canada (@TD_Canada) includes photos and initials of their service reps who handle Twitter on the background of its Twitter page. Even better, it's a fun tile of them laughing, clearly enjoying their work."[4]*

Extension Activity: *Ask students to craft responses to the celebrity complaints noted in the previous section. They can read their responses aloud and other students can offer feedback and/or edits.*

Twitter: Business

THE BUSINESS OF TWITTER

As noted in the infographic at the start of this chapter, in 2016 there were 310 million monthly active users on Twitter. This alone is perhaps the most obvious reason that Twitter is useful for business purposes. Like Facebook, Twitter is certainly an effective means through which a business can reach a large audience. In additon, the vast majority of Twitter users are accessing the platform through a mobile device. As a result, businesses can reach potential customers wherever they are at any given moment.[14] In the previous section, it was also noted that Twitter can be a good medium through which companies can respond to customer complaints and generally interact with their followers in real time. Twitter has some built-in mechanisms that make this interaction easier.

Take a look at the sample business profile page and the following notes.

#18: Business Uses Hashtags:

- **Organizing and Locating Conversations:** A brand needs to be able to recall previous conversations between the company (itself) and customers, as well as organize those conversations. The 'hashtag' allows customers to engage in this process.

#19: Business Thanks and Responds to Followers:

- **Thanking a Follower:** A couple of ways exist within Twitter to do this effectively. The first involves the mention. A business can include the follower's Twitter handle in its tweet, thanking him or her for a retweet, for example. Mentions are also useful if a company wants to ask a follower a question or bring his or her attention to something in particular. Another way to thank a follower is to 'like' a tweet.
- **Responding to a Follower:** Engaging in conversation with a follower is simple. All a business needs to do is click 'reply'.

TWITTER BUSINESS PROFILE

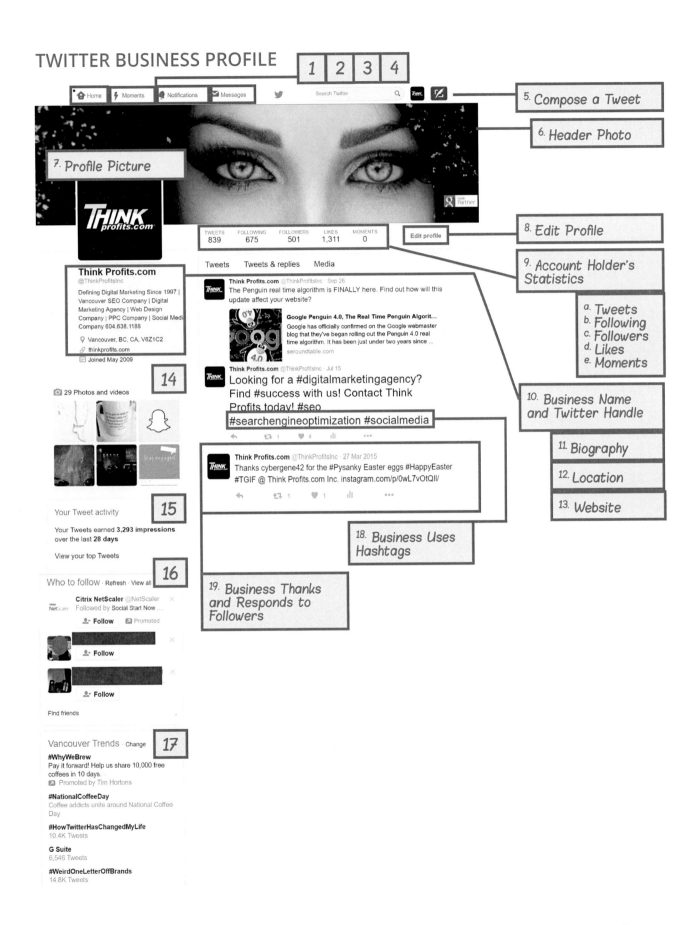

1 2 3 4

5. Compose a Tweet

6. Header Photo

7. Profile Picture

8. Edit Profile

9. Account Holder's Statistics

a. Tweets
b. Following
c. Followers
d. Likes
e. Moments

10. Business Name and Twitter Handle

11. Biography

12. Location

13. Website

14

15

16

17

18. Business Uses Hashtags

19. Business Thanks and Responds to Followers

MORE ABOUT HASHTAGS

It is important for a business to track discussions about relevant topics. A brand can interject a thought or pose a question in the context of these discussions, thus raising its profile and giving it an opportunity to further promote its products and/or services.

A business can also utilize a popular hashtag to promote its products and/or services. This can also be an effective way to pick up followers. However, it is important for a company to fully understand *why* a hashtag is popular. Not doing so, and hitching a ride along with a hashtag merely because it's gotten a bit of attention, can have disastrous results, as will be demonstrated in a Twitter fail example in the upcoming 'Twitter: Advertising Section'.

Any content a company attaches to a particular hashtag must be relevant to it. A brand will be entering into an established conversation, so its contribution can't stick out like a sore thumb. It would often be ideal for the brand to enter such conversations in an informational capacity and then market within that.

THE ESSENCE OF AN EFFECTIVE TWEET

Note for Teachers

Go through the Indigo Chapters example with students first, before discussing "The Essence of an Effective Tweet" (See 'Activity: Creating a Great Tweet').

An effective tweet must, in essence, be a hook. It must compel the reader to click on it. He or she needs to check out the link because it is so intriguing that it is impossible to resist the urge to read further and/or learn more about the content being presented. However, while it is great that a brand can participate in a discussion and inform a reader, its primary goal is conversion. Within one or two steps, it needs to link from the discussion to its conversion point.

🕐 ACTIVITY: CREATING A GREAT TWEET

1. Scroll through your Twitter feed.

2. Find a compelling tweet from a business that contains a link.

3. Click on the link. Locate a conversion point somewhere within the linked content, if there is one.

4. Note down why you found the tweet compelling. What motivated you to click on the link? Was it the text, image, or both?

5. Describe where that link led you.

Students could be asked to hand in this information, present it to the class, share with a partner, or a combination of all three.

EXAMPLE:

Business: Indigo Chapters @chaptersindigo

Tweet: "Red Notice is a compelling real-life thriller about an American financier #HeathersPicks indg.ca/74pX"[15]

Why the tweet was compelling: The text in the tweet wasn't particularly compelling, but the quotation from a reviewer next to the book's picture was:

"'A tale that makes the dirty dealings of **House of Cards** look like Snow White.'"

-**The Toronto Star**[16]

6. Indicate where the conversion point was and describe it.

It was clever of @chaptersindigo to include this quotation with the image of the book because it presents readers with two familiar references that they can now associate with the unfamiliar product the company is selling. Also, the stark juxtaposition between the two references is provocative. Thus, this is probably motivation enough for most readers to click on the link.

There were two conversion points when the link is clicked. The first was not, as might have been expected, a link to buy the book itself. Instead a box pops up and asks the Twitterer to:

"Get in on a Good Thing! **Yes! Sign me up** to receive emails from Indigo about exclusive offers, the newest and best in books, gifting & much more."[17]

Thus, the brand solicits the account holder's email address so it can continue to have additional conversion opportunities through **email marketing**, as well as Twitter. Then, once the account holder closes the box, the second conversion point to purchase the book is accessible.

Extension Activity: Ask students to create an effective tweet. It needs to have a hook (text and/ or image). Students should also describe what it would link to and the conversion point(s).

Twitter: Advertising

TWITTER FAILS AND WINS: CELEBRITY EDITION

Celebrities are brands. A large part of their earning capacity comes from their ability to maintain a certain public persona; anything that could tarnish that image should be avoided at all costs. Alternatively, anything that could boost a celebrity's profile is definitely sought after. In the following case studies, Twitter is the medium through which one celebrity's reputation took a serious nose dive, but the show of another became more popular than ever.

TWITTER FAIL

👓 CASE STUDY: Bill Cosby and "Meme Me!"

On November 10th, 2014, Bill Cosby, or someone in his employ, made a massive Twitter fail. The infamous tweet, "Go ahead. Meme me!"[18] was posted and accompanied by a meme generator link. Followers of the comedian could find 12 photos on Cosby's website that they could add text to and 'tweet'. "The memes had to be submitted for approval, but unfortunately for Cosby's PR team, most internet users know how to take a screenshot."[19] The result was a series of memes referencing allegations that the former TV dad had drugged and raped a series of women. For instance:

"14 Allegations of Rape?! Zipzopzubittybop! #CosbyMeme"[20]

"My two favorite things Jello pudding & rape #CosbyMeme"[21]

A few weeks prior to the "Meme Me!" debacle, Cosby and rape allegations were the subject of a comedy routine by Hannibal Buress. This routine went viral, making the allegations much more present in public consciousness than they had been in some time. Thus, this begs the question as to why Cosby or his people created a Twitter campaign that made them vulnerable to such attacks.

Two important takeaways from the Cosby Twitter disaster are:

1. Know what is being said about a brand online **before** initiating any social media campaign.

2. Get into the mindset of the target audience. What are all the possible ways people could respond to a particular strategy? If there is **any** possibility that the campaign could elicit some negative responses, is it really a good idea to launch it?

TWITTER WIN

ᴗᴗ CASE STUDY: Jimmy Kimmel and Mean Tweets

Jimmy Kimmel's mean tweets is one of the many successful social media-based segments of his late night talk show. Initially, Kimmel created the spot in anticipation of Twitter's sixth birthday. The concept was an ingenious, but relatively simple one. Kimmel's staff would scan Twitter to find mean tweets about celebrities and select one or two for each celebrity to read on air. The tweets could range from funny with a bit of mean rolled in:

"If you change the 'i' in Anna Faris' last name to a 't', you get 'Anna Farts.' Interesting."[22]

to a straight-up ouch:

"Dear God, give us 2pac back and we'll give you Justin Bieber"[23]

The mean tweets segment became hugely popular, with the original, also posted on YouTube, getting more than 41 million views.[24] Kimmel continued to air new mean tweets segments, adding ones focused on music acts, pro athletes, and even U.S. President Barack Obama. Soon, other people started posting their own mean tweets videos—professors reading mean tweets from their students and sports teams reading angry comments from their fans.

Takeaways from the Kimmel's success with mean tweets:

1. Learn what the target audience wants and give it to them. Prior to their exit from late night TV, competing talk show hosts David Letterman and Jay Leno were attracting a smaller share of the 18 – 49 demographic than Kimmel was.[25] Consequently, he knew that this more tech-savvy age group would respond to a Twitter-based bit on the show. For digital marketers, this is where doing an accurate buyer persona profile is a key activity before a campaign launch.

2. Be different, especially on social media. So many Twitter campaigns focus on 'retweeting' nice messages about a company and its products, when much of the Twitterverse is a very negative place. Kimmel shines a light on that aspect of the social network, making his segment seem more reflective of social media reality, rather than a sanitized version of it.

⏰ ACTIVITY: FINDING TWITTER WINS AND FAILS

Do some online research to find two companies who have utilized Twitter for marketing purposes. One company must have come up with a winning strategy, and the other an unsuccessful one. Refer back to the celebrity marketing examples on Twitter, and the examples of Facebook marketing wins and fails.

Include the following for the winning Twitter campaign:

1. The name of the company
2. The name of the campaign
3. The goal of the campaign
4. A description of the campaign
5. Facts that support the assertion that the campaign was successful
6. An explanation as to why the campaign was successful

Include the following for a Twitter campaign that failed:

1. The name of the company
2. The name of the campaign (if applicable)
3. The goal of the campaign
4. A description of the campaign
5. Facts that support the assertion that the campaign was a failure
6. An explanation as to why the campaign failed

Then, note what social media marketers can take away from both the winning campaign and the failed campaign. Discuss.

EXAMPLE OF A WINNING TWITTER CAMPAIGN:	EXAMPLE OF A FAILED TWITTER CAMPAIGN:
1. LG	1. DiGiorno Pizza
2. LG Ticket Hunter	2. N/A
3. "Boost smartphone sales amongst 16-24 year-olds."[26]	3. Promote its brand and sell more pizzas
4. "LG would set out a stall in a UK city and the first person to get to their stall won two tickets to a high profile concert. To help users and the stall, LG placed a map online that gradually zoomed in on the precise location whenever the hashtag #lgtickethunter was used."[27]	4. #WhyIStayed was a trending hashtag. DiGiorno didn't know why the hashtag was so popular, but decided to capitalize on that popularity and use it to promote its product anyway. The company 'tweeted':"'#whyistayed You had pizza.'"[29]
5. Day One: 5000 tweets, end of campaign: 50,000 Engagement rates: 38% from sponsored links Smart phone sales in target market: quadrupled after campaign end[28]	5. The company received many negative replies on Twitter that continued to keep rolling in once the tweet was pulled.
6. The challenge was fun and competitive. The prizes motivated people to participate.	6. It wasn't really a campaign. The company was just piggybacking on a popular hashtag. What it didn't check was the context that that hashtag referred to. In this case, it was domestic violence and a recent scandal involving domestic violence.

Social media marketers can learn to be inventive from the LG campaign. An exciting, somewhat unusual campaign will catch the attention of the target audience. Also, really good incentives, like highly desirable prizes will encourage members of that audience to participate. On the other hand, DiGiorno Pizza's Twitter fail teaches digital marketers not to initiate any kind of promotional effort online without first knowing exactly what they are getting into (e.g. know what a hashtag means).

Twitter: Running a Targeted Campaign

GETTING STARTED

Twitter, as has been discussed in previous sections, is all about conversation. Unlike some other social media channels, conversations can occur in near realtime. A company needs to understand that before it enters the Twitterverse. Its Twitter presence will be shaped largely by how it fits into the Twitter dialogue.

Most businesses will find establishing and maintaining a Twitter presence beneficial:

- **A startup company or a company without a Twitter presence:** brand awareness goal
    - » This can be accomplished through acquiring followers.
    - » A company can gain followers by directly marketing to its target audience (e.g. through promotions, specials, etc.).
- **An established company with followers:** goal is to maintain a positive image with its customer base and increase that base.
    - » A business can accomplish this by remaining in-the-know about what its customers are saying.
    - » It should also look at who else its followers are following. That way, it can interject, when appropriate, into threads. This tactic may result in more traffic, but it will certainly ensure that the business stays up-to-date on other happenings within the industry.

TWITTER CARDS

Imagine a cake. Ideally, it's a beautiful baked good that looks delicious. However, a cake that just looks delicious, but tastes terrible isn't much of a dessert. Good ingredients, on the other hand, make it taste as wonderful as it looks. In other words, the ingredients are more important than the cake's appearance. A Twitter card is kind of like a delicious looking cake. Of course, the card needs to look great. However, the ingredients in the Twitter Ads campaign, are, like the cake, more important than the appearance of the card. Those ingredients are essentially mechanisms through which a company reaches people, which is commonly referred to as a call to action [CTA].

What follows is an examination of this beautifully decorated piece of social marketing. However, in subsequent sections, the focus turns to what goes into making the Twitter card a marketing success. Also, consider that a good social media marketer will spend about ten minutes making a Twitter card, but an hour or more building the guts of the Twitter Ads campaign behind the scenes.

WHAT IS A TWITTER CARD?

It is an ad with several variations, including this example of a 'summary card with large image':

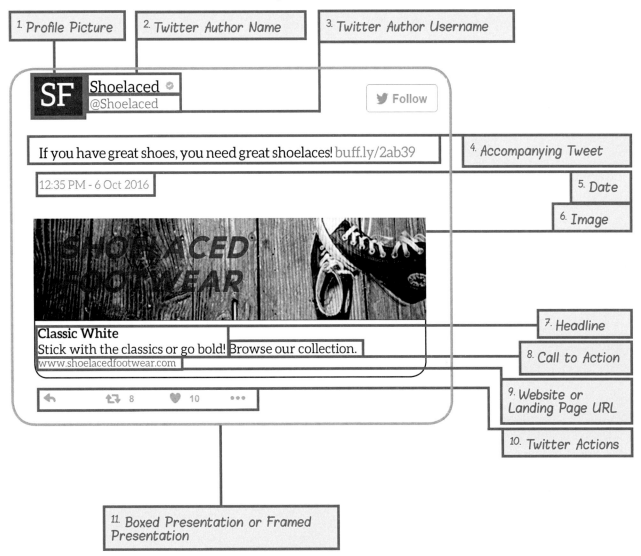

People can tell that it's an ad because of the boxed presentation, which along with the increased size, makes the ad stand out in the account holder's feed or timeline. This Twitter card also includes a big picture. Twitter emphasizes the importance of the images business account holders choose by stating, "Your card image communicates the value of your business and your offer."[30]

Different Twitter cards have different characteristics (text only, text and image, video, etc.) and restrictions, (headline/title length, image size, etc.). To learn more about the various card choices, consult Twitter's "Getting Started Guide". Your instructor will provide you with the link.

Note for Teachers

Provide students with the link to the: "Getting Started Guide": https://dev.twitter.com/cards/getting-started

A TWITTER CARD IS JUST AN ADVERTISEMENT?

As was noted earlier, growing a business' social media presence, getting followers and encouraging them to engage are often the goals of a Twitter Ads campaign, particularly for small businesses. This is not to say that a major brand could not benefit from this type of campaign. It could certainly be integrated in to generate buzz about a particular promotion or event. In addition, Twitter cards can be used to sell and generate leads, which along with other campaign efforts, may increase a business' bottom line.

Also mentioned earlier, marketers can integrate photos and videos into Twitter cards. When a business owner shares a Twitter card, images and multimedia can drive traffic to the company website. According to Twitter, all a business owner needs to do is "simply add a few lines of HTML to [his or her] webpage, and users who Tweet links to [the] content will have a 'Card' added to the Tweet that's visible to all of their followers."[31]

WHERE DO THEY APPEAR?

Twitter cards appear in account holders' timelines. A marketer will want to target specific people in a Twitter campaign. This naturally implies that demographic research will be done prior to the targeting process in order to find the best audience for a campaign. Also, hashtags, and keywords, which can be linked to particular interests, will be part of a well-targeted Twitter Ads campaign as well.

PEOPLE

- Competitors' followers
- Influential individuals, those with lots of followers and a significant social media presence

HASHTAGS

In earlier sections, it was established that hashtags help to organize information and make it easier to find. They enable brands to locate where their business has been mentioned, and help them to track online trends. What follows are two types of hashtags than can be useful to business owners and marketers:

- **Product-related**
    - » People look for familiar product tags. They also include them in their posts. When a

business posts its products, it needs to put itself in the consumer's mindset and use hashtags that connect its products and market.[32] For example, a cosmetics company might utilize the hashtag #lipstick to promote a new color. Or, a stationery store might use the hashtag #printerpaper, and so forth.

- **Trending** (those that represent trending topics)
    - » Ideally linked to events that are relevant to the campaign focus
    - » Obviously these will need to be monitored, as hashtags can be generated in a matter of seconds and can easily gain or lose momentum, but this is key if the marketer is to take full advantage of the platform

Note: Hashtags linked to trending topics can be especially beneficial to media and news organizations. They are useful mechanisms around which to organize tweets that focus on particular subjects.

KEYWORDS

- In order to understand how keywords function in Twitter advertising versus **Search Engine Optimization (SEO)**-based advertising, it is important to make a basic differentiation between how people interact with Twitter and Google. When an individual goes on Twitter, his or her purpose is generally to communicate, whereas on Google it is to find something.

- Thus, keywords on Twitter represent what people are 'tweeting' about, rather than searching for on Google (this is one way in which a Twitter Ads campaign differs from an SEO-based one). Therefore, a campaign's keywords should reflect what a business' audience is 'tweeting' about, as opposed to what a company would like them to be searching for.

Refer to Twitter's "Keyword Targeting" guide for more information about how to select keywords. Your instructor will provide you with the link.

TWITTER CARDS STEP-BY-STEP PROCESS

The following is a basic outline of what is involved in creating a Twitter card. It is important to remember that for a Twitter Ads campaign to be successful the copy written, image(s), and/or video(s) chosen must be attention-grabbing and compelling. Also, Twitter itself is always changing, so it is best to review current guidelines before initiating a campaign.

1. Sign in to "Twitter Ads" (a Twitter account is required).

Note for Teachers

Provide students with the link to "Keyword Targeting": https://business.twitter.com/help/keyword-targeting *and the link to "Twitter Ads":* https://ads.twitter.com/login *for the next activity.*

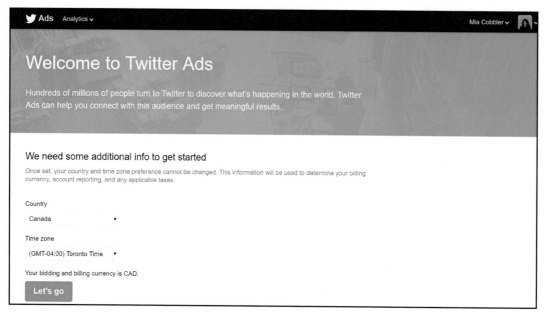

2. Select a campaign objective.

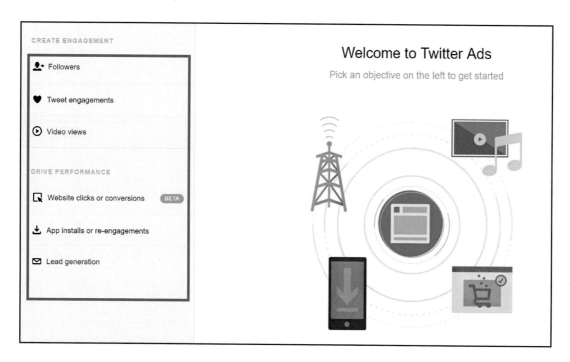

3. Enter the campaign name and dates.

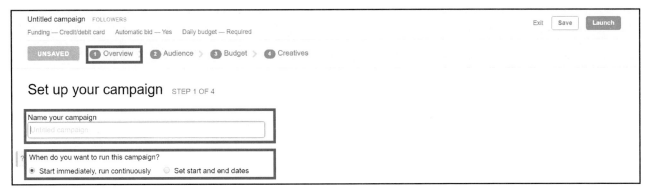

4. Select your audience.

Note: 'Add Interests' is a critical audience feature.

Anyone who has a Twitter account will notice that there are recommendations provided by the platform about who to follow. Also, ads will appear in a user's feed based on who or she already follows, searches for, likes, etc. Twitter shows account holders these ads and makes specific recommendations in the hope that it is presenting something the user is interested in, but hasn't found yet. This can be likened to a friend who knows you like Indian food because you have mentioned it in previous conversations. That friend gives you recommendations for Indian restaurants nearby, as a result.

Adding the right interests is key when it comes to ensuring that a campaign is appropriately targeted, and ultimately successful. When setting up a Twitter campaign, 'Interests refers to categories that might be attractive to certain kinds of followers that the campaign wants to target. According to the platform, "interest categories increase potential reach. We will target users interested in **any** of the categories you enter."[33]

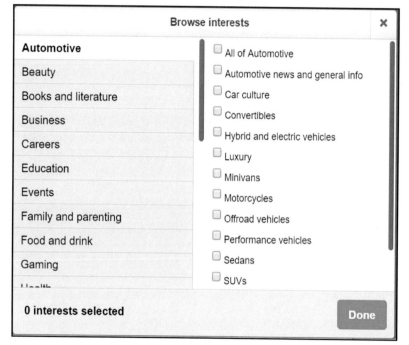

Extension Activity: Ask students to read "Twitter brands can now target ads based on the emoji you use": http://thenextweb.com/twitter/2016/06/15/twitter-brands-can-now-target-ads-based-emoji-use/#gref

Ask each student to select three emojis that could be tweeted out. Students could trade emojis with each other and answer the following question:

What kind of brands might want to advertise to the user who used each emoji (e.g. a broken heart emoji = ads for Tinder, ice cream, etc.)? Students can share responses.

5. Set your budget.

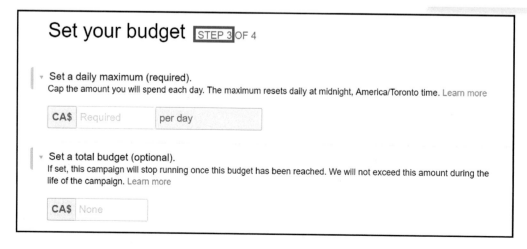

6. Choose your creatives.

⏱ ACTIVITY: MAKING A TWITTER ADS CAMPAIGN

The following activity does not involve the creation of an actual Twitter Ads campaign. It simply requires that you go through some of the steps in the process. However, if you were to actually create a campaign, it would be important to keep in mind that Twitter is a truly mobile-friendly platform. This must be taken into consideration **before** the components in any Twitter Ads campaign are assembled.

1. With a classmate(s), create a fictional B2C company.

2. Describe one product or service the company produces in a detailed paragraph. The paragraph should include:

   a. The target audience for the product or service

   b. The cost of the product or service

3. Describe a campaign focused on that product or service. The campaign should be easily relatable to an event or seasonal activity. Also, describe the message you will include to get the potential customer to respond to your CTA (i.e. describe how you'd like everything to look and function).

4. Create a mock-up of a Twitter card. Select a text-based or text- and image-based card type (e.g. the summary card, summary card with large image, etc.).

5. Note to whom you would target the campaign (Refer to Step 2 and think about the demographic features of your competitors' followers).

6. Note which hashtag(s) you could align your campaign with at the moment, if possible. Otherwise, if there are no trending hashtags, create product- or service-related hashtags. Remember: as you learned from the DiGiorno example, it is prudent to do some investigation as to how a particular hashtag is used because it can have negative connotations. See the notation that follows for some tools you can use to find hashtags.

7. List at least 20 keywords that you think your target audience would use in everyday speech.

8. Present your Twitter card and explain who you would target with your campaign.

Note: Finding Hashtags

1. Your best starting point is to look at Twitter itself and see what is on the list of current trending hashtags. Also, the search function will help uncover hashtags as well.

2. Trendsmap
This site allows people to see which hashtags are trending and breaking in regions around the world. You can look at the map and see trends in the region you are targeting. Registered users are able to obtain city-specific trends.

3. RiteTag
RiteTag requires people to sign up to use its service. The app can be used for Twitter, Facebook, Google+, and more. In its introductory tutorial, the site outlines a number of features, such as the ability to:

- Click on a word in a tweet and see what the currently associated hashtags with that word are,

- Click a hashtag in a post to see regularly updated impressions, retweetability, etc., and

- Get the hashtags most likely to result in link clicks, sharing, and views.[34]

Note for Teachers

Provide students with the link to "Trendsmap": http://trendsmap.com and the link to "RiteTag": https://ritetag.com

Twitter: Analytics

INTRODUCTION

Analytics for Twitter is internally-based. Unlike some other social media channels (e.g. Pinterest), Twitter offers its analytics to anyone with a personal or business account, rather than only to those with the latter. Once an account holder installs Twitter Analytics he or she arrives at a dashboard that allows him or her to access a plethora of information via 'Home', 'Tweets', and 'Audiences'. These three sections will be examined in-depth.

HOME

28 day summary with change over previous period

Tweets	Tweet impressions	Profile visits	Mentions	Followers
4 ↓42.9%	248 ↓66.9%	68 ↓54.7%	1 ↓50.0%	174 ↓-2

What the account holder sees at the top of the 'Home' dashboard is a summary of his or her activity on Twitter over the last 28 days. This is represented by the numbers in black. The numbers in red serve as a comparison to the previous 28-day summary of the account holder's activity. Now, in examining the example from left to right, it is clear that:

- The account holder has been tweeting significantly less.

- Her tweets have been appearing less frequently in other users' Twitter feeds.

- Fewer people have checked out her profile.

- The number of times the account holder's handle (e.g. @handle) was mentioned by other users (e.g. in a reply) has gone down.

- The account holder has lost two followers during this period.

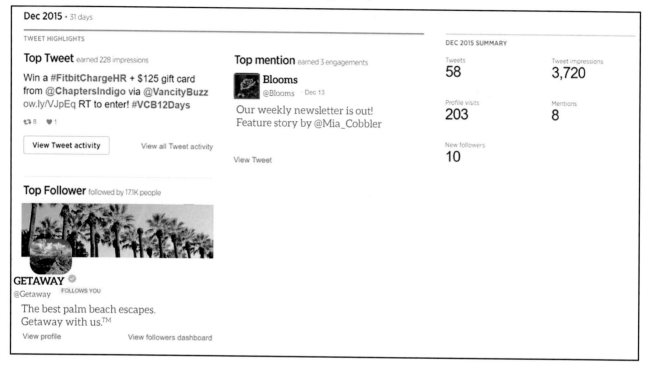

The account holder also receives 'tweet highlights' and a summary for every month. In this December 2015 example, the following is clear from the highlights:

- The account holder's top tweet earned 228 impressions, was retweeted eight times, and liked once.

- The top follower (in terms of the number of people following the account) was Getaway.

- The top mention was by Blooms, which earned three engagements.

The summary in this example shows:

- The account holder is engaging new individuals (e.g. She has received ten new followers).

- People are interested enough in her tweets to go further and visit her profile.

- The account holder tweeted at the rate of almost two tweets per day.

TWEETS (TWEET ACTIVITY)

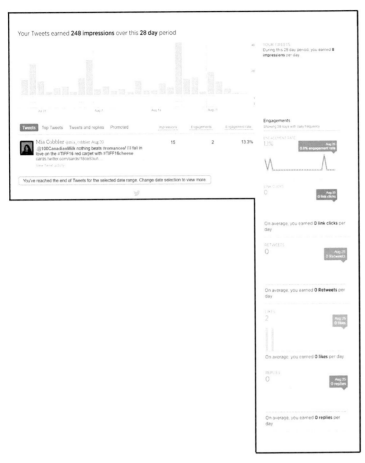

The purpose of the 'Tweets' section is to show the account holder how each tweet performed. The August 20th example demostrates this, as it shows Mia Cobbler the number of impressions and engagments the tweet has garnered, as well as its engagement rate. Twitter generates the engagement rate by taking the number of engagements and dividing them by the number of impressions.[35]

The graph above the example demonstrates how the rest of Mia Cobbler's tweets have performed in terms of impressions over a 28-day period. The time period can be adjusted to cover a longer date range if the account holder wishes.

The rest of the data on the far right compares Mia's August 20th performance in terms of link clicks, retweets, likes, and replies with her average Twitter activity in each of these respective areas.

AUDIENCES

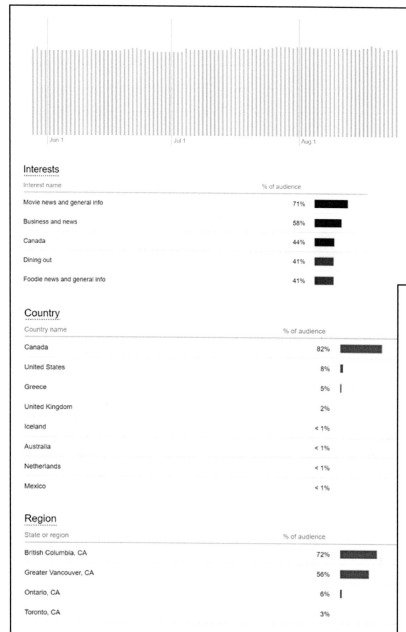

The 'Audiences' section of Twitter Analytics is designed to give the account holder more information about his or her followers. In this example, it is obvious from the top graph and its accompanying information that this account holder has had almost the same number of followers for the last three months.

The account holder also learns that she has 12% more female followers than male followers. The vast majority of her followers are interested in 'movie news and general info.', come from Canada, and live in British Columbia.

It is also possible for all account holders to "benchmark [their] audience against the average Twitter user, [their] tailored audiences, and other significant groups."[36]

Note for Teachers

Provide students with the link to "Twitter Account Analytics": https://analytics.twitter.com/

🕐 ACTIVITY: CHECK THE PULSE OF YOUR TWITTER ACCOUNT

Log in to your personal account. Find the following information:

1. **Your 28-day summary:** How many tweets did you post? How many impressions and profile visits did your tweets generate? How many followers did you lose or gain?

2. **Your tweet highlights last month:** What was your top tweet? How many engagements and link clicks did it receive?

3. **Your tweet highlights from the last six months:** Which month was your best in terms of profile visits? Number of new followers? Who was your top follower?

Discuss this information with a classmate(s), including why you think that certain months your Twitter profile got more clicks than others.

ANALYTICS FOR TWITTER CARDS

Twitter Ads are the same as **pay per click (PPC)**. In other words, every time someone clicks on a Twitter card it costs money. Promoted tweets can cost as little as tens of cents and as much as ten-plus dollars. This type of digital marketing tends to be cost-effective. Like other PPC platforms, Twitter Ads only charges per click. This means that when building a campaign, a marketer's objective is to make certain that the right people are clicking on the campaign. Not only does this ensure that a business is attracting the right audience, but it also keeps costs under control.

Read through 'Twitter Cards Analytics' to see what information account holders can receive about the performance of their campaigns. Your instructor will provide you with the link.

Note for Teachers

Provide students with the link to "Twitter Card Analytics": https://business.twitter.com/en/help/campaign-measurement-and-analytics/twitter-card-analytics-dashboard.html

Social Media Strategy Project

Guidelines

At this point, it is appropriate for instructors to go through the requirements for the students' final project. Then, the example project, along with the video interview, should be presented. Any remaining time can be used for students to research small businesses they might like to approach for an interview (students should be sure to select businesses with some social media presence).

CHAPTER REVIEW

1. How are most people accessing Twitter (e.g. via desktop or mobile device)?

2. What are two important takeaways from the Cosby Twitter disaster mentioned in this chapter?

3. What goal is a startup company likely to have on Twitter?

4. What two types of hashtags can be useful to business owners and marketers in a Twitter Ads campaign?

5. In Twitter analytics, what does 'tweet impressions' mean?

Chapter Review (Optional)

The following questions can be utilized in a variety of ways (e.g. Students can complete them for homework, in class with a partner, orally in a whole-class format, etc.).

1. *Via a mobile device*

2. *• Know what is being said about a brand online before initiating a social media campaign.*

   • Get into the mindset of the target audience.

3. *Increasing brand awareness*

4. *Product-related, trending*

5. *It refers to the number of times an account holder's tweets appeared in other users' news feeds.*

FOOTNOTES: CHAPTER 3

1   Parrack, Dave. "7 Reasons Why You Should Be Using Twitter." MakeUseOf. 03 Apr. 2013. Web. 17 Jul. 2015. http://www.makeuseof.com/tag/7-reasons-why-you-should-be-using-twitter/.
2   Ibid.
3   Berry, Megan. "5 Tips for Dealing with Complaints on Twitter." Mashable. 13 Aug. 2010. Web. 17 Jul. 2015. mashable.com/2010/08/13/twitter-complaints-tips.
4   McGovern, Michele. "3 great ways to handle customer complaints on Twitter." Customer Experience Insight. 16 Jan. 2015. Web. 17 Jul. 2015. www.customerexperienceinsight.com/3-top-ways-to-handle-customer-complaints-on-twitter/.

FOOTNOTES: CHAPTER 3

1   Casti, Taylor. "The History of Twitter, from Egg to IPO." *Mashable Infographic*. 04 Oct. 2013. Web. 09 Jul. 2015. http://mashable.com/2013/10/04/history-twitter/.

2   Hernandez, Brian Anthony. "Twitter Rewind: Big Highlights from 2012 to 2006." *Mashable Infographic*. 21 Mar. 2012. Web. 09 Jul. 2015. http://mashable.com/2012/03/21/history-of-twitter-timeline/.

3   Stricker, Gabriel. "The 2014 #YearOnTwitter." Twitter. 10 Dec. 2014. Web. 9 Jul. 2015. https://blog.twitter.com/2014/the-2014-yearontwitter.

4   Smith, Craig. "By the Numbers: 150+ Amazing Twitter Statistics." DMR. 05 Jun. 2015. Web. 09 Jul. 2015. http://expandedramblings.com/index.php/march-2013-by-the-numbers-a-few-amazing-twitter-stats/10/.

5   Newton, Casey. "Twitter launches Moments, its dead-simple tab for browsing the best tweets." The Verge. 06 Oct. 2015. Web. 05 Oct. 2016. http://www.theverge.com/2015/10/6/9457267/twitter-moments-project-lightning.

6   Frier, Sarah. "Snapchat Passes Twitter in Daily Usage." Bloomberg. 02 Jun. 2016. Web. 05 Oct. 2016. https://www.bloomberg.com/news/articles/2016-06-02/snapchat-passes-twitter-in-daily-usage.

7   Twitter, Inc. "About Moments." Twitter. 2016. Web. 28 Sept. 2016. https://support.twitter.com/articles/20174546.

8   Lui, Kevin. "Twitter's Revamped Character Limit is Finally Here." *Time*. 19 Sept. 2016. Web. 05 Oct. 2016. http://time.com/4488924/twitter-revamped-140-character-limit-unveiled/.

9   Ibid.

10 Ibid.

11 Jefferson, Whitney. "24 Utterly Annoying Celebrity Complaints on Twitter." BuzzFeed. 12 Jun. 2013. Web. 17 Jul. 2015. http://www.buzzfeed.com/whitneyjefferson/24-celebrity-complaints-on-twitter#.cy83ey1YK6.

12 Ibid.

13 Heaney, Katie. "Spare Us Your Customer Service Complaint Tweets." BuzzFeed. 03 Apr. 2013. Web. 17 Jul. 2015. http://www.buzzfeed.com/katieheaney/spare-us-your-customer-service-complaint-tweets#.qsAQnA8Pzo.

14 Twitter, Inc. "Learn Twitter." Twitter. 2015. Web. 20 Jul. 2015. https://business.twitter.com/basics/learn-twitter.

15 Indigo Chapters (@chaptersindigo). "Red Notice is a compelling real-life thriller about an American financier #HeathersPicks indg.ca/74pX." 20 Jul. 2015. 3:25 p.m. Tweet.

16 Indigo Chapters (@chaptersindigo). "'A tale that makes the dirty dealings of *House of Cards* look like Snow White.'" 20 Jul. 2015. 3:25 p.m. Tweet.

17 Indigo. "Red Notice: A True Story." Indigo. 2015. Web. 20 Jul. 2015. https://www.chapters.indigo.ca/en-ca/red-notice-a-true-story/9781476755717-item.html?s_campaign=Indigo.Social.Twitter:HeathersPicks@s_campaign=Indigo.Social.Twitter:.

18 Harmann, Margaret. "Bill Cosby Asks Internet to 'Meme' Him; Twitter Responds With Rape Allegations." *Vulture: Devouring Culture*. 10 Nov. 2014. Web. 10 Jul. 2015. http://www.vulture.com/2014/11/bill-cosby-asks-for-memes-twitter-focus-on-rape.html.

19 Ibid.

20 Paunescu, Delia. "Bill Cosby's massive social media fail." *New York Post*. 10 Nov. 2014. Web. 10 Jul. 2015. http://nypost.com/2014/11/10/bill-cosby-twitter-hasthag-meme-immediately-backfired/.

21 Ibid.

22 Jimmy Kimmel Live, "Celebrities Read Mean Tweets #1." *YouTube*. Online Video Clip, https://www.youtube.com/watch?v=RRBoPveyETc (accessed 10 Jul. 2015).

23 Jimmy Kimmel Live, "Celebrities Read Mean Tweets #2." *YouTube*. Online Video Clip, https://www.youtube.com/watch?v=Hcmz74AaXHs (accessed 16 Jul. 2015).

24 Ibid

25 Rawden, Jessica. "Jimmy Kimmel Live Continues to Improve in the Ratings." *Cinema Blend*. 2013. Web. 10 Jul. 2015. http://www.cinemablend.com/television/Jimmy-Kimmel-Live-Continues-Improve-Ratings-51316.html.

26 Hawes, Alex. "5 Intriguing Twitter Marketing Case Studies." Our Social Times. 15 Jul. 2013. Web. 13 Jul. 2015. http://oursocialtimes.com/5-intriguing-twitter-marketing-case-studies/.

27 Ibid.

28 Ibid.

29 Griner, David. "DiGiorno Is Really, Really Sorry About Its Tweet Accidentally Making Light of Domestic Violence." *Adweek*. 09 Sept. 2014. Web. 13 Jul. 2015. http://www.adweek.com/adfreak/digiorno-really-really-sorry-about-its-tweet-accidentally-making-light-domestic-violence-159998.

30 Twitter, Inc. "Card Content." Twitter. 2015. Web. 29 Jul. 2015. ads.twitter.com.

31 —. "Twitter Cards." Twitter. 2015. Web. 22 Jul. 2015. http://dev.twitter.com/cards/overview.

32 Bunskoek, Krista. "How to Market Your Business & Content." Wishpond. 2015. Web. 05 Aug. 2015. http://blog.wishpond.com/post/62253333766/3-key-hashtag-strategies-how-to-market-your-business.

33 Twitter, Inc. "Followers." Twitter. 2015. Web. 29 Jul. 2015. ads.twitter.com.

34 RiteTag. "About RiteTag." RiteTag. 2015. Web. 06 Aug. 2015. https://ritetag.com/about/.

35 Twitter, Inc. "Tweet activity dashboard." Twitter. 2016. Web. 28 Aug. 2016. https://support.twitter.com/articles/20171990.

36 —. "Audience Insights." Twitter. 2016. Web. 28 Aug. 2016. https://business.twitter.com/en/analytics/audience-insights.html.

#4 INSTAGRAM
MARKETING STRATEGIES

Instagram: History	Instagram: Personal	Instagram: Business	Instagram: Advertising	Instagram: Targeted Campaign	Instagram: Analytics
107	**108**	**113**	**120**	**123**	**128**

INSTAGRAM: HISTORY

Instagram is a photo and video sharing social network that allows users to connect with one another using multimedia in real time. People use hashtags to ensure that when users search for something (e.g. Justin Bieber, oak trees, hamburgers, etc.) they can find the applicable photos and videos. This practice also increases the likelihood that photos and videos will be 'liked' and seen by more people. Ultimately, an Instagrammer's account can increase in popularity because people will choose to become followers of it.

LAUNCHES

Sponsored photos and videos
OCT. 24, 2013

Instagram videos
JUN. 30, 2013

Photo tagging and 'Photos of You'
MAY 2013

Photo maps feature
AUG. 16, 2012

Bought by Facebook for 1 billion dollars
APR. 9, 2012

Named iPhone App of the Year
DEC. 9, 2011

Instagram Launched by Kevin Systrom and Mike Krieger
OCT. 6, 2010

START

Profiles for web
NOV. 5, 2013

Users able to share photos privately with Instagram Direct
DEC. 12, 2013

Internal Ad Analytics gradually rolled out
AUGUST 2014

Sneak peek at first image of Pluto; NASA's Instagram exclusive
JUL. 14, 2015

New API makes it easier for Business to Create Ad campaigns and buy ads
AUGUST 2015

Instagram Stories
AUG. 2, 2016

END

MILESTONES

JUNE 2016
500 Million Users

JULY 2015
300 Million Users

2014
35 Million Mobile Users; Close to 5 Million More than Twitter

JULY 26, 2012
Partly due to the Facebook acquisition, Instagram's users grew to 80 million

JULY 2011
100 million photos uploaded

DECEMBER 2010
1 million monthly users

1, 2, 3, 4, 5, 6, 7

Instagram: Personal

NAVIGATING INSTAGRAM

Instagram is a very visual social media channel that tends to encourage creativity through its photo- and video-sharing capabilities. It is also a mobile-only social platform, so in order to take full advantage of those capabilities and more, people need to become familiar with how to utilize this application as effectively as possible.

The following section will present a condensed version of Instagram's many features. For more detailed information, people can access the Instagram Help Center. Your instructor will provide you with the link.

A person can create an Instagram account "using the Instagram mobile app, not a computer"[8], but can access it from a computer once the account has been set up. Account holders will see various buttons on their profile page that will allow them to access a number of different functions.

Note for Teachers

Provide students with the link to the "Instagram, Help Center": https://help.instagram.com

Ideally, in this section, students with the Instagram app could refer to it during this explanation, and perhaps add additional information about photo and video sharing, gaining followers, etc.

INSTAGRAM PERSONAL PROFILE (MOBILE VIEW)

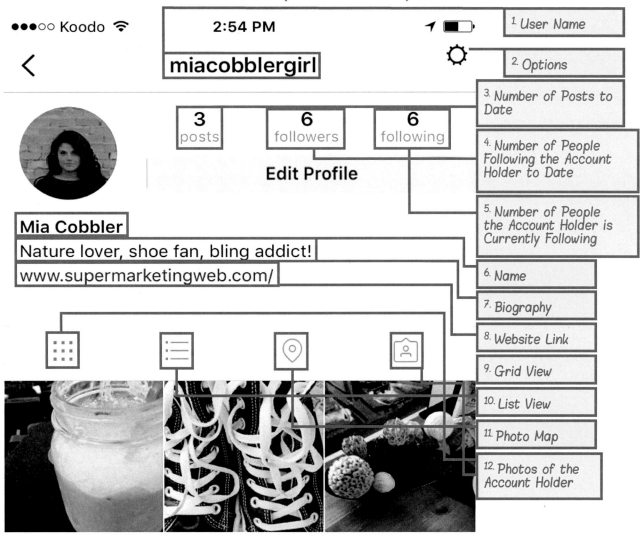

1. User Name
2. Options
3. Number of Posts to Date
4. Number of People Following the Account Holder to Date
5. Number of People the Account Holder is Currently Following
6. Name
7. Biography
8. Website Link
9. Grid View
10. List View
11. Photo Map
12. Photos of the Account Holder

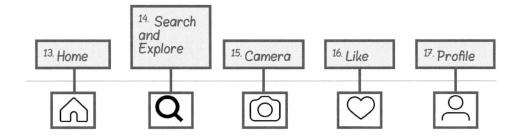

13. Home
14. Search and Explore
15. Camera
16. Like
17. Profile

INSTAGRAM PERSONAL PROFILE NOTES (MOBILE VIEW)

Note for Teachers

Go through all the elements of the Instagram Profile, as indicated on the graphic, stopping periodically to discuss the following notations:

#2: Options:
- Follow People: Facebook Friends; Contacts (if synced)
- Account: Edit Profile, Change Password, Change Privacy Settings, Posts You've Liked, etc.
- Settings: Linked Accounts, Push Notification Settings, Cellular Data Use, Option to Save Original Photos, etc.
- Support: Help Center, Report a Problem
- About
- Option to Clear Search History

#11: Photo Map:
Account holders can locate where they took their images and videos.

On the **bottom bar**, Instagrammers can monitor their activity:

#13: Home:
Account holders can:
- See their feed
- 'Like' and comment on posts
- Share posts on Facebook or Twitter
- Copy Share a URL
- Send a photo or video through Instagram Direct to another Instagrammer(s). This individual(s) is the only one who can see what the account holder posted using this function.

#14: Search and Explore:
This function allows account holders to:
- Find new people to follow
- Search hashtags
- Search places
- View their search history

#15: Camera:
Instagram offers account holders the option of taking photos or videos (3 to 60 seconds long) via the Instagram camera. Instagram has added a number of features that enable people to enhance their photos and videos. These include:
- A variety of filter options
- The ability to adjust photos in terms of size, brightness, contrast, etc.

When posting a photo, the account holder can tag people in it. This is not possible with a video, but the account holder can mention them in the comment section and they'll get a notification.[9]

When posting both photos and videos, it is possible to name the location and share them on other social media platforms.

#16: Like:
- The Account Holder
  - » Shows likes and comments on an Instagrammer's posts
  - » Shows new follows
  - » Notifies the account holder when his or her Facebook friends join Instagram
  - » Lists @ mentions
- Following: Allows the account holder to:
  - » See what the people he or she is following are 'liking'
  - » Read the comments people he or she is following are making
  - » Discover who people he or she is following are also following

"Note that the **Following** tab won't work for those who follow more than 1000 people."[10]

ACTIVITY: POINTS OF COMPARISON

Thus far, you have examined three social media channels in this text. In the following activity, you will be asked to make some comparisons between them and draw some conclusions.

Students can complete this activity in pairs or groups. Some suggested points of comparison for 6 – 10 are included in the chart. Also, see accompanying notes that follow the chart.

1. The first five features have been listed for you. If a particular social media channel allows account holders to access such a feature, put a check mark; if it doesn't put an 'x'.

2. Space has been provided following the chart for you to add additional notes and qualifiers.

3. Discuss with a classmate(s) what additional points of comparison you could make between the three social media channels. List them in spaces 6 –10.

4. Repeat Steps 1 and 2.

5. Discuss the comparisons you have made with the rest of the class and your instructor.

Features	Facebook	Twitter	Instagram
1. You are able to follow anyone you choose and anyone can follow you.	X	✓	✓
2. You can repost content.	✓	✓	✓
3. You can share photos.	✓	✓	✓
4. You must adhere to a character limit per post (Facebook), tweet (Twitter), or photo caption (Instagram)	X	✓	X, but…
5. The social media channel offers you suggestions or recommendations.	✓	✓	X
6. *The social media channel is a source of breaking news.*	✓	✓	✓
7. *The social media channel is more about creating original work than reposting someone else's work.*	X	X	✓
8. *Fans can connect with celebrities.*	X	✓	✓
9. *Unsolicited ads appear.*	✓	✓	✓
10. *People can set privacy settings.*	✓	✓	✓

Note: While it is easy to be anonymous on Instagram (by selecting a name and uploading images and/or videos that don't have any identifying features), it is advisable to keep all uploads of an appropriate nature. There is always the possibility that an Instagram account could be linked to a particular individual, or the account holder may want to publish his or her images on another platform(s). Like other social media channels, what an individual posts can make or break his or her online reputation.

Note for Teachers

1. Facebook is an invitation-based platform.

2. Facebook has a built-in share feature. Twitter has the built-in retweet feature. Instagram requires account holders to get the external repost app.

3. While all three social media channels allow you to post photos, Twitter and Instagram are more geared toward helping people look for photos of a particular thing. On Facebook, account holders are more likely to happen upon photos because their friends include them in their timeline or as part of particular albums.

4. Facebook: virtually no limit (60,000+ characters/post)[1]; Twitter: 140/post; Instagram: "For posts in feed, only the first three lines of a caption will be displayed. For captions longer than three lines, people can tap More to view the full caption. If you want your entire caption to display in feed, we recommend adding a caption of 125 characters or fewer."[2]

5. Facebook offers account holders suggested likes, Twitter offers suggested recommendations, but there is no feature like this in Instagram.

6. Twitter has become the major source of breaking news; Facebook to a lesser extent. However, Instagram is also starting to emerge as a channel that can be very useful when it comes to conveying images and information in emergency situations.

7. While people can and do post original content on Facebook and Twitter, there is a lot of reposting and copying and pasting of other people's content. The majority of the images on Instagram are user-generated. This is partially due to the fact that Instagram requires an external app to repost.

8. Generally, celebrities do not just invite members of the public to be their Facebook friends. However, some do have fan pages where they communicate with their fans directly, so there are some exceptions to the 'x' annotation.

Extension Activity:

Instagram Stories was launched on August 2nd, 2016. Ask students to research this and provide a basic description of what it allows the account holder to do. Then, for students who have Snapchat, ask them how Instagram Stories compares to that platform. Also, how could Instagram Stories be utilized for marketing purposes? Students could also view the link to "Instagram Stories: How 18 Brands And Influencers Are Using It (And You Can Too!)": https://blog.bufferapp.com/instagram-stories-who-to-follow to get inspiration when it comes to marketing ideas.

Instagram: Business

BEFORE PAID ADS

Instagram ads are a relatively new phenomenon. They were launched in the U.S. in late 2013 and in Canada about a year later. In a subsequent section, how businesses can utilize paid ads on this social channel will be examined. However, at this juncture, alternative forms of Instagram marketing will be discussed.

THE NATURE OF INSTAGRAM

To use Instagram effectively for business, it's important to understand the nature of the platform. One way to gain this insight is to recognize that 'Instagram' is in fact a blending of the words 'instant' and 'telegram'.[11] The 'instant' quality of Instagram implies that images and videos are being produced in realtime. The 'telegram' element means that the images and videos are being transmitted quickly to followers.

Thus, Instagram is a channel through which the public gets to see the face of a company at a given moment. Over time, if a business has posted a series of positive images and videos, followers will become comfortable with the brand, perceive it as a more human entity, rather than a faceless corporation, and even perhaps trust and gain more confidence in it.

Refer to the example business profile page.

INSTAGRAM BUSINESS PROFILE

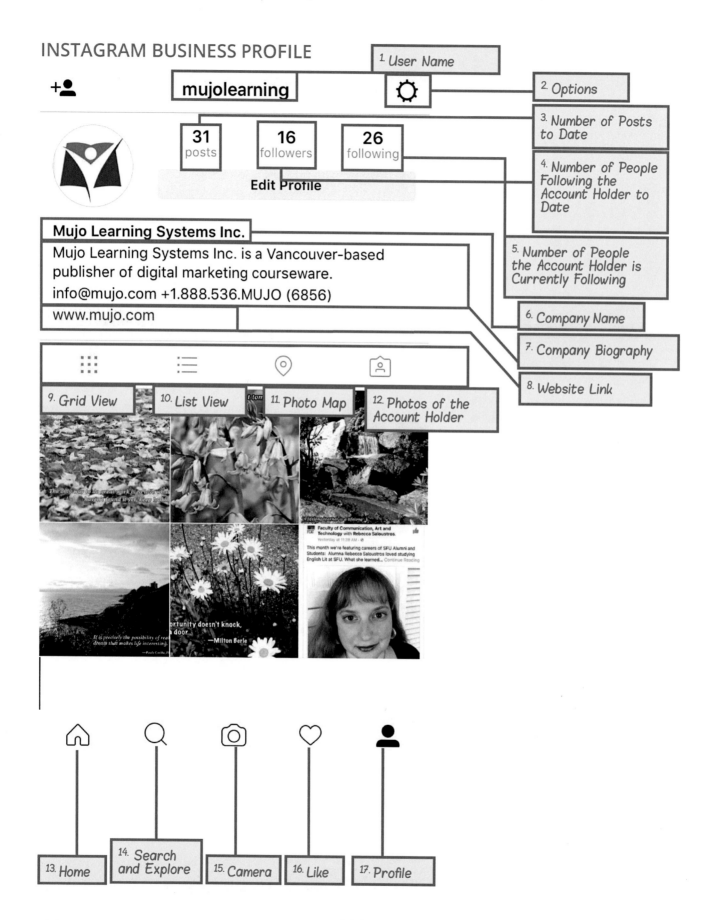

mujolearning

1. User Name

2. Options

31 posts

16 followers

26 following

Edit Profile

3. Number of Posts to Date

4. Number of People Following the Account Holder to Date

5. Number of People the Account Holder is Currently Following

Mujo Learning Systems Inc.

Mujo Learning Systems Inc. is a Vancouver-based publisher of digital marketing courseware.
info@mujo.com +1.888.536.MUJO (6856)
www.mujo.com

6. Company Name

7. Company Biography

8. Website Link

9. Grid View

10. List View

11. Photo Map

12. Photos of the Account Holder

13. Home

14. Search and Explore

15. Camera

16. Like

17. Profile

INSTAGRAM PHOTOS

Instagram is a medium that all businesses can use for marketing purposes, but given the channel's integral ability to help a corporation become more of a relatable entity, it clearly works most effectively in a B2C scenario. Even within that scenario, certain businesses will have an easier time utilizing Instagram's features to promote their products and/or services. For this section, the focus will be on static images.

It's easy for an airline to upload beautiful pictures. Most major carriers fly to picturesque, exotic locations. A clothing store has gorgeous outfits and accessories that look great on film too, and an interior design firm has one attractive room after another for the camera to capture.

On the contrary, it might not be as simple to imagine the kind of images a plumbing company or pest control service might include. This is where a digital marketer and business owner need to think outside the box. How about before and after photos (e.g. a flooded bathroom versus a clean and shiny one)? Maybe a member of staff with happy customers? Any one of these companies could also post images of corporate social events, making Instagram another way to implement persona-driven marketing.

Note for Teachers

Provide students with the links to "Content Strategy Tips": https://business.instagram.com/getting-started/ *and "Advertising on Instagram":* https://business.instagram.com/advertising/

🕐 ACTIVITY: GET THE PICTURE?

1. Visit Instagram's "Content Strategy Tips" and "Advertising on Instagram" pages. Your instructor will provide you with the links.
2. Choose three companies that you are familiar with, and do not have Instagram accounts.
3. Write each company name and a short description of its products and/or services in the spaces provided in the chart.
4. Select one of the following goals for each company (you may only use each goal a maximum of two times):
   - Increase Awareness
   - Shift Perception
   - Reach a new audience[12]
   - A place to store company pictures
5. Find an image that will help to promote the business and achieve that goal. You may select photos from the company website or other social media channels, stock photos, or even your own photos, if applicable.
6. Write a brief description of why you chose the photo or image; include why you think the subject and the look of the image are effective.
7. Include a caption and hashtag(s) that would accompany the image and be prepared to explain why they are appropriate and important.

Some generalized, short-form examples are included:

Company Name and Description	Goals	Image Description, Caption, and Hashtag(s)
Paper Clip Company	*Increase Awareness*	*Launch a contest in which participants have to use a company's paper clips to create a piece of art. The company can set up voting and offer a prize, generating online buzz and engagement from followers.*
Clothing Company	*Shift Perception*	*Show an image of the garment factory in which workers are performing their duties in a clean, safe environment, implying that the company treats its staff ethically.*
Running Shoe Company	*Reach a New Audience*	*Present a picture of a well-known athlete wearing a pair of the running shoes. This athlete would not have promoted the shoes before, so the athlete's fans would be new potential followers/buyers of the product.*

INSTAGRAM VIDEO

When Instagram introduced videos, it was like silent movies suddenly having sound. A new element and means of interaction with the audience became available. This is not to say that image-based marketing is ineffective. It is just that with video, digital marketers have another option when it comes to advertising products and/or services. For example:

1. Brands can, in 60 seconds or less, **tell** their audience a story, rather than just show it to them. With that story, companies could also share the core values behind their businesses.[13]

2. Companies can also demonstrate to their audience what great employers they are. A video can show employees having light-hearted conversations, while also demonstrating teamwork to achieve a common aim.

3. Businesses are able to give their audience a peek at a product launch. "They can make a series of short videos of the "staff behind the scenes preparing for the launch, and the actual launch with excited customers."[14]

What other ways could marketers use Instagram videos to promote a brand? Discuss your ideas with a classmate(s). Try to come up with at least three suggestions and then share them.

As with all videos posted on social media channels, it is advantageous if consumers 'like', repost, and/or leave positive comments on them. Brands need to be sure that they acknowledge this kind of engagement by thanking people.

Note for Teachers

Answers will vary, some suggested responses could be:

- *Use Instagram videos as part of a contest. For example, the client is Tourism Vancouver. A campaign to promote the organization could involve asking consumers to upload a video of them running with their dog in a pet-friendly tourist location. A hashtag(s) would need to be included, and a winner could be chosen at random or through a voting process.*

- *Include a customer testimonial, saying how wonderful a product or service is.*

- *Show customers utilizing a retail product a year after purchase to demonstrate that they are still pleased with it and that it is a quality item that lasts.*

LOOP GIVEAWAY

Note for Teachers

This activity is designed for the student to complete at home and then for an in-class discussion to happen in the following class. However, if extra time is available, it could be done in pairs or groups during class time

One way some companies engage in marketing on Instagram is through contests. A particular kind of contest, called 'the loop giveaway' has become popular. Basically, it works like this:

A company posts a picture. The picture's caption usually announces that there is a prize giveaway and explains how people can participate and any rules involved. Companies participating in the loop giveaway may each pay a portion of the cost of the prize(s), or each company might select one of its own products or services as a prize. In order to win the prize(s), the Instagrammer has to 'like' the picture and follow the company that posted it. However, the process is just getting started.

The individual then needs to click on the picture and go to the next account that is featured. That account will also post a picture connected to the giveaway. The individual must 'like' that picture and follow that account as well. This process of 'liking' and following continues until the individual finds himself or herself at the start of the loop again. The number of companies participating in the loop can be more than 30.[15]

Some giveaways also require the Instagrammer to tag another person every time he or she follows a new account and 'likes' its contest-related picture.

Once the loop giveaway ends, the Instagrammer can 'unfollow' and 'unlike' all the accounts that were part of the contest. However, it's very probable that some people won't bother to do this or may actually want to continue following at least some of the new accounts that were part of the giveaway. Given the potential for people to quickly click through, the loop campaigns may see less return than otherwise expected and the concept is likely to generate 'Instagram Follow Fatigue' driving people away from future endeavors. The advice here would be to use loop campaigns carefully.

QUESTIONS

1. What is your opinion of loop giveaways? Do you think they are a good strategy on the part of marketers and companies when it comes to achieving goals like increasing awareness and reaching a new audience?

2. How successful are they? Do some online research to answer this question.

3. How real are the followers garnered through these types of contests? Do some online research to answer this question.

Note for Teachers

Answers will vary, but the following points should be mentioned in the course of the discussion:

1. Yes, they can be a good marketing strategy when the goal of that strategy is to increase awareness and/or reach a new audience. However, a company with a small or non-existent Instagram following should try to partner with other businesses that are more established, "post professional images and have a sizable following."[3]

   The loop giveaway shouldn't only be publicized on Instagram either. It should be marketed on other social media channels the participants are on (cross-channel marketing). This strategy will increase the exposure of the contest and ensure that the companies are "pooling [their] followers across all social media platforms."[4]

2. Businesses can gain a large number of followers very quickly during an Instagram loop giveaway. However, the concern is that those followers will leave once the contest period has ended or may not be the kind of followers the business wants to attract. Here are a couple of ways a company can reduce the drop off:

   - It is better for the loop to be a short one. In other words, having less than ten companies involved is a good strategy. It's less frustrating for participants during the contest, and the likelihood that they will unfollow is lower. A few commercial accounts and promotional messages in the Instagrammer's feed are less irritating than the onslaught of many all of a sudden.

   - Contests need to be legitimate. Part of establishing that legitimacy rests on the company's publication of the winner's name (and photo, possibly) on the Instagram channel, and any other channels on which the contest was advertised.[5]

   - One way to publicize the winner's name **and** reduce the number of unfollows is to break the loop. "It's easy for new followers to run through the loop and unfollow each host. In order to keep as many followers as possible, [participating companies can untag] each other from the posts and edit the image caption to reveal the winner and announce the giveaway has closed."[6]

3.
   > At the end of the giveaway, there [is] no way to track the number of people who visited [a] site from Instagram during the giveaway period. Instagram isn't counted as a separate referrer in Google Analytics... It appears as a direct link. And the fact that Instagram only allows you to include a direct link in your profile makes the conversion rate lower. So, while the loop giveaway was beneficial for gaining followers, there isn't any hard and fast data to tell me how beneficial those new followers have been to my business [in terms of ROI].[7]

Instagram: Advertising

INSTAGRAM FAILS AND WINS

Compared to other major social networks, Instagram is the new kid on the block. Yet, it has already been the site of some significant flops and triumphs by major brands. Like any medium, **how** it is used will determine the effectiveness of any campaign. What follows are a couple of examples of Instagram campaigns that stand as testaments to some valuable dos and don'ts of marketing on this social media channel.

INSTAGRAM FAIL

CASE STUDY: Not Much McLovin' on Instagram

As stated earlier, advertising on Instagram is a relatively new phenomenon. When it was initially launched in the U.S. back in 2013, only a select number of brands could put out ads. McDonalds was one of them. Unfortunately, it didn't take long for one of the world's biggest brands to make one of the biggest thuds. In the summer of 2014, McDonalds initiated a campaign that focused on its bacon clubhouse burger. Although the ad generated a significant number of likes, it received resoundingly negative feedback.[16]

The primary reason for the negativity can be explained by citing a type of advertising that existed long before social media, the Internet, and even television—**interruption marketing**. This type of advertising forces the audience to encounter a brand and its message. The Instagram audience, primarily composed of millennials, resented this kind of interruption. "Instead of targeting, for example, only customers who follow food-related accounts or customers who previously tagged #McDonalds or even #bacon, the Instagram campaign is an untargeted bomb, detonated in a place where many image-conscious consumers are openly hostile to things like fast food."[17] In other words, the campaign went to the Instagram audience as a whole when it should have only gone to those who were likely to be receptive to it.

Some industry insiders argue that Instagram may be the wrong medium for fast food in general, and that it is better suited to showcasing "fashion brands, selfies and sports products"[18] While this is certainly an argument worthy of consideration, a spring 2015 McDonald's Instagram campaign hints at what may actually be another problem with the golden arches' strategy: its food doesn't always look great. Now, fast food is not gourmet, but it is possible to make it look appetizing. Unfortunately, when McDonald's posted pictures of its hamburgers with a "thick and juicy" header, neither adjective accurately described the flat, unappealing image the company presented.[19] A critical error, given that on Instagram, image is king.

QUESTIONS

1. Instagram, by its very design, gives brands a unique opportunity "to reveal a softer, less direct sales approach that supports customer relationship building and staying top of mind through transparency and humanizing of the brand."[20] With this in mind, how could McDonald's change its advertising to take full advantage of Instagram's best features?

2. Look through your Instagram feed and select a brand that you think presents the most appealing visuals. Describe why these visuals are appealing (e.g. attractive colors/filters used, evidence of food styling, etc.).

3. Now that more brands are able to advertise on Instagram, and people will start seeing more sponsored posts in their feeds, do you think Instagrammers will continue to resent the interruption marketing, or do you think they will adjust to it?

All answers will vary.

INSTAGRAM WIN

CASE STUDY: Starbucks' White Cup Challenge

In April 2014, Starbucks launched its white cup challenge in the United States and Canada. The 'white cup' refers to the reusable cups that Starbucks began selling for one dollar in January 2013. They look like Starbucks' regular, disposable cups, but have a 30-use lifespan.[21] Jim Hanna, Starbucks' director of environmental impact, called the iconic white cup Starbucks' billboard.[22]

Challenge participants were asked to put their own original art on these 'billboards'. They could then take pictures of their customized cups and post them on Instagram or Twitter with the hashtag #WhiteCupContest. Starbucks received almost 4000 entries, many of which can still be viewed on the company's Pinterest page, which long after the contest has closed, still has 120,000+ followers.[23] "The winning entry won [Starbucks] over with its expressive, iconic and handmade graphics . . . [The company] can't wait to launch future versions of the contest. The winning cup . . . will be printed on [Starbucks'] reusable cup and sold online in the fall."[24]

So why was this contest a good social media marketing move? Starbucks has millions of Instagram followers, and the company knew it would reach a huge audience by asking participants to post their entries on this social media platform, along with Twitter. The contest itself was very visual, and that helped the campaign to translate well on the image-based Instagram.

The challenge was also "a winning combination of crowd-sourced product design, increas[ed] reusable cup sales and reinforc[ed] Starbucks' environmental responsibility credentials."[25]

QUESTIONS

1. Think about other companies that advertise on Instagram. Could any of their products be considered 'billboards'?

2. How could one of those companies utilize its 'billboard' as part of an Instagram campaign?

All answers will vary.

Instagram: Running a Targeted Campaign

CAMPAIGN STRATEGY FOR BRANDED POSTS

There are a variety of ways to market products and services on Instagram. Many companies, especially up until August 2015 when ads became more easily accessible, have chosen to advertise on their own rather than purchase ads through Instagram. Earlier in the text, various ways to use images and videos for promotional purposes were examined.

Note for Teachers

At this point, ask students to recall what was mentioned in previous sections on this topic.

What follows are several additional ways brands can increase the effectiveness of their Instagram campaigns:

Cross-marketing on other social media sites: It makes sense for a company to promote its Instagram campaign on other channels where it has a social media presence. This is particularly true when it comes to Facebook, which owns Instagram. "Make an Instagram tab on your Facebook page – this enables you to instantly share your Instagram photos to your Facebook fans."[26]

Being Exclusive: The flipside of cross-marketing is using one platform, in this case Instagram, to show followers something they won't see anywhere else (not on your website, Facebook page, Twitter account, etc.). By doing this, Instagram followers will feel like they're getting a specific reward for engaging with a particular brand on this channel.[27]

Paying it Forward: If customers and other businesses engage with a brand through Instagram by 'liking', reposting, following, commenting, and/or participating in a contest, the brand should in turn engage with them. A brand can 'like' its target audience's posts and follow their pages. It can help promote other local businesses and perhaps try to link up its promotions with theirs.

EFFECTIVE USE OF HASHTAGS ON INSTAGRAM

Hashtags on Instagram are as important, if not more so, than on Twitter. "While the other sites give you a diminishing return if you use more than one or two, on Instagram the rule is the more the merrier. You can load up your pictures with an infinite number of hashtags, and the more you use the more likely you are to get them noticed, 'liked', and shared. The posts with the highest number of interactions have 22 or more hashtags attached."[28] Thus, it is critical that marketers utilize hashtags effectively in Instagram campaigns to ensure their promotions get seen by the right target audience and as many members of that audience as possible.

🕐 ACTIVITY: USING HASHTAGS ON INSTAGRAM

1. Do some research and find a brand that knows how to use hashtags on Instagram to boost its promotional efforts.

2. Describe the brand, its campaign, and how it incorporated hashtags.

3. Note at least one takeaway from the company's use of hashtags on Instagram that could be useful to other businesses when they are building their branded campaigns.

4. Share your research.

Answers will vary, but several examples are available on "3 Outstanding Use Cases for Branded Hashtags on Instagram": sproutsocial.com/insights/3-outstanding-use-cases-branded-hashtags-instagram

rsaloust One more reason why Syros is the hidden gem of The Cyclades #syros #greece #greek #greekislands #mediterranean #cave #caves #churchinacave #thecyclades #greektravel #travel #greekisland #sunset #sunsets #church #churchbell #europeantravel #europe #agiosstefanos #seaview #mediterraneansea #greece2015 #greece🇬🇷

ACTIVITY: THE EVOLUTION OF AND CAMPAIGN STRATEGY FOR PAID ADS

Individually, or in pairs/groups, ask students to respond to the questions in this section.

Instagram has made some significant strides in the past few years when it comes to introducing paid advertising on its platform. Conduct some online research to respond to the questions within this article.

When Instagram ads were launched in the U.S. and Canada, only select brands were allowed to access the paid ads feature. Which six brands were the first to advertise on Instagram Canada?

Instagram chose these brands "based on the quality of their current presence on the platform".[29]

Answers

- *Hudson's Bay*
- *Target Canada*
- *Sport Chek*
- *Air Canada*
- *Mercedes Benz Canada*
- *Travel Alberta*[8]

A standard Instagram ad can be recognized by the word 'sponsored' in the upper right-hand corner of the post. Otherwise, the ad looks like any other posting a regular Instagrammer would make.

Why does Instagram want standard ads like this to blend in so seamlessly with the rest of an account holder's feed?

Note for Teachers

"Because the ads will blend in to organic posts, users won't feel like they are being inundated with flashy ads. And according to **The Guardian**, *Instagram will take additional steps to ensure that ads don't become spammy or annoying: 'Instagram will manage volume, frequency and creative integrity, ensuring that users are not spammed with offer-based advertising.'"[9]*

Note: *At this point, it is worth reminding students that there was still a backlash against the McDonalds ads, despite how blended in they were. Also, students previously answered a question about how the Instagram audience was reacting to more frequent 'interruption-style' ads in their feeds. Revisit that discussion.*

THE CAROUSEL AD

In 2015, Instagram introduced a new kind of ad, first to the U.S., then to the Canadian market. It was called the 'carousel ad'. Search online and define what a carousel ad is and how a company or marketer could use one advantageously.

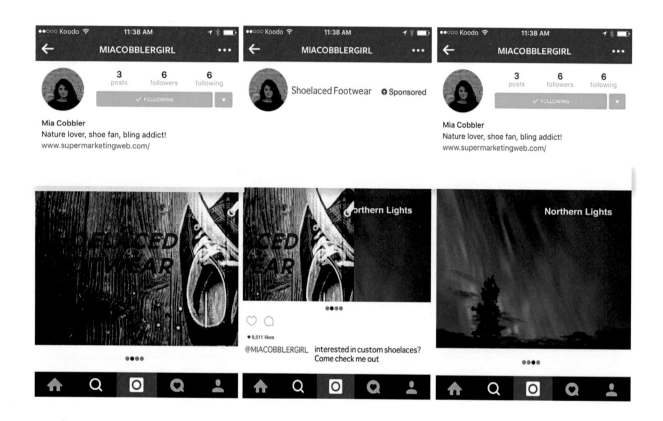

Note for Teachers

A carousel ad allows marketers to include three to five images or videos in a single post. They can create an entirely image- or video-based ad, or one that includes any combination of the two. Advertisers can sequence them accordingly.[10]

"Carousel ads give brands more flexibility in telling their stories by allowing people to view their ads to swipe left to see additional images [or videos] and link to a website of the brand's choice. One way to look at it is carousel ads bring the potential of multi-page print campaigns to mobile phones."[11]

For additional information, provide students with the link to, "Adding Video to Carousel Ads":
http://blog.business.instagram.com/post/144613122511/video-carousel-ads

CALL-TO-ACTION BUTTONS

In addition to introducing carousel ads, Instagram changed its policy of not permitting "links that took users outside the app to buy the products in the pictures."[30] Incorporated into Instagram ads include call-to-action (CTA) buttons like:

- Shop Now
- Book Now
- Download
- Learn More
- Sign Up[31]

Then, on August 4th, 2015, Instagram "officially switched on its advertising API to a wider audience (application programming interface)".[32]

What was the significance of Instagram's move?

Note for Teachers

"Ads can now be purchased by just about anyone, using online ad-buying tools offered by official Instagram partners."[12] Prior to this, ads were very expensive, or as mentioned earlier, only an available option for select companies.

Note: *Students can now be asked to discuss what campaign strategies might make paid ads more attractive to Instagrammers. Make note of their suggestions and ask them to continue to keep looking for paid ads in their feeds. What brands are advertising? Are their ads effective? What is the goal of their Instagram advertising and are the strategies being utilized by marketers working?*

Check back with students periodically, asking what they've noticed regarding this new development in Instagram marketing.

Instagram: Analytics

Prior to August 2014, Instagram had no internal analytics. Marketers had to rely on their own methods or utilize external tools to track brand and ad performance. However, the introduction of Instagram's three analytics tools, account insights, ad insights, and ad staging,[33] changed all that.

ACCOUNT INSIGHTS

It is very simple, and free, for a business to change its personal Instagram account into a business account, and thus enable account insights. The process begins by clicking 'Switch to Business Profile'. Then, Instagram invites the account holder to select 'View Features'.

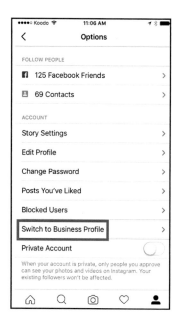

The platform makes suggestions about what to add to a business profile, and recommends using Account Insights to gain demographic data about followers and check post performance.

The account holder needs to log in with his or her Facebook information because Instagram business profiles are linked to Facebook pages. The account holder adds his or her information and clicks 'Done'.

Once the business profile has been set up, it may take time before the account holder will be able to see all the data from account insights. For example, in order to see demographic information, the account holder must have at least 100 followers.

Note for Teachers

To see an example of demographic data, students can refer to, "Instagram's analytics will offer audience demographics, post impressions, reach & more": https://techcrunch.com/2016/05/16/instagrams-analytics-will-offer-audience-demographics-post-impressions-reach-more/

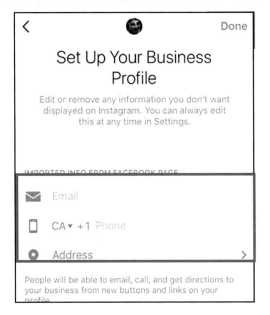

METRICS FROM ACCOUNT INSIGHTS

On an individual post, it is possible to get insights after the post has gone live, though that information may not be available immediately. The example that follows is the data provided for a post dated September 27th, 2016, that had been live for almost five and a half hours. Instagram makes it very clear what the data means. The first two kinds of data, impressions and reach, are what is referred to as 'brand metrics'. The third, engagement, is a 'social-specific metric', which is linked to how many likes and comments a post gets.[34]

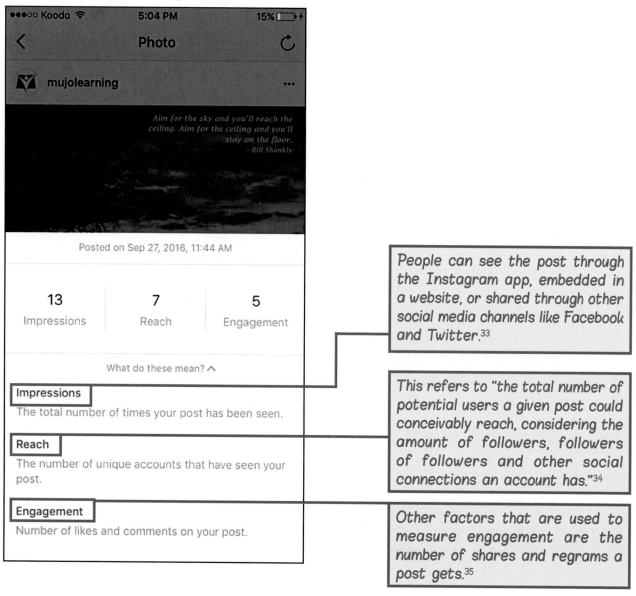

People can see the post through the Instagram app, embedded in a website, or shared through other social media channels like Facebook and Twitter.[33]

This refers to "the total number of potential users a given post could conceivably reach, considering the amount of followers, followers of followers and other social connections an account has."[34]

Other factors that are used to measure engagement are the number of shares and regrams a post gets.[35]

On the total number of posts, it is also possible for an account holder to see impressions, reach, and engagement. Instagram separates engagement into likes and comments so they can be viewed individually too. This information can be filtered by media type (e.g. photos only or videos only), as well as by time span (e.g. 7 days, 30 days, 3 months, 6 months, 1 year, 2 years). Instagram will list the account's top posts too.

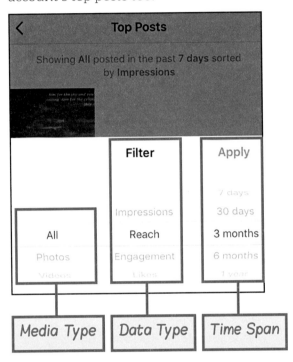

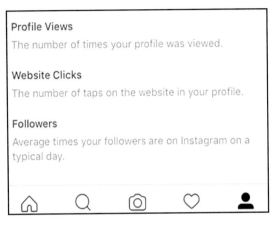

The Instagram account holder can learn about his or her profile as a whole in terms of profile views, website clicks, and followers. He or she can also view a profile summary in the same way that a personal account holder can. This summary includes: the number of posts made, followers acquired, and how many accounts he or she is following.

Which number do you think is most important when it comes to increasing brand awareness? Explain your answer.

Note for Teachers

The number of followers a brand has is the most important number when it comes to increasing brand awareness. Two reasons for this are:

1. *Followers = Influence (i.e. The more followers a brand has the more influential it will be on Instagram. The channel will be more likely to show its ads to more people if it has more followers, for example.)*
2. *An Increase in Followers = An Increase in Other Numbers (e.g. impressions, reach, social-specifics)*

AD INSIGHTS

Ad Insights "shows the performance of paid campaigns with brand analytics (impressions, reach, and frequency) for each individual ad delivered to the target audience."[35]

Again, more specifically, within this analytics tool a business owner or marketer can set the:
- Ad campaign's objective or goal
- Time period or dates when the campaign will be running
- Target demographic (e.g. location, gender, age range)
- Target impressions

He or she can also list the ad(s) that will be running during the campaign.

The analytics provide the business owner or marketer with information about the paid campaign's:
- Current impressions
- Reach
- Average frequency

Brand and social metrics will also be noted for each of the listed ads.

⏰ ACTIVITY: UNDERPERFORMING INSTAGRAM ADS

Suppose a marketer or business owner uses this tool and discovers that an ad or an entire campaign is underperforming. What could be the reasons? Consider everything you have learned about Instagram thus far before answering. List at least five reasons.

Answers could include:

1. *Too broad a demographic target (Note: At this point, it should be mentioned that the Instagram sample demographic target has a wide age range and geographic area. A real campaign would have a narrower age range and would likely focus on specific States.)*
2. *Poor content that isn't compelling*
3. *Content that isn't relevant to the target demographic*
4. *Poorly chosen hashtags*
5. *Poor quality image or video that may not be compelling or relevant enough to attract the target audience*

AD STAGING

This third Instagram tool is more relevant when it comes to facilitating the creative process in general. It "allows advertisers and their creative teams to preview, save, and collaborate on ad creative for upcoming campaigns."[36]

Ad staging can be compared to a preview movie screening for a test audience or a new product being tried out by a focus group. These kind of processes work out glitches, catch mistakes etc., giving those responsible an opportunity to make changes. The ad staging process allows business owners or marketers a chance to refine a campaign before it goes live.

⏱ ACTIVITY: IMPROVING AN INSTAGRAM AD

1. With your classmate(s), take a look at an Instagram ad.
2. Pretend the ad has not gone live yet, and that you are tasked with evaluating it.
3. Give constructive feedback to the advertiser about:
   - The image or video
     » Its quality
     » How compelling it is
     » How relevant
   - Any written content
     » How compelling it is
     » How relevant
4. Suggest at least one way the advertiser could improve the image, and one way he or she could improve the content. Share your feedback.

Note for Teachers

Show each pair or group of students a screenshot of an Instagram ad. Have them go through the process that follows. Then, show each ad to the class and ask each pair or group to present its feedback.

TIME MANAGEMENT

These three tools give a marketer "access to a real-time campaign summary and data showing how their target audience is responding to each of their sponsored photos. Also, brand marketers will be able to better understand the best time of day to post a photo or video."[37]

Do some online research and find some general information about when are the best and worst times to post on Instagram. Share your findings.

Note for Teachers

Answers may vary, given how this information may change for the Instagram platform as time passes. Thus, students should be encouraged to find the most up-to-date information possible. The following links contain information from 2015:

"The Best Times to Post on Facebook, Instagram, and Twitter":

www.businessinsider.com/best-times-to-post-on-facebook-instagram-twitter-2015-7

"Here's the Best Time to Post a Photo on Instagram":

www.huffingtonpost.com/2015/02/25/get-instagram-likes_n_6751614.html

Extension Activity: Provide students with the link to "This Social Network Engages Audiences Better Than the Rest": https://www.entrepreneur.com/article/279827

Ask them to read the article and note the following:
- Which social network gets the best engagement
- Which channel was best in terms of engagement for each of these industries: music, sports and entertainment, airlines and aviation, luxury items, and wine and spirits

Ask students to hypothesize as to why certain channels are better for certain industries.

CHAPTER REVIEW

1. Which of the following is **not** true of Instagram?

    a. Instagrammers can share photos.

    b. Instagrammers can repost content.

    c. Instagram offers account holders suggestions or recommendations.

    d. Instagram allows account holders to follow whomever they choose.

2. A retailer of slippers wants to shift consumers' perceptions about where and how his product is made. What kind of image and accompanying caption and hashtag could he post on Instagram to achieve this?

3. How long can Instagram videos be? What could a company show in a video that would bolster its public image?

4. How has paid advertising changed on Instagram?

5. What four factors are associated with engagement on Instagram?

Chapter Review (Optional)

The following questions can be utilized in a variety of ways (e.g. Students can complete them for homework, in class with a partner, orally in a whole-class format, etc.).

Answers

1. c. Instagram offers account holders suggestions or recommendations.

2. Answers will vary.

3. 60 seconds; answers will vary

4. Initially, only a few brands could advertise on Instagram. They had to go through the social platform to do so and ads were very expensive. Instagram introduced the carousel ad. Analytics programs were also added so that marketers could see how well their ads were performing. As of August 4th, 2015, Instagram ads became accessible to almost anyone, and brands no longer needed to go through Instagram. Instead, they could access online ad tools through official Instagram partners.

5. Likes, comments, shares, and regrams

    Note: At this point, if not already done so, the instructor should prepare students for the upcoming midterm exam (e.g. explaining topics to be covered, question styles, length of time, etc.).

MIDTERM EXAM   /30

The following exam should take 30 – 45 minutes to complete if administered 'closed book'. An 'open book' exam may require additional time. All students will need to complete the exam is a pen or pencil. Do not permit students to use smart phones or other electronic devices during the exam.

SECTION ONE: MULTIPLE CHOICE   /10

Circle the correct answer to each multiple-choice question. All questions are worth one mark.

1. Which of the following social media networks is known to appeal to the female demographic?
   a. Twitter
   b. **Pinterest**
   c. Google +
   d. LinkedIn

2. Which of the following is an example of a 'brand metric'?
   a. **impressions**
   b. comments
   c. likes
   d. none of the above

3. A person can tell that a Twitter post is an ad because of its:
   a. hashtags
   b. URLs
   c. **boxed presentation**
   d. all of the above

4. Instagram is owned by:
   a. **Facebook**
   b. Twitter
   c. Google
   d. Pinterest

5. Marketers can utilize which of the following to create an accurate buyer persona?
   a. questionnaires
   b. analytics
   c. social media listening
   d. **all of the above**

6. Which of the following is **not** true about Instagram?

   a. It has been a source of breaking news.

   b. Unsolicited ads appear.

   c. It allows Instagrammers to share photos.

   d. It offers Instagrammers suggestions or recommendations.

7. What is the main goal of the following ad?

   A toy store owner posts the same image on Facebook, Twitter, and Instagram. It is a picture of a local woman making puppets in her home. These puppets are sold in the owner's toy store. Before the owner posted the image, he knew many of his customers believed the puppets were made in China.

   a. To increase brand awareness

   b. To shift perception

   c. To generate likes

   d. None of the above

8. How long can an Instagram video be?

   a. 30 seconds or less

   b. 15 seconds or less

   c. 45 seconds or less

   d. 1 minute or less

9. If a brand puts an Instagram button on its Facebook page, the business is engaging in:

   a. Persona-driven marketing

   b. Cross-marketing

   c. A loop giveaway

   d. None of the above

10. Which of the following is most important when it comes to increasing brand awareness on Instagram?

    a. Weekly impressions

    b. Monthly reach

    c. Number of followers

    d. Number of positive comments

SECTION TWO: FILL IN THE BLANKS   /10

Complete each statement with the correct word(s). Write in the space(s) provided.

1. A carousel ad allows a marketer to put up to *five* images in one post.   (1 mark)

2. Account insights and ad insights allow Instagram advertisers to track *brand* and *social-specific* metrics.   (2 marks)

3. The three kinds of Facebook advertising mentioned in the text are: *promoted or suggested posts*, *right-hand column ads*, and *contest apps*.   (3 marks)

4. *Product-related* and *trending* hashtags can be useful to business owners and marketers.   (2 marks)

5. Regrams, shares, likes, and comments help a marketer to measure *engagement* on an Instagram post.   (1 mark)

6. *Brand awareness* is the kind of goal a startup company would want to achieve on Twitter.   (1 mark)

FOOTNOTES: CHAPTER 4

1   Buck, Stephanie. "10 Things You Can Fit Into Your 63,206-Character Facebook Status." Mashable. 04 Jan. 2012. Web. 07 Aug. 2015. mashable.com/2012/01/04/facebook-character-limit/.
2   Instagram, Inc. "Instagram Help Centre." Instagram. 2016. Web. 23 Sept. 2016. https://www.facebook.com/help/instagram/375691319209377.
3   Hooker, Lauren. "What I Learned from Gaining 3,000 Instagram Followers in One Day." Elle & Co. 17 Feb. 2015. Web. 12 Aug. 2015. www.elleandcompanydesign.com/blog/2015/2/16/what-I-learned-from-gaining-3000-instagram-followers-in-one-day.
4   Ibid.
5   PromoSimple, Inc. "What to Do After a Giveaway Ends to Increase Your Credibility." PromoSimple. 2015. Web. 12 Aug. 2015. blog.promosimple.com/promoting-giveaways/what-to-do-after-a-giveaway-ends.
6   Hooker, Lauren. "What I Learned from Gaining 3,000 Instagram Followers in One Day." Elle & Co. 17 Feb. 2015. Web. 12 Aug. 2015. www.elleandcompanydesign.com/blog/2015/2/16/what-I-learned-from-gaining-3000-instagram-followers-in-one-day.
7   Ibid.
8   Martin, Russ. "Instagram Rolls Out Ads in Canada." **Marketing**. 10 Nov. 2014. Web. 18 Aug. 2015. www.marketingmag.ca/media/instagram-ads-now-live-in-canada-129555.
9   Garst, Kim. "Instagram Ads Are Now Open to Everyone." Boom Social. 16 Aug. 2015. Web. 19 Aug. 2015. kimgarst.com/Instagram-ads-are-now-open-to-everyone.
10 Instagram, Inc. "Adding Video to Carousel Ads." Instagram. May 2016. Web. 23 Sept. 2016. http://blog.business.instagram.com/post/144613122511/video-carousel-ads.
11 Instagram, Inc. "A New Way for Brands to Tell Stories on Instagram." Instagram. April 2015. Web. 19 Aug. 2015. blog.business.instagram.com/post/112707530471/carousel-ads.
12 Holmes, Ryan. "Why an Instagram Tweak Spells the Beginning of a Multibillion-Dollar Industry." Re/code. 19 Aug. 2015. Web. 19 Aug. 2015. recode.net/2015/08/19/why-an-instagram-tweak-spells-the-beginning-of-a-multibillion-dollar-industry/.

SECTION THREE: SHORT ANSWER   /10

Respond to the following questions in the space provided. You may write in point form.

1. What does the following quotation mean, and teach people about social media?

(2 marks)

"Aim to have content on the web be 'professional' not 'confessional'"[39]

—E. Chandlee Bryan

Answers will vary, but essentially it means that people should not give too much away on social media (e.g. post information that is too personal). It teaches people that what they post is not private and can harm their reputation and personal brand.

2. Why do Facebook account holders often follow and 'like' small, local businesses' pages? (1 mark)

They have community appeal, and if they do well, money stays in the community and benefits it.

3. What are three reasons why an Instagram ad might be underperforming?   (3 marks)

Answers could include:
- *The hashtags were poorly chosen.*
- *The image quality is poor.*
- *The content isn't relevant to the target demographic.*

4. What does Instagram's ad staging help marketers to do?   (1 mark)

Refine a campaign before it goes live.

5. How do keywords function differently on Twitter advertising versus SEO-based advertising?

(3 marks)

When an individual goes on Twitter, his or her purpose is generally to communicate, whereas on Google it is to find something.

Keywords on Twitter represent what people are 'tweeting' about, rather than searching for on Google.

A campaign's keywords should reflect what a business' audience is 'tweeting' about, as opposed to what a company would like them to be searching for.

*See the Appendix for a reproducible print-version of the test that is available for teachers to duplicate and distribute to their students.

FOOTNOTES: CHAPTER 4

1   Rakos, Mikaela. "The History of Instagram." Dashburst. 12 May. 2014. Web. 15 Jul. 2015. https://blog.dashburst.com/history-of-instagram/.

2   Desreumaux, Geoff. "The Complete History of Instagram." We Are Social Media. 03 Jan. 2014. Web. 15 Jul. 2015. http://wersm.com/the-complete-history-of-instagram/#!prettyPhoto.

3   Alba, Davey. "NASA Teams Up with Instagram to Debut Pluto Surface Photo." **Wired**. 14 Jul. 2015. Web. 15 Jul. 2015. http://www.wired.com/2015/07/nasa-teams-instagram-debut-pluto-surface-photo/.

4   Instagram, Inc. "Announcing a New Suite of Business Tools for Brands on Instagram." Instagram. 2014. Web. 18 Aug. 2015. blog.business.instagram.com/post/95314562151/businesstools.

5   Dirks, Brent. "Instagram opens the advertising floodgates by launching its new API." AppAdvice. 04 Aug. 2015. Web. 21 Aug. 2015. appadvice.com/appnn/2015/Instagram-opens-the-advertising-floodgates-by-launching-its-new-API.

6   Instagram, Inc. "Introducing Instagram Stories." Instagram. 02 Aug. 2016. Web. 08 Oct. 2016. http://blog.instagram.com/post/148348940287/160802-stories.

7   —. "Instagram Today: 500 Million Windows to the World." Instagram. 21 Jun. 2016. Web. 08 Oct. 2016. http://blog.instagram.com/post/146255204757/160621-news.

8   —. "Creating an Account & Username." Instagram. 2015. Web. 06 Aug. 2015. http://help.instagram.com/182492381886913/.

9   —. "Instagram Help Centre." Instagram. 2016. Web. 23 Sept. 2016. https://www.facebook.com/help/instagram/375691319209377.

10 —. "Exploring Photos and Videos." Instagram. 2015. Web. 07 Aug. 2015. https://help.instagram.com/441951049195380.

11 —. "FAQ." Instagram. 2015. Web. 13 Aug. 2015. https://instagram.com/about/faq?hl=en.

12 —. "Content Strategy Tips." Instagram. 2015. Web. 10 Aug. 2015. https://business.instagram.com/gettingstarted/.

13 Bunskoek, Krista. "52 Tips: How to Market on Instagram." Wishpond. 2014. Web. 19 Aug. 2015. blog.wishpond.com/post/59612395517/52-tips-how-to-market-on-instagram.

14 Ibid.

15 Callan, Nadine. "What You Need to Know About Instagram Loop Giveaways." Blog Brighter. 08 Jun. 2015. Web. 10 Aug. 2015. blogbrighter.com/what-you-need-to-know-about-instagram-loop-giveaways/.

16 "Social Media Fail: McDonald's (Again)." Social Media Knowledge. 21 Aug. 2014. Web. 22 Jul. 2015. smk.co/article/social-media-fail-mcdonalds1.

17 Malatesta, Irene. "How to Fail at Instagram: McDonald's." Irene Kaoru Malatesta. 12 Aug. 2014. Web. 22 Jul. 2015. irenekaoru.com/?p=90.

18 "Social Media Fail: McDonald's (Again)." Social Media Knowledge. 21 Aug. 2014. Web. 22 Jul. 2015. smk.com/article/social-media-fail-mcdonalds1.

19 Lattin, Pace. "McDonalds Fails with Instagram Campaign." Performance Marketing Insider. 18 May 2015. Web. 22 Jul. 2015. performinsider.com/2015/05/mcdonalds-fails-with-instagram-campaign/.

20 Box, Toni. "Instagram Advertising: Consumer's Aren't Loving It...Yet." PM Digital. 07 Aug. 2014. Web. 22 Jul. 2015. www.pmdigital.com/blog/2014/08/instagram-advertising-consumers-arent-loving-yet/.

21 Starbucks Newsroom. Starbucks. Starbucks Corporation. 2015. Web. 24 Jun. 2015. https://news.starbucks.com/news/starbucks-invites-you-to-decorate-its-iconic-white-cup.

22 Ibid.

23 Pinterest, Inc. Starbucks. "Starbucks Cup Art." Pinterest. n.d. Web. 15 Jul. 2015. https://www.pinterest/com/starbucks/starbucks-cup-art/.

24 Starbucks Newsroom. Starbucks Corporation. 2015. Web. 24 Jun. 2015. https://news.starbucks.com/news/starbucks-invites-you-to-decorate-its-iconic-white-cup.

25 Gross, Max. "5 marketing campaigns that had real world impact." Marketing Eye Atlanta. 16 Feb. 2015. Web. 25 Jun. 2015. http://www.marketingeyeatlanta.com/blog/marketing/5-marketing-campaigns-that-had-real-world-impact.html.

26 Bunskoek, Krista. "52 Tips: How to Market on Instagram." Wishpond. 2014. Web. 19 Aug. 2015. blog.wishpond.com/post/59612395517/52-tips-how-to-market-on-instagram.

27 Ibid.

28 Pindoriya, Vishal. "How to Effectively Use Hashtags for Maximum Engagement." Sendible. 30 Jul. 2014. Web. 19 Aug. 2015. sendible.com/insights/how-to-effectively-use-hashtags-for-maximum-engagement/.

29 Martin, Russ. "Instagram Rolls Out Ads in Canada." 10 Nov. 2014. Web. 23 Sept. 2016. http://www.marketingmag.ca/media/instagram-ads-now-live-in-canada-129555.

30 Sloane, Garett. "Instagram Unleashes a Fully Operational Ad Business." **Adweek**. 02 Jun. 2015. Web. 18 Aug. 2015. www.adweek.com/news/technology/instagram-just-unleashed-fully-operational-ad-business-165117.

31 Ibid.

32 O'Reilly, Lara. "Instagram just made a major move that will turn it into a huge advertising business." Business Insider. 04 Aug. 2015. Web. 19 Aug. 2015. www.businessinsider.com/instagram-switches-on-ads-api-2015-8.

33 Instagram, Inc. "Announcing a New Suite of Business Tools for Brands on Instagram." Instagram. 2014. Web. 18 Aug. 2015. blog.business.instagram.com/post/95314562151/businesstools.

34 Kalra, Achir. "Instagram Bolsters Ad Analytics Offerings - Are More Advertisements to Follow?" **Forbes**. 21 Aug. 2014. Web. 20 Aug. 2015. www.forbes.com/sites/achirkalra/2014/08/21/instagram-bolsters-ad-analytics-offerings-are-more-advertisements-to-follow-ssas/.

35 Butzbach, Alex. "Want Instagram marketing data? Brands can now see impressions, reach and engagement." Brafton. 27 Aug. 2014. Web. 20 Aug. 2015. www.brafton.com/news/want-instagram-marketing-data-brands-can-now-see-impressions-reach-engagement.

36 Ibid.

37 Ibid.

5 LINKEDIN
MARKETING STRATEGIES

LinkedIn: History	LinkedIn: Personal	LinkedIn: Business	LinkedIn: Advertising	LinkedIn: Targeted Campaign	LinkedIn: Analytics
141	142	149	154	156	160

LinkedIn: History

Founded by Reid Hofman, Allen Blue, Konstantin Guericke, Eric Ly, and Jean-Luc Valliant more that a decade ago, LinkedIn has become the go-to network for working professionals. The site has changed how people look for jobs and how employers hire. "'It's not what you know, it's who you know.' LinkedIn is proof of that. Simply finding an appealing job and submitting a resume isn't enough—now companies are looking for personalized approaches and recommendations from networks."[1] LinkedIn has also "slowly evolved into more of a contact relationship management service...for individuals."[2]

LAUNCHES

2016
LinkedIn Learning

2015
Global Display Ad Network (B2B)

2013
LinkedIn Contacts

2012
SlideShare acquired; iPad App Launched

MAY 19, 2011
IPO First Publicly Traded Social Network

2008
Recruiter Corporate Teams Can Source Candidates Across Network

2007
Photos Now Addable to Profiles

2006
Recommendations and People You May Know

2005
Jobs and Subscriptions

2004
Groups

MAY 5, 2003
LinkedIn Launched

MILESTONES

2016
450+ Million Users

2015
350+ Million Users

2014
300+ Million Users

MAY 12, 2013
10th Anniversary

2011
100 Million Users

2008
50 Million Users

2007
Company Achieves Profitability

2006
5 Million Users

2005
2 Million Users

MAY 12, 2003
2708 Users

1, 2, 3, 4, 5, 6, 7, 8, 9

LinkedIn: Personal

 Discussion Questions

1. How is LinkedIn different from other social media channels?
2. What kind of content and images would you post on other platforms that you wouldn't on LinkedIn?
3. How have you used LinkedIn in the past?
4. How do you think LinkedIn could be used for marketing purposes?

Answers

1. Answers will vary, but the primary difference is:
   LinkedIn is a professional networking platform, rather than a social networking one.

2. Answers could include:
   - Frivolous content
   - Pictures of a more personal nature (e.g. a wedding anniversary dinner)
   - Anything that could polarize your network (e.g. a request to sign a petition to stop the sale of meat)

   All of these examples come with exceptions, of course. If an individual were an activist, then posting a petition might be in keeping with his or her personal brand, for example.

3. Answers could include:
   - To get a job
   - To post and share content of a professional nature
   - To network and connect with others in a similar or complementary field
   - To stay in touch with former classmates, coworkers, etc.

4. *Collect students' ideas and responses to this question. Explain that this topic will be the main focus of this chapter. At this point, however, the purpose is to gauge the students' pre-knowledge of this particular platform, and to get them to refer back to what they have already learned about marketing on social media.

LINKEDIN PERSONAL PROFILE

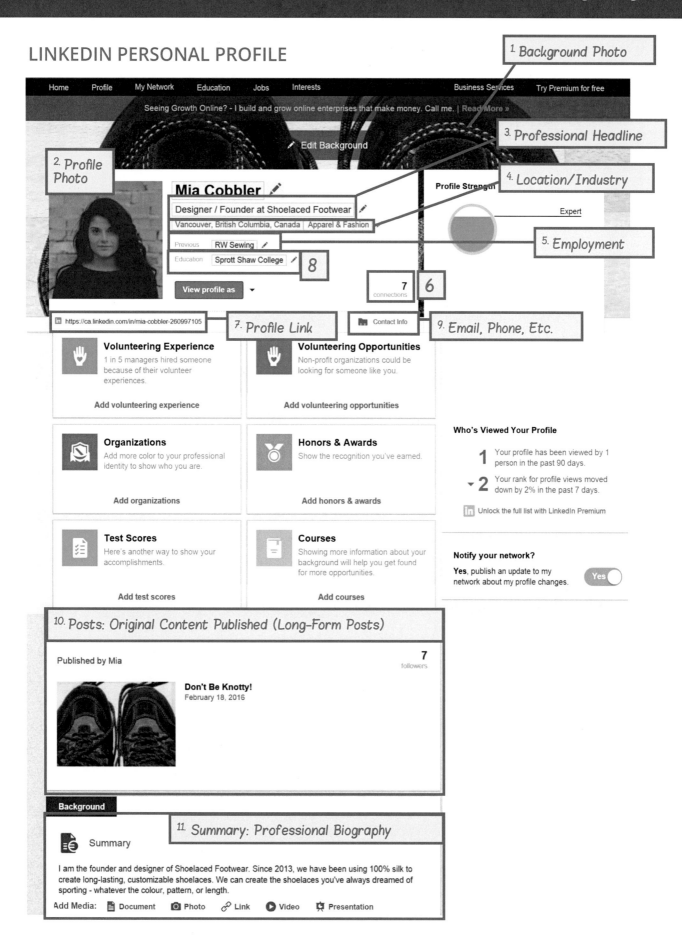

1. Background Photo

2. Profile Photo

3. Professional Headline

4. Location/Industry

5. Employment

6.

7. Profile Link

8.

9. Email, Phone, Etc.

10. Posts: Original Content Published (Long-Form Posts)

11. Summary: Professional Biography

Mia Cobbler

Designer / Founder at Shoelaced Footwear

Vancouver, British Columbia, Canada | Apparel & Fashion

Previous   RW Sewing

Education   Sprott Shaw College

View profile as

https://ca.linkedin.com/in/mia-cobbler-260997105

Profile Strength — Expert

7 connections

Contact Info

Volunteering Experience
1 in 5 managers hired someone because of their volunteer experiences.

Add volunteering experience

Volunteering Opportunities
Non-profit organizations could be looking for someone like you.

Add volunteering opportunities

Organizations
Add more color to your professional identity to show who you are.

Add organizations

Honors & Awards
Show the recognition you've earned.

Add honors & awards

Test Scores
Here's another way to show your accomplishments.

Add test scores

Courses
Showing more information about your background will help you get found for more opportunities.

Add courses

Who's Viewed Your Profile

1 Your profile has been viewed by 1 person in the past 90 days.

2 Your rank for profile views moved down by 2% in the past 7 days.

Unlock the full list with LinkedIn Premium

Notify your network?
Yes, publish an update to my network about my profile changes.

Yes

Published by Mia

7 followers

Don't Be Knotty!
February 18, 2016

Background

Summary

I am the founder and designer of Shoelaced Footwear. Since 2013, we have been using 100% silk to create long-lasting, customizable shoelaces. We can create the shoelaces you've always dreamed of sporting - whatever the colour, pattern, or length.

Add Media: 📄 Document   📷 Photo   🔗 Link   ▶ Video   📌 Presentation

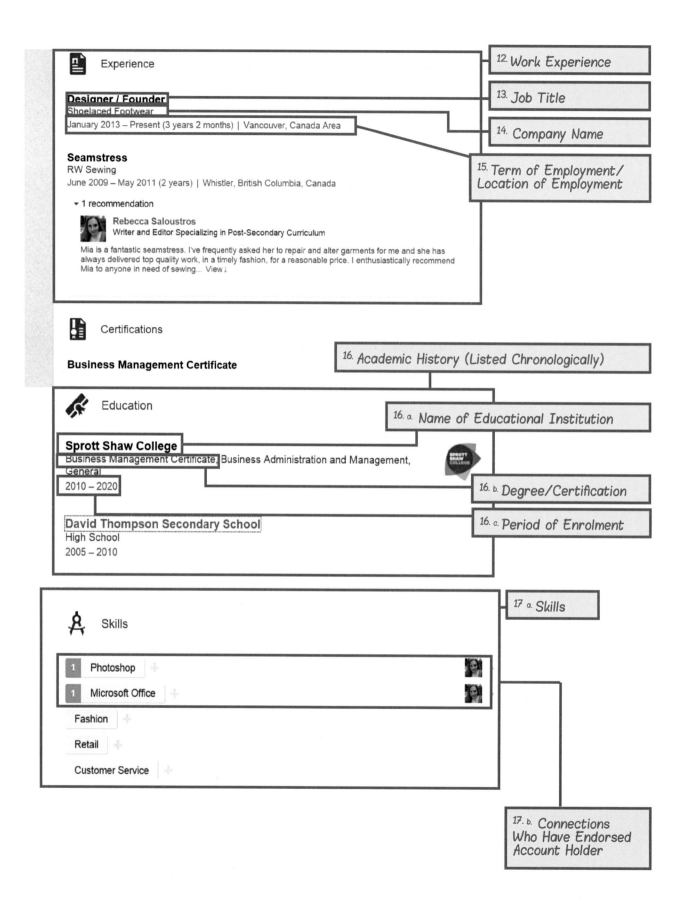

Experience

Designer / Founder
Shoelaced Footwear
January 2013 – Present (3 years 2 months) | Vancouver, Canada Area

Seamstress
RW Sewing
June 2009 – May 2011 (2 years) | Whistler, British Columbia, Canada

▾ 1 recommendation

Rebecca Saloustros
Writer and Editor Specializing in Post-Secondary Curriculum

Mia is a fantastic seamstress. I've frequently asked her to repair and alter garments for me and she has always delivered top quality work, in a timely fashion, for a reasonable price. I enthusiastically recommend Mia to anyone in need of sewing... View↓

Certifications

Business Management Certificate

Education

Sprott Shaw College
Business Management Certificate, Business Administration and Management, General
2010 – 2020

David Thompson Secondary School
High School
2005 – 2010

Skills

1 Photoshop ✦

1 Microsoft Office ✦

Fashion ✦

Retail ✦

Customer Service ✦

12. Work Experience

13. Job Title

14. Company Name

15. Term of Employment/ Location of Employment

16. Academic History (Listed Chronologically)

16. a. Name of Educational Institution

16. b. Degree/Certification

16. c. Period of Enrolment

17. a. Skills

17. b. Connections Who Have Endorsed Account Holder

Causes Mia cares about:

• Arts and Culture
• Education

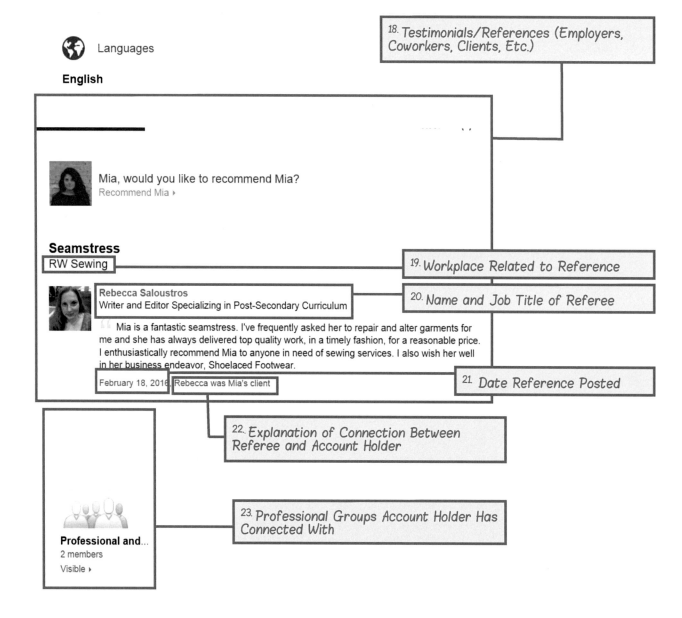

Languages

English

18. Testimonials/References (Employers, Coworkers, Clients, Etc.)

Mia, would you like to recommend Mia?
Recommend Mia ›

Seamstress
RW Sewing

19. Workplace Related to Reference

Rebecca Saloustros
Writer and Editor Specializing in Post-Secondary Curriculum

20. Name and Job Title of Referee

Mia is a fantastic seamstress. I've frequently asked her to repair and alter garments for me and she has always delivered top quality work, in a timely fashion, for a reasonable price. I enthusiastically recommend Mia to anyone in need of sewing services. I also wish her well in her business endeavor, Shoelaced Footwear.

February 18, 2016 Rebecca was Mia's client

21. Date Reference Posted

22. Explanation of Connection Between Referee and Account Holder

23. Professional Groups Account Holder Has Connected With

Professional and...
2 members
Visible ›

^{24.} *Companies, Schools, and More That The Account Holder Follows*

Following

Customize news   Customize companies

News

Leadership & Manag...
17,228,945 followers
Unfollow

Big Ideas & Innovation
14,912,906 followers
Unfollow

Technology
13,490,283 followers
Unfollow

Entrepreneurship
10,878,129 followers
Unfollow

Social Media
10,562,366 followers
Unfollow

Pulse
438,578 followers
Unfollow

Companies

Sprott Shaw College
Higher Education
Unfollow

Blanche Macdonald...
Higher Education
Unfollow

Schools

Sprott Shaw College
Canada
Unfollow

LINKEDIN PERSONAL PROFILE PAGE NOTES

PROFILES ARE PUBLIC

LinkedIn is how people present themselves as professionals to the world. Thus, it is perhaps most important on this of all platforms that the content and images on a LinkedIn profile be appropriate and enhance an individual's public persona. Also, profiles need to be as complete as possible and contain all pertinent details associated with education, work history, and other relevant experience. If an individual wants to work in marketing, for example, it's important that he or she have a significant number of connections. Naturally, an individual who is well-networked will be an asset to the industry.

Go through all the elements of the LinkedIn Profile, as indicated on the graphic, stopping periodically to discuss the notations that follow.

#1: Background Photo:

In 2014, LinkedIn gave members the option of including a background photo. This image is another way individuals and companies can ensure they stand out in the crowd and enhance their brand image. There are various ways to do this, including using graphic design techniques and color effectively.[10]

#2: Profile Photo:

LinkedIn offers its account holders some suggestions when it comes to including the right kind of profile photo. Refer to: "5 Tips for Picking the Right LinkedIn Profile Picture". Your instructor will provide you with the link.

#6: Connections:

Account holders should look at who their connections are. The quality of those connections should be much more business-oriented than they would be on Facebook, for instance. They should include:

- People within the same industry (commonality will exist on the basis of similar services offered by these individuals)
- Prospective and existing clients
- Former classmates
- Family members

Note: It is still important to include family members, as they can help to support the LinkedIn member's professional endeavors.

As mentioned earlier, it is advantageous for LinkedIn members to grow the number of connections they have, particularly if they are in an industry like marketing where being well-networked is key. However, it is important when soliciting more connections to make it clear **why** a connection is desired. Individuals should touch on something of significance that goes beyond just a shared personal connection (e.g. look for a commonality in industry).

Note for Teachers

Provide students with the link to "5 Tips for Picking the Right LinkedIn Profile Picture":
talent.linkedin.com/blog/index.php/2014/12/5-tips-for-picking-the-right-linkedin-profile-picture

🕐 ACTIVITY: IMPROVING THE PROFILE

1. Compare your profile with a classmate's.

2. How could you each improve your personal brand on LinkedIn? Make suggestions to one other and note down ideas.

3. Compare your personal profiles to a LinkedIn company page. How are they similar? Different?

4. Share your ideas.

Note for Teachers

For question three, students should just be noting down their observations. In the upcoming sections, they will discover what elements of a business profile are similar to and different from a personal profile. However, this activity gives them an opportunity to do some inductive learning.

LinkedIn: Business

SETTING UP A LINKEDIN COMPANY PAGE

A LinkedIn company page is another representation of a brand's image. Therefore, it needs to reflect a business' values and project a positive image of the company. LinkedIn walks businesses through a quick tutorial on how to begin that process by setting up a company page.

Your instructor will show you the video, "How to Set Up Your LinkedIn Company Page"now. Respond to the following questions in point form, based on what you learn from the video, and can see noted in the business profile page diagram.

Note for Teachers

Show students "How to Set Up Your LinkedIn Company Page" (02:08), available on Mujo's YouTube playlist.

Extension Activity: *Ask students to view the Think Profits' LinkedIn page and Showcase pages online as well:* http://www.linkedin.com/company/think-profits-com-inc

LINKEDIN BUSINESS PROFILE

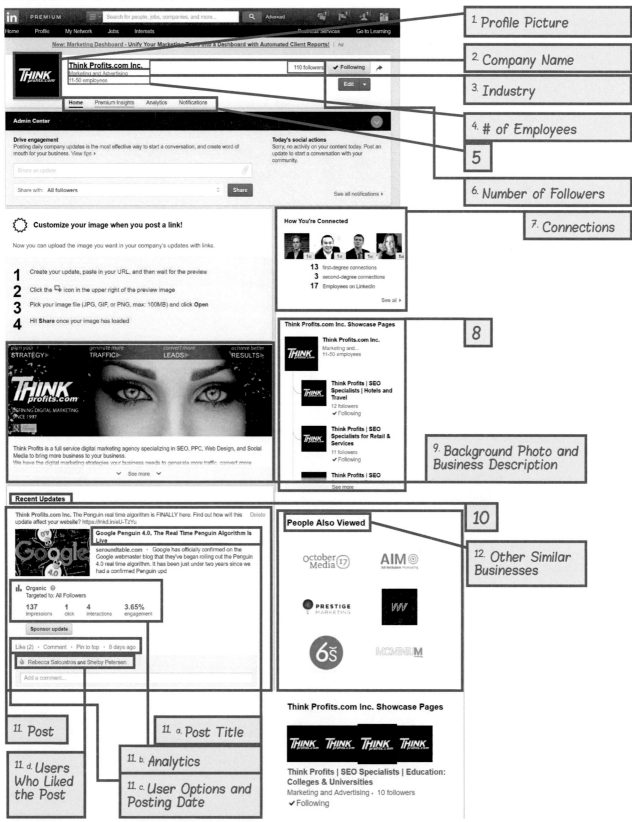

1. Profile Picture
2. Company Name
3. Industry
4. # of Employees
5.
6. Number of Followers
7. Connections
8.
9. Background Photo and Business Description
10.
12. Other Similar Businesses
11. Post
11. a. Post Title
11. b. Analytics
11. c. User Options and Posting Date
11. d. Users Who Liked the Post

QUESTIONS

1. What kind of information does a business include when it sets up a LinkedIn company page?

2. What are the first things people see when they visit a company page?

3. What kind of content needs to be expressed concisely in the company description?

Answers

1. • Type of company it is
   • Size of the company
   • Industry the business is in
   • Operating status of the business
   • Business' founding year[1]

2. • Company image
   • Company logo[2]

3. • What the company does
   • What makes the company unique[3]

UPDATES AND POSTS ON A BRAND'S COMPANY PAGE

Like on personal LinkedIn pages, businesses on LinkedIn can share or post content. Shared content could be a short update, similar to a tweet on Twitter. Followers can 'like' what a business shares by giving it a thumbs up. On the other hand, a company can also publish a post. A post is much more substantial than a quick update, and not just because it is longer. It comes from the brand's profile, establishing that it is authored by someone who has been sanctioned by the company to produce content. It too can be 'liked' and shared.

Both company updates and posts are important and should be created with care and attention to detail. LinkedIn provides guidelines as to how a brand can create meaningful content through either form.

Note for Teachers

1. Give students this link to "LinkedIn Company Pages": https://business.linkedin.com/marketing-solutions/company-pages/best-practices. Students should click on links within the page, as well.

2. Ask them to fill in the required information on the following page. They could work individually, in pairs, or in groups.

3. Ask them to share their responses with the class.

🕐 ACTIVITY: EXPANDING ON UPDATES AND POSTS ON A BRAND'S COMPANY PAGE

Add in the relevant information that you accessed from the webpage.

1. A business should include images on its page. Its two main images should be _the company logo and a cover image[4]_ .

2. Updates should be about:
   - _Company news[5]_
   - _Industry articles[6]_
   - _Thought Leadership pieces or_
   - _Followers' opinions on hot topics[7]_

3. It is best to post at least once every _weekday_ , and the highest engagement time is usually in the _morning[8]_ .

4. The best headlines are optimized and snappy. Good introductions are concise and contain a clear _call to action[9]_ .

5. Company page analytics show _"changes in the size and composition of your follower community, as well as activity on your page"[10]_ .

6. Sponsored content pricing offers a choice of _CPC_ or _CPM[11]_ to the business owner.

7. Turn your company page into a _recruitment[12]_ portal.

8. A showcase page can spotlight a _brand, business unit, or initiative[13]_ .

9. The purpose of showcase pages is to build _relationships with LinkedIn members[14]_ .

10. Note two other pieces of key information you discovered in this resource.
   - _Answers will vary, but could include: "If your business has a global presence, you can set up your Company Pages and Showcase Pages in more than 20 different languages".[15]_
   - _Stand out in the news feed by posting rich media; images generate more comments and YouTube videos more shares. [16]_

FOLLOW-UP

This activity could be started in class, but completed for homework. Students could also share their articles with one another and/or the class, as well as their responses to question two.

1. Based on what you have learned about what makes a brand's posted content effective, take a look at various posts made by companies on their LinkedIn Company pages. **Ensure that these are B2C businesses.**

2. Select one post that you think is well-written and would resonate well with the company's target audience. Explain in one to two paragraphs why it is effective, making reference to the LinkedIn articles you read in order to complete the previous activity.

OR

Select one post that you think is poorly written and would not resonate well with the company's target audience. Explain in one to two paragraphs why the post is ineffective, making reference to the LinkedIn articles you read in order to complete the previous activity.

Recent Updates

Think Profits.com Inc. When Google Makes a Mistake – how can an average person "fix" Google? Check out our new blog post "Google Makes Mistakes": http://bit.ly/1tsxWsq

When Google Makes a Mistake

thinkprofits.com · What do you do when Google is wrong? A man from Northern BC has been battling Google to get his address disassociated with a provincial park entrance.

Like (2) · Comment · Share · 1 month ago

LinkedIn: Advertising

LINKEDIN WIN

🕶 CASE STUDY: Cushy Jobs, Courtesy of Fruit of the Loom

About Fruit of the Loom

Fruit of the Loom is an American retailer that has been in business for more than 160 years. The company is known worldwide as a provider of affordable underwear, T-shirts, socks, and more.[11] Fruit of the Loom emphasizes that its garments are comfortable and fit well. The business tends to take this more pragmatic approach, rather than a fashion-forward one.

Getting Hired Never Felt So Good

'Start Happy' is Fruit of the Loom's overriding campaign. It "has a theme that is based on the idea that putting on well-fitting and comfortable undies can lift the spirits and, thus, help people start their day in a great mood."[12] Within that campaign, Fruit of the Loom initiated a promotion called 'Fresh Gigs' that focused on giving freebies to certain LinkedIn members. The process was as follows:

Step 1: A U.S.-based LinkedIn account holder got hired during a five-week period that started on October 15th, 2013.

Step 2: That individual was chosen by Fruit of the Loom to receive a free pair of cotton underwear. He or she was one of 25,000 (5,000 per week) selected by the company.

Step 3: The LinkedIn account holder got a message from Fruit of the Loom. The company told the individual that he or she would be getting "a complimentary pair of underwear to help kickstart their workday of their 'new gig.'"[13] Each person was also able to pick his or her preferred style and size of men's or women's underwear. Recipients of the free underwear were asked "to share the promotion on LinkedIn, Facebook, and Twitter."[14]

Step 4: A gift box would arrive at the LinkedIn account holder's home stating, "Fresh Fruit for Your Fresh Gig" on top of the box. Inside the box was the free pair of underwear and a coupon for five dollars off an underwear multipack.[15]

The Numbers, In Brief

Fruit of the Loom created a page that included some notable statistics about the Fresh Gigs promotion:

1. A map of America that showed, from least to most, where the underwear was sent

2. What percentage of men versus women got jobs and received underwear

3. Which industry sector employees were receiving the most pairs of underwear

4. Which styles of underwear were chosen by recipients (this was delineated by gender and industry in which the individuals were hired)[16]

QUESTIONS

1. What do you think the goal of the Fresh Gigs promotion was?

2. Re-read "The Numbers, in Brief". Why do you think Fruit of the Loom chose to post these particular numbers online?

3. Do you think the promotion utilized the LinkedIn platform effectively? Explain your answer.

Answers

1. *The goal was to change the public's perception of underwear. Many people don't consider underwear an important purchase. Yet, a competitor of Fruit of the Loom, Freshpair President Matthew Butlein, thinks they should, and likes the Fruit of the Loom campaign:*

   "'The 'Start Happy' tagline speaks to the fact that the wrong pair of underwear can really bum you out,' said Mr. Butlein, pun apparently unintended. 'Underwear is not just the first thing you put on or the last thing you take off, but rather the most important thing that you wear every day.'"[17]

2. *The statistics show which Fruit of the Loom styles are the most popular. Other consumers will see them and be motivated to purchase those particular styles. This can be compared to C&A's strategy, mentioned earlier in the text, where people could see Facebook 'likes' for particular outfits on coat hangers. Thus, they could choose the ones that were 'liked' most or choose a more niche product. In the Fruit of the Loom promotion, people became aware of what people in their industry are wearing under their clothes. Consequently, they can make the leap that a particular style of underwear is comfortable and will work for them as they perform similar duties in a similar job.*

3. *Answers will vary, but yes, the promotion was very creative and attention-grabbing. It also provided information about which industries were hiring, got people sharing the promotion on other social networks, etc.*

LinkedIn: Running a Targeted Campaign

GOALS BEFORE STRATEGY

Although this point has been mentioned before in the text, it is worth reiterating here: goals need to be set ***before*** strategies are put in motion. In the case of LinkedIn, "most marketers' goals tend to cluster into two categories:

- Brand building through **Thought Leadership**

- **Lead Generation**"[17]

'Thought Leadership' refers to creating compelling and relevant content that the target audience wants to access. As content creation for LinkedIn has been dealt with in some detail earlier in the chapter, the focus in this section will be on a range of LinkedIn ads.

⏰ ACTIVITY: LEAD GENERATION

Discuss the following questions with your classmate(s). Answer them using your own knowledge and by conducting online research. Present your findings.

1. What is 'lead generation'?

2. What is the key(s) to a successful lead generation campaign?

3. The majority of B2B and B2C marketers view lead generation as a primary goal.[18] Why?

4. How could the LinkedIn platform be used to generate leads? Note down two ideas.

Have students complete the following activity in pairs or groups. Suggested responses are provided.

Answers

1. *According to BusinessDictionary.com, 'lead generation' is defined as "the process of collecting names and contact information about qualified prospects which will be contacted by the salespeople for generating orders."[18]*

2. *According to LinkedIn, "the key to successful lead gen campaigns is to engage prospects in relevant conversations throughout their purchase consideration process. Because buyers are up to 90 percent of their way through the 'buyer's journey', or purchase decision, before making contact with your company, it is critical to build a relationship early through compelling content."[19]*

   Note: *This presupposes that the marketer has first researched and developed a good understanding of the target market and understands what niche his or her product and/ or service is going to fill within the marketplace.*

3. *Essentially, there has to be someone to sell to. Great marketing ideas and pitches have little or no purpose if there is no one to hear them. Also, the greater the number of ears that hear the pitches, the higher the chances of converting.*

4. *Join a group and participate in discussions, or host a group and initiate discussions and/ or sponsor events.*

   Note: *Private groups can designate a moderator who will approve any joining requests. This is a form of quality control, and also ensures that competitors can't infiltrate the group.*

   • *Utilize sponsored updates.*

   Example: HSBC Bank Canada utilized sponsored updates to establish key global connections. The company stated to LinkedIn that "'Sponsored Updates allowed us to select content that we feel has greatest relevance at a particular time or on a particular topic, and then highlight it to an interested audience by placing it in the LinkedIn feed.'"[20]

   Additional examples in "13 Creative Ways to Use LinkedIn for Lead Generation":

   smallbiztrends.com/2014/02/ways-use-linkedin-for-lead-generation.html

 ACTIVITY: A RANGE OF LINKEDIN ADS

Note for Teachers

Provide students with the following link: "Market to Who Matters":

https://business.linkedin.com/marketing-solutions

Marketers and business owners have many different LinkedIn ad options. Different ad styles will align better with a company's goals, than others. Your instructor will give you a link to a LinkedIn page that describes the types of ads that are available. Complete the following once you have read the article:

1. Define each type of ad in your own words.
2. Go to your LinkedIn page (Home, Profile, Mail, etc.). See how many different types of ads you can find.
3. Look at the ad that follows, and its various labeled components.
4. Note what type of ad it is and what you think the goal behind it is.
5. Comment on whether you think the ad was effective or not. Give reasons why. If you think that the ad was ineffective, suggest some ways it could be improved.

Answers

1. *Sponsored Content, Sponsored InMail, Dynamic Ads, Display Ads, Text Ads*

2. *Answers will vary.*

4. *Sponsored InMail ad; increase brand awareness*

5. *Answers will vary.*

Never Have Knotty Laces Again

Dear Charlie

Shoelaced Footwear is a Vancouver-based company offering stylish laces that will not leave you in knots. Our laces are made from 100% pure silk, and this high quality fabric makes them easy to tie and untie. They also will not fray even if worn in wet weather conditions.

Buy Now

Along with ease of use and durability, Shoelaced Footwear also offers a range of colors and patterns for customers to choose from. Match your shoes and laces for a subtle, classy look, or put your laces front and center with a bold pattern that will command attention.

Visit our website: http://shoelacedfootwear.com/ and select the shoelaces you've been looking for all your life.

Sincerely,

Mia Cobbler
Designer/Founder
shoelacedfootwear@gmail.com
(604) 123-4567

SHOELACED FOOTWEAR

Custom durable shoelaces!

1. Salutation to Targeted User

2. Body Copy

6. Ad Unit

4. Closing to Targeted User

3. Call to Action

5. Sender's Name and Contact Info.

LinkedIn: Analytics

1. *Go through the following information with students, but ask them to ignore the blank areas, until you show them the video clip.*
2. *Show students the video: "A Quick Walkthrough of LinkedIn Company Page Analytics"(03:12), available on Mujo's YouTube playlist. Ask them just to watch the video without writing down anything, so that they can focus only on understanding the material.*
3. *Show students the video a second time and ask them to fill in the blanks.*
4. *Go through the answers with students.*

COMPANY PAGE ANALYTICS

Earlier in this chapter it was established that if a brand has a well-composed LinkedIn company page, it can help ensure that its target audience views it positively. One way a business accomplishes this is to post and share content that will be relevant and useful to its audience. But, how does a business owner or marketer know if his or her content is resonating with the target audience? Beyond just looking at the number of likes and followers, and the nature of the comments, a business is able to access LinkedIn's analytics tab for company pages.

Through the analytics tab, a business owner or marketer can view data about updates, followers, and visitors.

UPDATES

In the updates section, LinkedIn shows its business account holders what posts they have uploaded. It also identifies what kind of post each one was: _a regular link post_ or _an image_ [19]. Brand metrics like impressions, clicks, and reach are examined too, along with the more social-specific metric of engagement. LinkedIn specifically defines what these terms mean for this particular platform and company pages:

"**Impressions**: The number of times each update was shown to LinkedIn members.

Clicks: The number of clicks on your content, company name, or logo. This doesn't include interactions...

Reach: A graph showing a trend on the number of times your updates were seen both organically and through paid campaigns on a daily basis."[20]

What are 'interactions'? Basically, this is what LinkedIn defines as the number of times each update was 'liked', commented on, and shared.[21]

Engagement is represented by a percentage that "shows the number of interactions plus the number of clicks and followers acquired, divided by the number of impressions."[22] And, like with reach, LinkedIn provides its company page account holders with a graphic representation of the data. In terms of engagement, the graph displays the number of times members clicked, 'liked', commented on, and shared your content in both organic and sponsored campaigns."[23]

FOLLOWERS

The followers section provides business owners and marketers with:

- Daily updates on the number of LinkedIn account holders following the company, and where those followers came from (organically or through sponsored updates and/or company follow ads)

- Follower demographics (_seniority, industry, company size, function, employee[21]_)

- Follower trends (whether the number of followers has gone up or down within a specified date range)

- How many followers a particular company has in comparison to _like companies_ and _competitors_ [24]

VISITORS

The visitors section gives business owners and marketers the following information through various graphs:

1. Page views

2. Career page clicks (only applicable if a company has a career page): a company would want a career page if it was _looking to gain some employees_ .[25]

3. Unique visitors (similar to page views, except that it "removes duplicate visits to a single page such as when a member refreshes your Company Page or navigates away from it, but returns later"[26])

4. Visitor demographics[27]

Note for Teachers

Return to the video and pause it at various points. Ask students questions related to the data presented (When did the company have the lowest engagement in the month of July? How would you describe the type of followers the company is attracting? How does the company compare to its competitors in terms of follower numbers?). Ask students to evaluate how the business' page is performing overall.

ᴗᴗ CASE STUDY: ABC Digital Agency Analytics

What follows is an example of the kind of analytics a company can access about its page through LinkedIn. ABC Digital Agency maintains a premium account with the social media network.

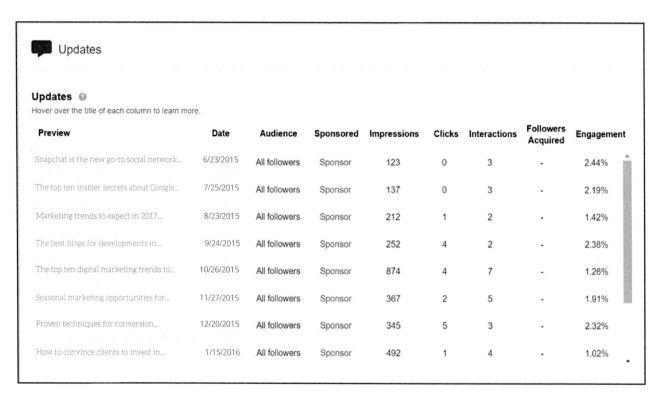

Preview	Date	Audience	Sponsored	Impressions	Clicks	Interactions	Followers Acquired	Engagement
Snapchat is the new go-to social network...	6/23/2015	All followers	Sponsor	123	0	3	-	2.44%
The top ten insider secrets about Google...	7/25/2015	All followers	Sponsor	137	0	3	-	2.19%
Marketing trends to expect in 2017...	8/23/2015	All followers	Sponsor	212	1	2	-	1.42%
The best blogs for developments in...	9/24/2015	All followers	Sponsor	252	4	2	-	2.38%
The top ten digital marketing trends to...	10/26/2015	All followers	Sponsor	874	4	7	-	1.26%
Seasonal marketing opportunities for...	11/27/2015	All followers	Sponsor	367	2	5	-	1.91%
Proven techniques for conversion...	12/20/2015	All followers	Sponsor	345	5	3	-	2.32%
How to convince clients to invest in...	1/15/2016	All followers	Sponsor	492	1	4	-	1.02%

Note: The first column lists the partial title of the update. The fourth column makes it clear that the updates are not sponsored, as the link to do so is still active.

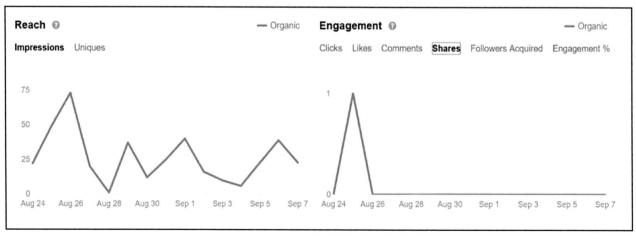

Note: These graphs indicate the reach and engagement that has occurred during a 15-day period.

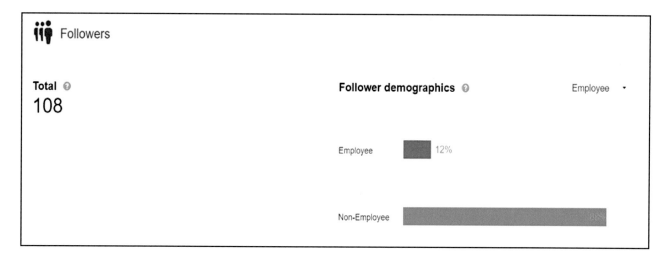

Note: It is common for employees to follow their company's LinkedIn page. This graph helps the business owner to see the ratio of employee to non-employee in terms of followers.

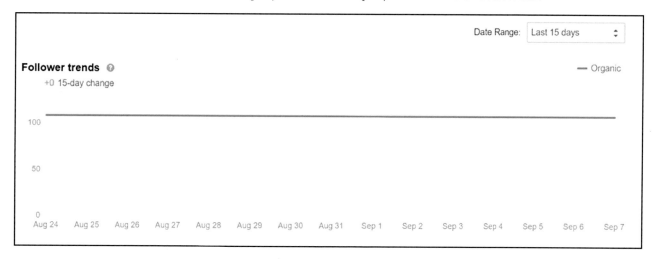

Note: Here it is obvious that the company's followers have not experienced any change over this specified time period (i.e. It hasn't lost or gained any followers). Notice that the date range can be modified.

	Followers	Grow Your Follower Base
MacDonald Digital Agency	712	**Attract More Followers**
Red Rock Agency	244	Followers are your brand advocates - driving word of mouth, recommendations, and referrals. Learn some simple but effective techniques for growing this important community.
Baines & Morgan	152	Learn more
Essence Agency	112	
ABC Digital Agency	108	

Note: This graphic compares the account holder with its competitors in terms of how many followers it has, and then presents a CTA to encourage that account holder to grow its follower base.

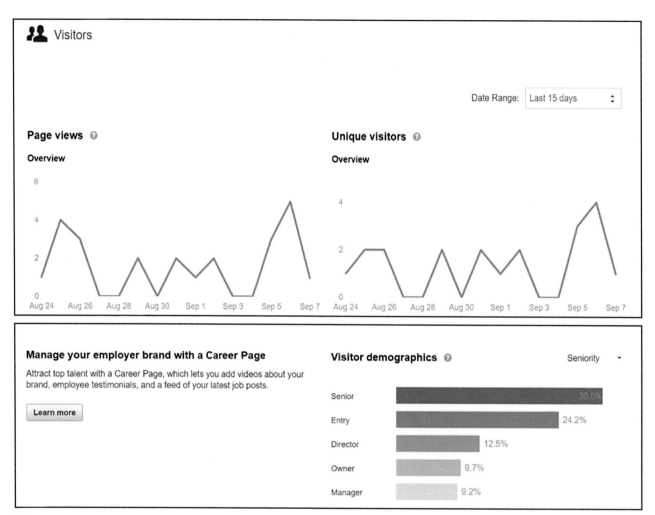

Note: These graphs tell the account holder about its visitors, including what career levels they have attained within their own companies. It is possible to drill down into even more detail as the following graphs demonstrate.

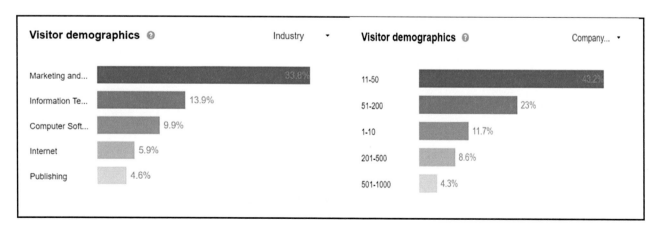

Note: The graph on the left tells the account holder what industries visitors are employed in. The graph on the right shows the size of companies the visitors are employed in.

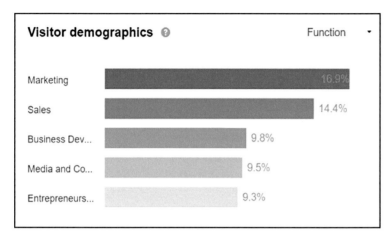

Note: This graph specifies what type of roles visitors are employed in within their industries.

ADDITIONAL ANALYTICS EXAMPLES

If analytics are enabled by the account holder and he or she just wants to see a quick snapshot of page engagement, it is possible to go to 'notifications' and get that information.

Earlier, it was noted that the account holder can look at a list of page updates and see how they are performing. It is also possible to click on each post and see more details about its performance over a particular date range. What follows is an example of just this. The date range can be adjusted.

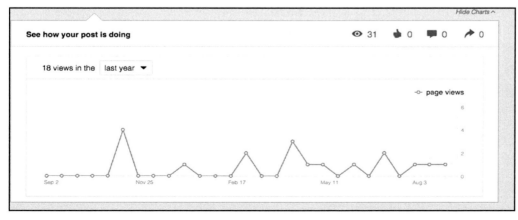

Extension Activity: In June 2016, Microsoft bought LinkedIn for more than 26 billion dollars. Ask students: Based on everything you have learned about LinkedIn, do you think Microsoft made a wise decision to purchase the social network at such a high price? This could be an excellent debate topic that students could research ahead of time to bolster their positions. Sample articles for them to review include:

"This is the Real Reason Microsoft Bought LinkedIn" (Yes, LinkedIn was worth it): http://www.forbes.com/sites/grantfeller/2016/06/14/this-is-the-real-reason-microsoft-bought-linkedin/#6d1f0cca4acd

"LinkedUp" (No, LinkedIn was not worth it): http://www.economist.com/news/business-and-finance/21700605-it-one-most-expensive-tech-deals-history-it-may-not-be-smartest-making-sense

CHAPTER REVIEW

1. What kind of content should be included on a LinkedIn company page in the description?

2. What images should appear on a company's LinkedIn page?

3. Describe the Fresh Gigs promotion and what marketers can learn from it.

4. What goals do marketers have when it comes to LinkedIn?

5. What kind of LinkedIn ad encourages a business' followers to share messages and write product recommendations?

Chapter Review (Optional)

The following questions can be utilized in a variety of ways (e.g. Students can complete them for homework, in class with a partner, orally in a whole-class format, etc.).

1. • What the company does
   • What makes the company unique[22]

2. Its logo and a cover photo[23]

3. Answers will vary. Some takeaways could include:
   1. Be creative.
   2. Grab the audience's attention.
   3. Understand the social media platform and the people utilizing it; adjust the style, tone, and look of the campaign accordingly.

   Note: Although all kinds of people are on LinkedIn, it is a more professional and conservative platform than other social media channels. Smart brands will understand this and tailor their campaigns accordingly.

4. Brand building and lead generation[24]

5. Social ads[25]

FOOTNOTES: CHAPTER 5

1   LinkedIn Marketing Solutions, "How to Set Up Your LinkedIn Company Page." **YouTube**. Online Video Clip, https://www.youtube.com/watch?v=VoZt5_77nsI (accessed 27 Aug. 2015).
2   Ibid.
3   Ibid.
4   LinkedIn Corporation. "Company Page Best Practices." LinkedIn. 2017. Web. 02 Jun. 2017. https://business.linkedin.com/marketing-solutions/company-pages/best-practices.
5   Ibid.
6   Ibid.
7   Ibid.
8   Ibid.
9   Ibid.
10 Ibid.
11 Ibid.
12 Ibid.
13 —. "Showcase Pages." LinkedIn. 2017. Web. 02 Jun. 2017. https://business.linkedin.com/marketing-solutions/company-pages/showcase-pages.
14 Ibid.
15 LinkedIn Corporation. "Company Page Best Practices." LinkedIn. 2017. Web. 02 Jun. 2017. https://business.linkedin.com/marketing-solutions/company-pages/best-practices.
16 Ibid.
17 Newman, Andrew Adam. "Fruit of the Loom Sees Workers in Their Underwear." **The New York Times**. 03 Oct. 2013. Web. 14 August 2015. http://www.nytimes.com/2013/10/04/business/media/fruit-of-the-loom-sees-workers-in-their-underwear.html?_r=0.
18 WebFinance, Inc. "Lead Generation." BusinessDictionary.com. 2015. Web. 02 Sept. 2015. www.businessdictionary.com/definition/lead-generation.html.
19 LinkedIn Corporation. "The Sophisticated Marketer's Product Showcase Series: LinkedIn Sponsored Updates." LinkedIn. 06 Aug. 2015. Web. 02 Sept. 2015. https://business.linkedin.com/content/dam/business/marketing-solutions/global/en_US/campaigns/pdfs/LMS_SophGuideSponUpdates_eB-final_08.06.15.pdf.
20 Ibid.
21 VerticalResponse, "A Quick Walkthrough of LinkedIn Company Page Analytics" **YouTube**. Online Video Clip, https://www.youtube.com/watch?v=gPYOma26kkE (accessed 27 Aug. 2015).
22 LinkedIn Marketing Solutions, "How to Set Up Your LinkedIn Company Page." **YouTube**. Online Video Clip, https://www.youtube.com/watch?v=VoZt5_77nsI (accessed 27 Aug. 2015).
23 LinkedIn Corporation. "Company Page Best Practices." LinkedIn. 2017. Web. 02 Jun. 2017. https://business.linkedin.com/marketing-solutions/company-pages/best-practices.
24 —. "The Sophisticated Marketer's Product Showcase Series: LinkedIn Sponsored Updates." LinkedIn. 06 Aug. 2015. Web. 02 Sept. 2015. https://business.linkedin.com/content/dam/business/marketing-solutions/global/en_US/campaigns/pdfs/LMS_SophGuideSponUpdates_eB-final_08.06.15.pdf.
25 Prodromou, Ted. "9 Ways to Advertise on LinkedIn." **Entrepreneur**. 28 Apr. 2015. Web. 26 Aug. 2015. www.entrepreneur.com/article/243440.

FOOTNOTES: CHAPTER 5

1 Yeung, Ken. "LinkedIn is 10 years old today: Here's the story of how it changed the way we work." The Next Web. 05 May 2013. Web. 27 Jul. 2015. http://thenextweb.com/insider/2013/05/05/linkedin-10-years-social-network/.
2 Ibid.
3 LinkedIn Corporation. "A Brief History of LinkedIn." LinkedIn. 2015. Web. 16 Jul. 2015. http://ourstory.linkedin.com.
4 Priestley, Theo. "LinkedIn Is Not Facebook, But It Clearly Wants To Be And It's Turning Away Users." **Forbes**. 25 Jul. 2015. Web. 27 Jul. 2015. http://www.forbes.com/sites/theopriestley/2015/07/25/linkedin-is-not-facebook-but-it-clearly-wants-to-be-and-its-turning-away-users/.
5 Conner, Cheryl. "New Research: 2014 LinkedIn User Trends (And 10 Top Surprises)." **Forbes.** 04 May 2014. Web. 29 Jul. 2015. http://www.forbes.com/sites/cherylsnappconner/2014/05/04/new-research-2014-linkedin-user-trends-and-10-top-surprises/.
6 Smith, Craig. "By the Numbers 125+ Amazing LinkedIn Statistics." DMR. 21 Jul. 2015. Web. 29 Jul. 2015. http://expandedramblings.com/index.php/by-the-numbers-a-few-important-linkedin-stats/.
7 O'Reilly, Lara. "LinkedIn has launched an audience network, its first big leap into ad tech." **Business Insider**. 19 Feb. 2015. Web. 29 Jul. 2015. http://www.businessinsider.com/linkedin-launches-an-ad-network-2015-2.
8 Smith, Craig. "By the Numbers: 133 Amazing LinkedIn Statistics." DMR. 16 Aug. 2016. Web. 08 Oct. 2016. http://expandedramblings.com/index.php/by-the-numbers-a-few-important-linkedin-stats/.
9 Roslansky, Ryan. "Introducing LinkedIn Learning, A Better Way to Develop Skills and Talent." LinkedIn. 22 Sept. 2016. Web. 08 Oct. 2016.
10 Arruda, William. "5 Easy Ways to Create a Brilliant Background for Your LinkedIn Profile." **Forbes**. 09 Nov. 2014. Web. 24 Aug. 2015. www.forbes.com/sites/williamarruda/2014/11/09/5-easy-ways-to-create-a-brilliant-background-for-your-linkedin-profile/.
11 Fruit of the Loom, Inc. "The Fruit Story." Fruit of the Loom. 2015. Web. 14 Aug. 2015. http://shop.fruit.com/info/The_Fruit_Story.
12 Gonzalez, Leah. "Fruit of the Loom and LinkedIn Team Up for Ad Campaign." PSFK. 07 Oct. 2013. Web. 13 Aug. 2015. www.psfk.com/2013/10/fruit-of-the-loom-linkedin-underwear.html.
13 Ibid.
14 Ibid.
15 Ibid.
16 Fruit of the Loom, Inc. "Fresh Gigs." Fruit of the Loom. 13 Aug. 2015. Web. 13 Aug. 2015. starthappy.fruit.com/fresh-gigs.
17 LinkedIn Corporation. "The Sophisticated Marketer's Product Showcase Series: LinkedIn Sponsored Updates." LinkedIn. 06 Aug. 2015. Web. 02 Sept. 2015. https://business.linkedin.com/content/dam/business/marketing-solutions/global/en_US/campaigns/pdfs/LMS_SophGuideSponUpdates_eB-final_08.06.15.pdf.
18 —. "The Sophisticated Marketer's Product Showcase Series: LinkedIn Sponsored Updates." LinkedIn. 06 Aug. 2015. Web. 02 Sept. 2015. https://business.linkedin.com/content/dam/business/marketing-solutions/global/en_US/campaigns/pdfs/LMS_SophGuideSponUpdates_eB-final_08.06.15.pdf.
19 VerticalResponse, "A Quick Walkthrough of LinkedIn Company Page Analytics" **YouTube**. Online Video Clip, https://www.youtube.com/watch?v=gPYOma26kkE (accessed 24 Aug. 2015).
20 LinkedIn Corporation. "Analytics Tab for Company Pages." LinkedIn. 18 Aug. 2015. Web. 03 Sept. 2015. https://help.linkedin.com/app/answers/detail/a_id/26032/~/analytics-tab-for-company-pages.
21 Ibid.
22 Ibid.
23 Ibid.
24 Ibid.
25 VerticalResponse, "A Quick Walkthrough of LinkedIn Company Page Analytics" **YouTube**. Online Video Clip, https://www.youtube.com/watch?v=gPYOma26kkE (accessed 24 Aug. 2015).
26 LinkedIn Corporation. "Analytics Tab for Company Pages." LinkedIn. 18 Aug. 2015. Web. 03 Sept. 2015. https://help.linkedin.com/app/answers/detail/a_id/26032/~/analytics-tab-for-company-pages.
27 Ibid.

 # #6

YOUTUBE
MARKETING STRATEGIES

YouTube: History	YouTube: Personal	YouTube: Business	YouTube: Advertising	YouTube: Targeted Campaign	YouTube: Analytics
170	171	174	177	181	184

YouTube:History

Before YouTube, home entertainment consisted of whatever was on the TV schedule or available at the video store. Crazy antics by ordinary people were the stuff of *Candid Camera* and *America's Funniest Home Videos*. YouTube changed all that and now almost anything from anywhere is viewable all the time.

LAUNCHES

FEB. 14, 2005
Paypal employees Chad Hurley, Steve Chen, and Jawed Karim start YouTube

MAY 28, 2005
YouTube in Beta

APRIL 2009
Vevo Music Service

DECEMBER 2008
HD Video

AUGUST 2007
Advertisements

JANUARY 2010
Movie Rental Service

APRIL 2011
YouTube Live

JUNE 2015
YouTube Newswire

SEPT. 13, 2016
YouTube Community

MILESTONES

APRIL 23, 2005
The first YouTube video is uploaded.

OCTOBER 2006
Google buys YouTube for $1.65 billion.

DECEMBER 2012
Psy's "Gangnam Style" is the first video to get 1 billion views.

SEPT. 1, 2016
YouTube reaches 1,325,000,000 users.

SEPTEMBER 2005
A Nike ad is the first to get 1 million views.

2011 - ARAB SPRING
YouTube becomes the medium through which pro-democracy messages are sent.

MAY 28, 2015
YouTube turns 10.

1, 2, 3, 4, 5, 6, 7, 8

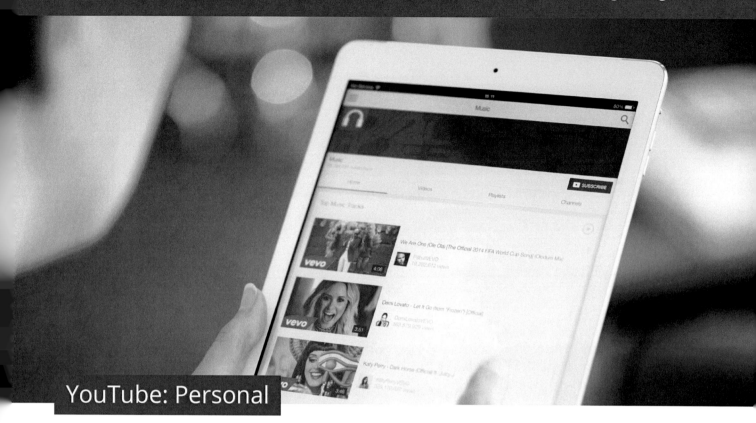

YouTube: Personal

 Discussion Questions

1. What do you utilize YouTube for?
2. Have you ever uploaded a YouTube video? If so, how successful was it in terms of views, likes, etc.?
3. Do any of your videos contain advertising? If so, what kind?

INTRODUCTION

YouTube is the medium through which two primary activities happen: video viewing and video uploading. People, it seems, will watch videos of almost anything; from the superficial (cats riding robot vacuums) to the significant (political elections). It also seems that people will create and upload videos of almost anything as well. "For some it is a way of sharing the latest video of the kids (or cats). For others, it is a way of making a living."[9] The sequence goes something like this:

- Content creators upload videos, and some choose to allow ads.

- YouTube sells ad space on those videos.

- Content creators whose videos are sufficiently popular can earn real money.

What follows is a video tutorial that will show in part one what features are available to YouTube viewers. In part two, the world of video uploading, which some YouTube viewers never access, is also explained.

VIDEO TUTORIAL: YOUTUBE FOR VIEWERS AND UPLOADERS

Note for Teachers

Show students the video, "YouTube for Viewers and Uploaders" (02:41), available on Mujo's YouTube playlist, perhaps stopping at various spots to show additional examples online.

TRANSCRIPT:

PART ONE

So, here is the YouTube homepage. On the left, you can choose from several video categories: music, sports, gaming, and so on. If you have an account, you will be able to access 'subscribed-to' channels and personalized recommendations. Let's stop here for a moment and define those terms.

A 'channel' is the name of a YouTube account. In the next section, 'YouTube: Business', we're going to look at exactly what the components of a YouTube account are. At this point, though, we are going to talk about what it means to subscribe to a YouTube account.

By subscribing to a channel, a separate individual is asking to be notified every time the account holder uploads content. This doesn't mean, however, that the content from other similar channels, (account holders) will appear in the subscription feed. That will come in the form of recommendations, as YouTube keeps a history of the kind of videos a person watches.

How do people give feedback on videos? "YouTube, unlike a lot of other sites with social networking features, explicitly allows users to like or dislike a video. These simple votes are anonymous."[1] However, a like cannot be 'unliked', in the way that it can on Facebook. An individual really needs to commit to his or her opinion on YouTube. "Comments are different. You must log in with a valid YouTube account to leave a comment, so they're never anonymous. However, you can remove a comment that you've made."[2]

PART TWO

Uploading a video to YouTube isn't difficult. The first step is being an account holder. Then, naturally, there needs to be a video to upload. It's possible to create, edit, and upload the video on a mobile phone using YouTube's Capture app. Here is the app recording a video. Then, the account holder can make a few edits, adjust privacy settings, create a title and description, and finally share the video to YouTube and other social media platforms, if desired. On a desktop, a video can be downloaded and then edited using an external software app. All the account holder needs to do after that is go to the YouTube website and upload it from there.

⏰ ACTIVITY: VIRAL VIDEOS

In Course 1, **Digital Marketing Fundamentals**, viral advertising videos were discussed briefly. Recall some of the ideas you and your classmates came up with regarding why a video goes viral.

1. With your classmate(s), select a product that one of you has with them (e.g. a cell phone, pen, backpack, etc.).
2. Pretend that you can make a 30-second YouTube video to sell that product.
3. Think about all the viral videos you have seen, particularly the example your instructor just showed you, and the elements that made them so popular.
4. Brainstorm some ideas that you could include in your YouTube video that might have a chance of making it go viral, thus improving the sales of your product.
5. Present your ideas.

Note for Teachers

Lead the discussion with students and then present the following information on the whiteboard.

Unfortunately, there's no exact science when it comes to predicting what will and will not go viral. However, some general tips would include:

- Be entertaining.
- Create a good quality video.
- Produce videos regularly.

Being entertaining is the most important of these and the most difficult to achieve.

Case Study: Psy's "Gangnam Style" (04:12)

Show students the music video, available on Mujo's YouTube playlist.

Ask students why they think this particular video went viral. Note their reasons on the whiteboard. They could include:

- The song is over-the-top and its creators don't take themselves too seriously. Thus, the audience knows that it's okay to laugh at it.

- Psy and the other performers do dance moves that are easy to imitate, so again the audience can also join in.

- The song has an upbeat tempo with some repetitive lyrics in English that people can sing along to. It's not necessary to understand Korean to enjoy the song. Once more, this demonstrates the importance of recognizing that YouTube is a global platform.

- The performers wear some outlandish clothing in bright colors, which is in keeping with the overall fun, upbeat nature of the song.

- The scenes in the video keep changing and the song isn't particularly long, demonstrating that the creators are aware that today's audiences, particularly the YouTube viewing audience, have short attention spans.

Students can also refer to a more detailed analysis of why "Gangnam Style" became popular by accessing: "Why Gangnam Style Became So Popular – The Reasons Behind Its' Horse-Riding Success!": http://blog.socialmaximizer.com/why-gangnam-style-became-so-popular/

Extension Activity: Have students create a 30-second YouTube video selling the product. Have them post it online and see how many views it gets. Ask other students to view the video and give one another feedback regarding how to make it more popular.

YouTube: Business

VIDEO TUTORIAL:
THE COMPONENTS OF A BUSINESS' YOUTUBE CHANNEL

Show students the video, "Components of YouTube for Business" (02:38), available on Mujo's YouTube playlist, perhaps stopping at various spots to show additional examples online.

TRANSCRIPT:

Anyone can get a channel on YouTube. All that's required is a Google or Google My Business account. Businesses large and small often opt to do so, as it's free and very easy to set one up. There are lots of online videos showing YouTubers how to do that, but in this video we are just going to focus on the components of the channel itself.

Here is an example of one company's channel. Let's start at the top of the page:

This is the business' channel art. It looks really similar to a Facebook cover photo and other banner-like art at the top of various profile pages on multiple social media platforms. Don't underestimate the importance of this image. It, like Facebook cover photos, helps to put forth the brand's desired persona.

Below the channel name there is the menu bar with 'home', 'videos', 'playlists', 'channels', and 'about', as well as the search function. After looking at the components of this home page, we'll return to these other items.

The video you see under the menu is the channel's featured video. It could take the form of either the company's most recent upload or could be a fixed video that serves as an introduction to what the business has to offer consumers. Next to the featured video is some information including: the video's title, the number of views it has, when it was uploaded, and a description. It's important that video titles and descriptions are accurate. People who click on the video thinking it is about one thing will be annoyed if they start watching and find out that it is about something else.[3] So, this is a rule of thumb for personal and business-oriented videos uploaded on YouTube.

Now, below this featured video are a series of other videos grouped by categories. Each one has the same type of information as the featured video provided below it. If we return to the channel's menu and click the 'videos' tab, we see more videos the company has uploaded. There are three tabs that can be used to customize how they are displayed, like so **[demo grid, date added, and uploads]**.

The business can also create playlists **[click tab]** and feature additional channels **[click tab]**. The 'about' page shows account holders the total number of views, when the account holder joined YouTube, a brief description of the business itself, and other links to the business' social media and website.

Note for Teachers

Students can complete the following activity in pairs or groups. Students could be asked to present their findings to the class and/or submit them to the instructor for evaluation.

ACTIVITY: EVALUATING A BUSINESS' YOUTUBE CHANNEL

1. With your classmate(s), select a business' YouTube channel. It should be a company or brand with which you are familiar.

2. Your task is to evaluate how well the business is utilizing its channel to market itself.

3. Use the following checklist to help you reach an overall conclusion about the effectiveness of the channel as a whole:

CHECKLIST FOR BUSINESS' YOUTUBE CHANNELS

√ Cover art is visually appealing and presents a positive image of the brand.

√ Channel name is concise and accurately describes what the channel is about.[3]

√ Featured video is compelling and can be linked to a business goal(s).

√ Range of videos is available, showing viewers a complete brand picture.

√ "YouTube channel layout [is] clear and easy for fans to navigate. Playlists help your audience find all of your videos on a certain topic, improving the user experience."[4]

√ Video titles, video descriptions, and the company description all contain keywords.

OPTIMIZING A YOUTUBE CHANNEL

Business owners and marketers want people to view their YouTube channel. They also want their YouTube viewers to become subscribers. The more popular a channel is, the higher it will rank on YouTube. The question is: how do business owners and marketers ensure their channel is popular? What follows are some strategies that can help a brand achieve this:

1. **Integrate Google My Business with YouTube.**
   Note: The YouTube channel integrated in Google My Business allows Google to see the brand's content offerings and **relevance** in rich media such as videos.

   Show students the videos, "Introducing Google My Business" (01:25) and "Google My Business" (05:12) available on Mujo's YouTube playlist.

2. **Link. Link. Link.**
   - Ensure that the YouTube video being viewed contains links to the brand's other social media channels. Also, ensure that the video's description contains links to company landing page(s) and/or the website.
   - Add a YouTube button to the company website.
   - Add a YouTube button or link on the company's other social media channels.

3. **Solicit Subscriptions.**
   - Add a 'subscribe' pop-up that appears ahead of all videos.

   Show students some examples in this section.

4. **Insert keywords.**
   - A video title can include a few keywords, ensuring that it doesn't make the title too long.
   - All video descriptions should be search-engine optimized.

   Note: "Make sure you're targeting keywords that relate to the content of your video. The goal is to make the best video to answer those keyword queries, not to game the system."[10]

5. **Upload a video's transcript.**
   - The purpose of doing this is twofold:
     » To assist the video's viewers when it comes to following the brand narrative
     » To present additional keywords that the search engine can pick up on

   Show students some examples in this section.

6. **Include tags.**
   - The purpose of tags is to help the search engine find a video creator's videos. YouTube provides video creators with suggested tags that they can add for a video as well.

   Note: They are only visible to the video creator, not the video's viewers. However, it still isn't advisable to go overboard. Only "use as many tags as necessary to accurately describe your video."[11]

🕐 ACTIVITY: TAGGING

1. Refer back to the previous activity.
2. Select a video from the channel you examined.
3. Come up with at least five tags that you would include if you were the content creator and wanted your video to be found by the search engine.

Ask students to submit their work for homework or present some examples in class.

YouTube: Advertising

YOUTUBE FAILS AND WINS

Death. It's one of the more evocative words in the English language. Say it to one person and he or she is thinking about the tearful funeral of a beloved relative. Yet, mention it to another and Halloween costumes and spine-tingling scary movies come to mind. As an advertising theme, death isn't off limits to marketers, but context is everything. What follows are two ad campaigns that took on the grim reaper and met with very different fates.

YOUTUBE FAIL

CASE STUDY: Hyundai's Pipe Job

About Hyundai

The Hyundai Motor Company was started in Korea back in 1967. In the 1980s, cars like the Hyundai Excel and Sonata became very popular in North America. A decade later, the Korean auto giant began developing fuel cell electric vehicles and solar-powered cars. The company's eco-friendly automotive ventures continued into the new millennium with the launches of hybrids and more electric cars. In 2012, the Korean brand was even "named the most fuel efficient and least CO_2 emitting brand by the U.S. Environmental Protection Agency."[12]

Hyundai's Pipe Dream Becomes a Nightmare

In April 2013, a Hyundai advertisement produced in Europe surfaced online.[13] It showed a depressed man attempting to kill himself in his garage while breathing in the exhaust fumes produced by his

SUV, the ix35. He does not succeed because Hyundai's ix35 produces water-only emissions.[14]

Hyundai's ad was also unsuccessful. In fact, the one-minute spot received scathing criticism on social media and some people took to their blogs to express their outrage.[15] The ad was particularly upsetting to individuals who had loved ones who had killed themselves in this manner.[16]

Hyundai's Response to the Controversy

Hyundai Motor Europe attempted to quell public outrage by doing three things: apologizing, taking down the video, and promising not to include it in any future marketing.[17] Suicide prevention activists responded positively to the company's decision to pull the ad, "'We know from research that graphic depictions of suicide in the media can inadvertently lead to further suicides, a phenomenon known as contagion,' said Robert Gebbia, executive director for the American Foundation for Suicide Prevention. 'This advertisement was particularly graphic and potentially dangerous. We are pleased that Hyundai has decided to pull this campaign.'"[18]

Note for Teachers

Ask students to watch the video, "Hyundai: Pipe Job" (01:01) available on Mujo's YouTube playlist.

QUESTIONS

1. Why did "Pipe Job" fail?

2. How did the fact that the ad was launched on YouTube, rather than TV affect the public response?

3. Many would argue that suicide should never be used as the subject matter of an advertisement. It is one of those topics that people worldwide will respond negatively to. Are there any other topics or subject matter that you think would have a similar impact and should be taboo? Discuss this with your classmates, thinking about YouTube as the advertising platform.

Answers

1. Answers could include:
   - It evoked bad memories for its target audience.
   - It also evoked concern that others might copy the dangerous behavior it depicted.
   - It made light of suicide, which is a serious topic.
   - The audience's focus wasn't on the car or the zero emissions feature; it was on the suicide attempt.

2. By launching an ad on YouTube, Hyundai Europe reached a global audience. If the ad had been broadcast on TV, it would probably have stayed within the continent. Thus, because people worldwide saw the ad, shared, and linked to it across the Internet it went viral, resulting in a global outcry. This is why American experts discussed the ramifications of the ad, for example.

3. Answers will vary.

YOUTUBE WIN

PUBLIC SERVICE ANNOUNCEMENTS (PSAS)

Public Service Announcements (PSAs) are designed to educate the public about important issues. They are created by ad agencies for clients like the government, activist groups, and charitable organizations. These ads remind people to avoid drinking and driving, put out campfires, stop smoking, and generally adopt a healthy, safe lifestyle. However, these ads often feature gory images of worst-case scenarios or upsetting realities that can turn off their target audience.

Note for Teachers

Explain to students that this anti-smoking commercial (or one like it, if you prefer to show something else) is an example of this kind of PSA. Ask students to watch the video, "Effects of Smoking on Human Body" (00:33) available on Mujo's YouTube playlist.

⌐◎ CASE STUDY: Metro Trains

Metro Trains Reinvents the PSA

However, not all PSAs are cut from the same cloth. When McCann Melbourne was asked to create one for rail safety by Metro Trains, the agency went for entertaining, creative, and cute, rather than morbid and depressing. This decision was not simply based on a desire to amuse the public. It was a carefully thought-out strategy, engineered to promote sharability and virality and spawn parodies and tributes.[19] The result was "Dumb Ways to Die". The video became an Internet phenomenon by:

* Creating cute and likeable characters
* Making the video inclusive (The characters don't have a particular gender, age, cultural background, or ethnicity; the animals aren't kangaroos and koalas, they're creatures that would be familiar to people worldwide)
* Structuring the video so that YouTube viewers could break it up into smaller segments and share them, rather than the entire three-minute ad
* Including a catchy song and launching it on various music sharing platforms
* Putting the video on other channels, as well as a karaoke version
* Introducing a video game app based on the ad, once the video's virality waned[20]

The Aftermath of "Dumb Ways to Die"

To say the ad campaign was a success is an understatement. As of October 2016, the original ad has received more than 140 million views on YouTube.[21] It has received tens of millions of impressions, and in one month the campaign reached 46% of its target audience. Subsequent videos have been made, including parodies. The ad's song "charted on iTunes in 28 countries and sold more than 100,000 copies."[22]

In the ad's extended poster campaign at train stations, over a million people pledged to be safer around trains, and there was a significant reduction in train accidents after the campaign's run.[23]

Note for Teachers

Show students the "Dumb Ways to Die" videos in the following order (all are available on Mujo's YouTube playlist):

Original: "Dumb Ways to Die" (03:02)

Parody: "Dumb Movie Ways to Die - Dumb Ways to Die Parody" (03:06)

Minecraft: "Dumb Ways To Die (Minecraft Edition)" (03:12)

Dumb Ways to Die Video Game ad: "Dumb Ways to Die 2 - Leg Training" (00:31)

Dumb Ways to Die Video Game ad: "Dumb Ways to Die 2 - Spin Training" (00:31)

QUESTIONS

1. How does the "Dumb Ways to Die" ad differ from other PSAs?

2. How did McCann Melbourne demonstrate that it had an excellent understanding of the YouTube platform?

3. What takeaways can be made about YouTube advertising, based on this example?

Answers

1. It did not feature realistic, gory images of worst-case scenarios that could turn off the target audience. Instead, it was entertaining, creative, and cute.

2. McCann Melbourne designed the video and campaign to promote sharability. It did this by understanding that YouTube's audience is worldwide, and thus the characters had to be generic-looking or familiar to a global audience. It ensured that the video could easily be broken down into smaller segments and shared that way.

3. Answers will vary, but this case study does demonstrate that:
   - Cross-platform social media marketing works effectively.
   - Being unique and breaking a traditional marketing formula will catch people's attention.
   - Parodies and tributes also help to keep the momentum going for an original ad.
   - YouTube marketing needs to factor in how things are shared (e.g. in short segments) and why things are likely to go viral.

YouTube: Running a Targeted Campaign

 Discussion Questions

In the previous sections, YouTube channels and full-length YouTube ads were examined. However, other advertising options exist on the platform that marketers can use to increase the effectiveness of a campaign.

1. What other ways have you seen YouTube used as a marketing platform?

2. Do you think certain forms of YouTube marketing (recall your responses to the previous question) are more effective than others?

3. What specific examples of YouTube marketing can you recall?

Different Kinds of YouTube Ads

Ask students to read about display ads, overlay ads, skippable video ads, non-skippable video ads and long, non-skippable video ads, and bumper ads. Students can ignore 'sponsored cards' for now. Share this link with them: "YouTube Advertising Formats": https://support.google.com/youtube/answer/2467968?hl=en

For homework, ask students to find an example of three of the ad types and take screenshots (three in total). They should then reassess their answer to question two, explaining in writing (approximately half a page) why a specific ad style(s) would be more effective than another.

Note: All of these ads are forms of interruption marketing. Consequently, students should first look at them as viewers only, not as future marketers. Chances are, they will respond to them negatively, albeit to varying degrees. Thus, the question may become: would they want to use any of them? Are stand-alone ads, and possibly YouTube cards (to be discussed in the next section) better alternatives?

YOUTUBE CARDS

In 2015, YouTube introduced YouTube cards, which replaced annotations. Annotations enabled an account holder to "layer text, links, and hotspots over [his or her] video".[24]

Now, a YouTube card is composed of an image, title, and call-to-action text that essentially makes the video an interactive experience for the audience. A user will be able to identify a video with a YouTube card because a teaser will be visible for a few seconds. However, even after the teaser disappears, the card will be accessible until the video ends. A marketer can incorporate up to five cards in a single video, but they will be more effective if they make sense within the context of that video and aren't displayed one right after another (i.e. spacing them out is better).[25]

YouTube will determine which account holders see which YouTube cards based on three factors: the performance of a particular card (which a marketer can track in YouTube Analytics), the behavior of the viewer, and the device the viewer is using.[26]

Have you seen YouTube cards? Clicked on them? Are they a good marketing option?

TYPES OF CARDS

As of October 2016, YouTube offered six kinds of cards:

1. **Donation card:** used when fundraising for a U.S. non-profit organization
2. **Channel card:** added when recommending or linking to another YouTube channel
3. **Fan Funding card**: enabled so that fans can contribute to a YouTube creator's channel
4. **Link card:** can refer to an associated website, crowdfunding, or merchandise card
5. **Poll card:** added so that viewers can vote
6. **Video or Playlist card:** used to link to another public YouTube video or playlist of viewer interest, a specific point in the video, or a specific video in the playlist by entering a URL directly.[27]

Example:
Business selected: Safeway
Video description: A chef prepares a simple salmon recipe using fish purchased at Safeway.

CARD ONE	CARD TWO	CARD THREE
Type: Channel card **Links to:** the chef's channel	**Type:** Link (Merchandise) card **Links to:** a special on salmon in Safeway's online flyer	**Type:** Video or Playlist card **Links to:** a video that shows various side dishes that pair well with salmon **Note:** It would be beneficial to include the original video in an original playlist that follows an applicable theme.

🕐 ACTIVITY: SELECTING YOUTUBE CARDS

1. Read about each type of card on YouTube's Help Page, "Add Cards to Videos". Your instructor will provide you with the link.
2. Select a business and choose three types of cards that could be featured on its page.
3. Describe what each card would link to.

YouTube provides internal analytics for both videos and cards. It is important that business owners and marketers are able to interpret the data garnered from You Tube's analytics correctly. This information is critical in helping them make data-driven, rather than subjective decisions, which can ultimately make or break a social media campaign.

Note for Teachers

Provide students with the link to "Add Cards to Videos": https://support.google.com/youtube/answer/6140491?hl=en

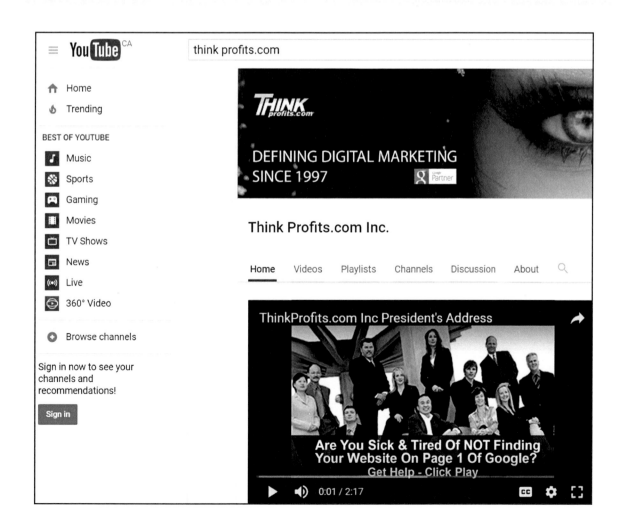

YouTube: Analytics

🕐 ACTIVITY: YOUTUBE ANALYTICS AND CARDS ANALYTICS

PART ONE
1. Your instructor is going to split your class into two large, 'expert' groups. One group will be responsible for examining YouTube Analytics and the other will be responsible for taking a close look at Cards Analytics. He or she will give you all the resources you need to understand your assigned analytics program.
2. You will have 25 minutes to become an 'expert'. Take notes, keeping in mind what will be required of you in part two of this activity.

PART TWO
1. Now that you know all about your assigned analytics program, you need to partner with a classmate who was in the other group.
2. You will now teach him or her what you learned in your expert group. You have ten minutes maximum to do this, so while you may utilize online resources, the best way to do so is to use your own words and perhaps one example.
3. Switch roles.

Note for Teachers

The most efficient way to set up this activity is to either split the class down the middle or number students as ones or twos and get them to sit together. If you have an especially large class, you may want to create multiple Group Ones (YouTube Analytics) and multiple Group Twos (Cards Report/Analytics).

Please see the Appendix for the resources packages you will be giving students: 'YouTube Analytics Resource Package' and 'Cards Report/Analytics Resource Package'. Photocopy/ share them, as needed.

CHAPTER REVIEW

1. How is a YouTube like different from a Facebook like?

2. List three ways a brand can optimize its YouTube channel.

3. What should marketers learn from Hyundai's "Pipe Job" fail?

4. Explain how the Metro Trains ad, "Dumb Ways to Die", promoted sharability, virality, parodies, and tributes. List at least three explanations.

5. The following describes a _____ card:

    This type of card allows a business owner or marketer to promote his or her licensed products directly from the video.[28]

    a. Fundraising

    b. Link (Merchandise)

    c. Channel

    d. Fan Funding

Chapter Review (Optional)

The following questions can be utilized in a variety of ways (e.g. Students can complete them for homework, in class with a partner, orally in a whole-class format, etc.).

1. • A YouTube like is anonymous, but a Facebook like isn't.
    • A YouTube like cannot be retracted in the way a Facebook one can.

2. Answers could include: Integrate Google My Business with YouTube.
    • Insert keywords.
    • Include tags.

3. Answers will vary, but suggested responses could be:
    • Consider all possible ways the target audience could respond to an ad before launching it on social media. Stay in tune with their feelings.
    • Err on the side of caution and exercise good judgement, rather than taking a risk that could harm the brand's reputation.

4. Answers could include:
    • Structuring the video so that YouTube viewers could break it up into smaller segments and share them, rather than the entire three-minute ad
    • Including a catchy song and launching it on various music sharing platforms
    • Putting the video on other channels, as well as a karaoke version

5. b. Link (Merchandise)

FOOTNOTES: CHAPTER 6

1   Smith, Matt. "The YouTube Guide: From Watching to Production." MakeUseOf. 08 Feb. 2012. Web. 29 Aug. 2015. http://www.makeuseof.com/tag/using-youtube-from-consumption-to-production/.
2   Ibid.
3   Wisuri, Rachel. "How to Boost Your YouTube Visibility." Social Media Examiner. 04 Jun. 2015. Web. 09 Sept. 2015. www.socialmediaexaminer.com/youtube-visibility/#more-84239.

FOOTNOTES: CHAPTER 6

1   Dickey, Megan Rose. "The 22 Key Turning Points in the History of YouTube." Business Insider. 15 Feb. 2013. Web. 24 Aug. 2015. www.businessinsider.com/key-turning-points-history-of-youtube-2013=2?op=1.
2   ColdfusTion, "The Surprising History of YouTube!" **YouTube**. Online Video Clip, http://www.youtube.com/watch?v=P4dT-IW9260 (accessed 24 Aug. 2015).
3   O'Neill, Megan. "An Infographic Timeline of YouTube's First 8 Years." **Adweek**. 06 Feb. 2013. Web. 24 Aug. 2015. www.adweek.com/socialtimes/infographic-timeline-youtube/119333.
4   Perez, Sarah. "YouTube Launches YouTube Newswire, A Channel Featuring Verified Eyewitness Videos." TechCrunch. 18 Jun. 2015. Web. 24 Aug. 2015. techcrunch.com/2015/06/18/youtube-launches-youtube-newswire-a-channel-featuring-verified-eyewitness-videos/#.de6ohx:0es2.
5   Rediff.com. "20 milestones in the history of YouTube." Rediff.com. 19 Feb. 2013. Web. 24 Aug. 2015. www.rediff.com/business/slide-show/slide-show-1-tech-20-milestones-in-the-history-of-youtube/20130219.htm#9.
6   YouTube Spotlight, "The A-Z of YouTube: Celebrating 10 Years." **YouTube**. Online Video Clip, https://www.youtube.com/watch?v=Wwokkq685Hk (accessed 24 Aug. 2015).
7   Google. "YouTube Community goes beyond video." **YouTube**. 13 Sept. 2016. Web. 08 Oct. 2016. https://youtube-creators.googleblog.com/2016/09/youtube-community-goes-beyond-video.html.
8   Statistics Brain. "YouTube Company Statistics." Statistics Brain. 01 Sept. 2016. Web. 08 Oct. 2016. http://www.statisticbrain.com/youtube-statistics/.
9   Smith, Matt. "The YouTube Guide: From Watching to Production." MakeUseOf. 08 Feb. 2012. Web. 29 Aug. 2015 http://www.makeuseof.com/tag/using-youtube-from-consumption-to-production/.
10 Wisuri, Rachel. "How to Boost Your YouTube Visibility." Social Media Examiner. 04 Jun. 2015. Web. 09 Sept. 2015. www.socialmediaexaminer.com/youtube-visibility/#more-84239.
11 Ibid.
12 Hyundai Motor Company. "History." Hyundai. 2015. Web. 28 Aug. 2015. http://worldwide.hyundai.com/WW/Corporate/CorporateInformation/History/index.html.
13 CBC/Radio-Canada. "Hyundai apologizes for offensive suicide ad." CBC News. 25 Apr. 2013. Web. 29 Aug. 2015. http://www.cbc.ca/news/business/hyundai-apologizes-for-offensive-suicide-ad-1.1403848.
14 Adsoftheworldvideos, "Hyundai: Pipe Job." **YouTube**. Online Video Clip, https://www.youtube.com/watch?v=jgffnYlAe9c (accessed 28 Aug. 2014).
15 CBC/Radio-Canada. "Hyundai apologizes for offensive suicide ad." CBC News. 25 Apr. 2013. Web. 29 Aug. 2015. http://www.cbc.ca/news/business/hyundai-apologizes-for-offensive-suicide-ad-1.1403848.
16 Ibid.
17 Ibid.
18 Woodyard, Chris and Fred Meier. "Hyundai yanks suicide ad." **USA Today**. 25 Apr. 2013. Web. 29 Aug. 2015. http://www.usatoday.com/story/money/cars/2013/04/25/hyundai-suicide-ad-commercial/2113461/.
19 Diaz, Ann-Christine. "How 'Dumb Ways to Die' Won the Internet, Became the No. 1 Campaign of the Year." **Advertising Age**. 11 Nov. 2013. Web. 24 Jun. 2015. http://adage.com/article/special-report-the-awards-report/dumb-ways-die-dissected/245195/.
20 Ibid.
21 DumbWays2Die. "Dumb Ways to Die." **YouTube**. Online Video Clip, https://www.youtube.com/watch?v=IJNR2EpS0jw (accessed 14 Oct. 2016).
22 Diaz, Ann-Christine. "How 'Dumb Ways to Die' Won the Internet, Became the No. 1 Campaign of the Year." **Advertising Age**. 11 Nov. 2013. Web. 24 Jun. 2015. http://adage.com/article/special-report-the-awards-report/dumb-ways-die-dissected/245195/.
23 Ibid.
24 Google. "Create and edit annotations." YouTube Help. 2015. Web. 10 Sept. 2015. https://support.google.com/youtube/answer/92710?hl=en.
25 Viper Gaming Central. "Youtube Tips: An Overview of Cards on YouTube" **YouTube**. Online Video Clip, https://www.youtube.com/watch?v=vtST3vOcZP8 (accessed 09 Nov. 2015).
26 Ibid.
27 Google. "Add Cards to Videos." YouTube. 2016. Web. 11 Oct. 2016. https://support.google.com/youtube/answer/6140493?hl=en.
28 Ibid.

#7 YELP
MARKETING STRATEGIES

Yelp: History	Yelp: Personal	Yelp: Business	Yelp: Advertising	Yelp: Targeted Campaign	Yelp: Analytics
188	189	193	198	201	205

Yelp: History

Before review sites like Yelp existed, people would ask their friends, relatives and neighbors for recommendations. Now, any time individuals want to know where to eat, get an oil change, or even what church to attend, they have that information at their fingertips.

Launches

- **2016**
  Yelp Knowledge

- **2015**
  Yelp's First TV and Digital Ad Campaign

- **2014**
  Yelp Reservations

- **2012**
  Direct from Site Ordering Platform for Takeout and Delivery

- **2009**
  Public Commenting for Business; Owners Can Respond Publicly to Reviews

- **2008**
  Business Owner Accounts; Owners Can Connect with Reviewers Privately

- **2005**
  Revamped Site, Allowing Review sharing

- **October 13, 2004**
  Yelp Launched By Former PayPal Employees, Jeremy Stopelman and Russel Simmons

Milestones

- **2016**
  102 Million Reviews

- **2015**
  83 Million Reviews

- **October 13, 2014**
  Yelp's 10th Anniversary

- **November 17, 2011**
  Yelp files for IPO

- **2011**
  20 Million Reviews

- **2010**
  15 Million Reviews

- **November 2008**
  4 Million Reviews over the Previous 30 Days

- **2006**
  100,000 Reviews

- **2004**
  First Restaurant Review Posted

1, 2, 3, 4, 5, 6

Yelp: Personal

Discussion Questions

1. Have you ever reviewed a business on Yelp?

   If so, think of one review you wrote and answer the following questions:
   a. What kind of business was it?
   b. How many stars did you give the business?
   c. What did you write in the body of your review?
   d. What motivated you to write the review?

   Answers will vary. Ask students to share their Yelp reviews, if they are comfortable doing so.

   If not, respond to the following questions:
   a. Why haven't you written a Yelp review?
   b. Have you written a review on any other social media site, blog, etc.? If so, respond to the questions noted earlier about that review(s).

2. Why do you think review sites are important? Give two reasons.

Note for Teachers

Answers will vary, but it is important to establish that review sites are important, regardless of whether people like them or not. Once students have given their responses, explain the following:

Yelp and other online review sites are important and powerful because:

• There's strength in numbers. Yelp has a large audience:

83 million reviews in 2015 from 32 countries that were seen by 162 unique individuals every month[1]

• Takeaway: It's important that businesses and marketers are where the audience is.

• Good reviews can increase a business' bottom line. "A Harvard researcher estimated that a one-star increase in a restaurant's average rating — the maximum is five stars — yields a 5 percent to 9 percent rise in sales."[2]

• Takeaway: Businesses that make improvements based upon what they hear from consumers will have a higher chance of success.

YELP PERSONAL PROFILE

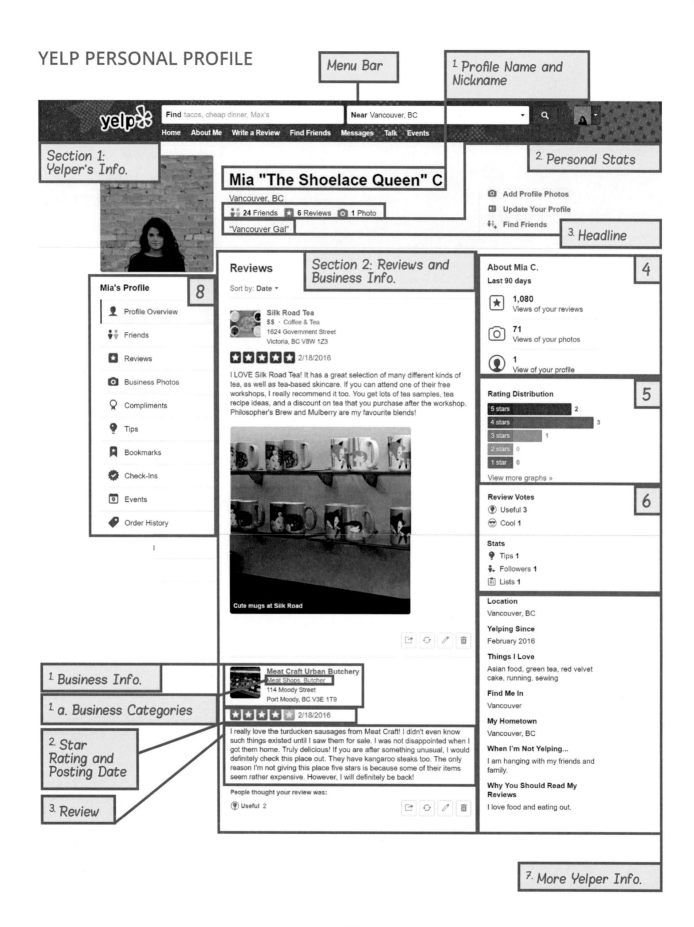

Menu Bar

1. Profile Name and Nickname

Section 1: Yelper's Info.

2. Personal Stats

Mia "The Shoelace Queen" C

Vancouver, BC

24 Friends　6 Reviews　1 Photo

"Vancouver Gal"

Add Profile Photos
Update Your Profile
Find Friends

3. Headline

Reviews
Sort by: Date

Section 2: Reviews and Business Info.

About Mia C.
Last 90 days

4

Mia's Profile

8

Profile Overview
Friends
Reviews
Business Photos
Compliments
Tips
Bookmarks
Check-Ins
Events
Order History

Silk Road Tea
$$ · Coffee & Tea
1624 Government Street
Victoria, BC V8W 1Z3

★★★★★ 2/18/2016

I LOVE Silk Road Tea! It has a great selection of many different kinds of tea, as well as tea-based skincare. If you can attend one of their free workshops, I really recommend it too. You get lots of tea samples, tea recipe ideas, and a discount on tea that you purchase after the workshop. Philosopher's Brew and Mulberry are my favourite blends!

Cute mugs at Silk Road

★ 1,080
Views of your reviews

71
Views of your photos

1
View of your profile

Rating Distribution

5

5 stars　2
4 stars　3
3 stars　1
2 stars　0
1 star　0

View more graphs »

Review Votes

6

Useful 3
Cool 1

Stats
Tips 1
Followers 1
Lists 1

Location
Vancouver, BC

Yelping Since
February 2016

Things I Love
Asian food, green tea, red velvet cake, running, sewing

Find Me In
Vancouver

My Hometown
Vancouver, BC

When I'm Not Yelping...
I am hanging with my friends and family.

Why You Should Read My Reviews
I love food and eating out.

1. Business Info.

1 a. Business Categories

2. Star Rating and Posting Date

3. Review

Meat Craft Urban Butchery
Meat Shops, Butcher
114 Moody Street
Port Moody, BC V3E 1T9

★★★★☆ 2/18/2016

I really love the turducken sausages from Meat Craft! I didn't even know such things existed until I saw them for sale. I was not disappointed when I got them home. Truly delicious! If you are after something unusual, I would definitely check this place out. They have kangaroo steaks too. The only reason I'm not giving this place five stars is because some of their items seem rather expensive. However, I will definitely be back!

People thought your review was:
Useful 2

7. More Yelper Info.

PERSONAL PROFILE PAGE NOTES

Note for Teachers

Go through all the elements of the Yelp Profile, as indicated on the graphic, stopping periodically to discuss the following notations:

SECTION ONE: YELPER'S INFORMATION

This section is similar to Facebook's 'About' and 'Timeline' tabs. It gives other Yelpers some personal information about the account holder and some statistics about his or her friends, ratings, etc. Also similar to Facebook, the platform lets the account holder decide how much or how little he or she wishes to include.

#2 Personal Stats:

Reviews: After a Yelper posts a review, he or she can update it. According to Yelp, the account holder's update will appear above his or her original review, "and both will be visible to the public and the business owner. Only the newest star rating will be factored into the overall star rating of the business."[7]

#4 About Mia Analytics: The Yelper learns how many people have viewed his or her reviews, photos, and profile.

#5 Rating Distribution: A bar graph represents how many five-star, four-star, etc. reviews the Yelper has completed in total. Yelp also provides graphs that show the Yelper's 'Top Reviewed Categories' and 'Top Reviewed Neighborhoods'.

#6 and #8 Review Votes, Stats, and Profile:

Tips: Specific recommendations about a particular aspect(s) of a business, as opposed to a detailed examination of the business as a whole (i.e. a review)

Compliment: One Yelper can give another a compliment on his or her review. The compliment can be personalized or selected from a compliment type list (e.g. Great Photo, You're Funny, Good Writer, etc.).[8]

Lists: The lists feature enables the account holder to organize his or her reviews into categories (e.g. Best British Pubs, Winning Late-Night Eateries, etc.).

SECTION TWO: REVIEWS AND BUSINESS INFO.

This section really gets down to the nitty-gritty of what Yelp is all about: reviews. It's here that the account holder tells other Yelpers what he or she really thinks about a particular business.

#1 Business Info:

a. **Business Categories:** This informs the account holder about what kind of services and products the business provides, or in the case of a restaurant, the type of cuisine it serves.

Note: Yelp sometimes uses dollar signs to indicate where a business falls in its pre-determined pricing scale:

» $ = inexpensive
» $$ = moderate
» $$$ = pricey
» $$$$ = ultra high-end[9]

#2 Star Rating and Posting Date:

Star Rating: Yelp allows the reviewer to give a business a five- to one-star rating. The star equivalence is as follows:

» 5 stars: "Woohoo! As good as it gets!"
» 4 stars: "Yay! I'm a fan."
» 3 stars: "A-OK."
» 2 stars: "Meh. I've experienced better."
» 1 star: "Eek! Methinks not."[10]

Note: Contrary to popular belief, most people don't only use Yelp to leave negative reviews; "79% of the reviews on the site are 3 stars or higher."[11]

Social Media Strategy Project Consultations

Remind students that their final projects are due on the last day of the course. Spend a couple of minutes meeting with each student, responding to any questions they may have. While consultations are going on, students can work on their final projects and/or seek feedback from one another. Also mention that on the final day of class there will be some time set aside to debrief and share experiences incurred while doing the project.

Yelp: Business

INTRODUCTION

Yelp is composed of two main elements: personal and business. As was discussed in the previous section, 'personal' refers to Yelp as a platform for the posting of reviews. In Canada, this is accessed through yelp.ca and in the United States through yelp.com. The business side of Yelp encompasses how businesses describe, build, and optimize their profiles through biz.yelp.ca or biz.yelp.com. Many businesses are on Yelp whether they choose to be or not. A listing for a business can be created by any Yelp account holder, so it's important that the company itself claims its listing. That way, the business can build out its profile, enabling users not only to find it, but see the images and information the business wants to convey.

Note for Teachers

Go through all the elements of the business page, as indicated on the graphic, stopping periodically to discuss the following notations:

YELP BUSINESS PROFILE

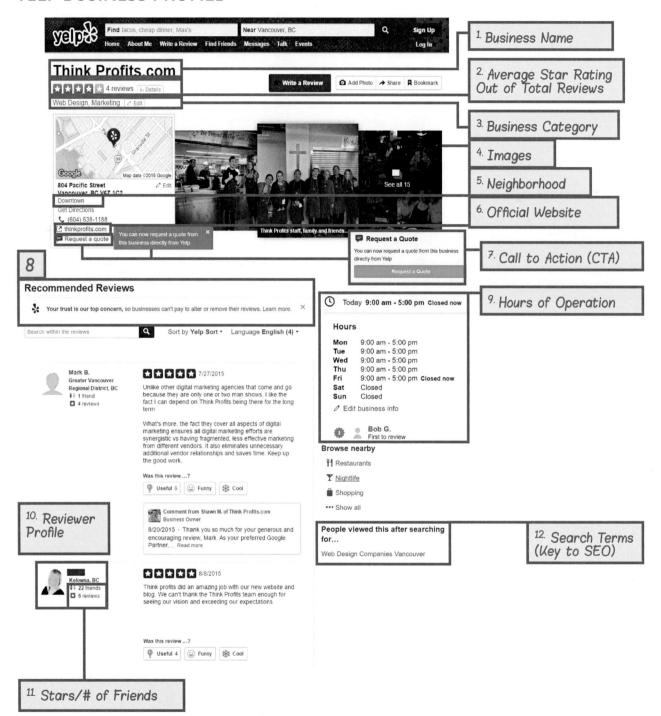

1. Business Name
2. Average Star Rating Out of Total Reviews
3. Business Category
4. Images
5. Neighborhood
6. Official Website
7. Call to Action (CTA)
8.
9. Hours of Operation
10. Reviewer Profile
11. Stars/# of Friends
12. Search Terms (Key to SEO)

Page 1 of 1

2 other reviews that are not currently recommended ▾

From the business

Specialties

Think Profits is a Vancouver based SEO company and digital marketing agency that brings Page 1 visibility to your business.

If you want more leads, a better search result, a brand new look or a more dynamic website, the team at Think Profits has the know-how.

We specialize in the Hotelier, Education, Manufacturing and Real Estate Development industries. We deliver proven results in reducing OTA's for Hoteliers, increasing lead generation, conversion and growing revenue for our more than 1,600 clients in Canada and the United States.

Our full range of digital marketing services is designed to get you to the place you want to be online. Turn your website into a source of revenue with Think Profits.

History

Established in 1997.

Shawn Moore started Think Profits in 1997 with a mission to make "the Internet profitable for his clients" through Internet marketing and search engine friendly web development.

With over 18 years of Internet marketing breakthroughs under their belt, Think Profits has implemented effective online strategies for a number of companies to help them successfully expand into a global market, harnessing the power and reach of the Internet to achieve outstanding profits and business growth.

Meet the Business Owner

 Shawn M.
Business Owner

Shawn Moore is a pioneering expert in the field of Digital Strategy, SEO, PPC, and Web Analytics Consulting.

In 1997 Shawn founded Think Profits, one of Western Canada's leading digital marketing agencies. Think Profits specializes in developing profitable digital marketing strategies which, when implemented with search engine optimized web development, achieve page 1 positioning on Google and Bing. By utilizing internet search, email, social media, content, and other digital marketing approaches, Shawn's proven methods continue to help his clients generate hundreds of millions of dollars in sales and revenue.

His 30 years of experience includes working with over 1600 clients across North America, in Education, Manufacturing & Distribution, Retail & Services, and Hotels & Travel markets.

13. Hidden Reviews

Note for Teachers

Ask students to read Yelp's explanation on "Does Yelp recommend every review?" and view the featured video, "Why Does Yelp Recommend Reviews?" (01:53): http://www.yelp-support.com/article/Does-Yelp-recommend-every-review?l=en_US

14. Description from the Business:

'Specialties' Note: Focus on what the business does best and what sets it apart from the competition. Be descriptive because "the more descriptive you are, the more likely consumers are to find you."[12]

BUSINESS PAGE LAYOUT AND COMPONENTS

#2 Average Star Rating Out of Total Reviews: If a business owner or Yelper clicks on the 'details' button, he or she will see a bar graph that shows how many stars the business has received in each star category (e.g. 14 five-star reviews, 3 four-star reviews, etc.). Yelp calculates the average star rating only using reviews that have been recommended using its software (this will be discussed later in the chapter).[13]

#3 Business Category: A business can select up to three categories on its Yelp page. They are listed in order too. The first one is how the business owner primarily identifies his or her operation. The second and third are secondary and tertiary.[14]

#4 Images: On this business page, there are images. Pictures are important; "the more high quality photos the more interesting [a] page is going to be. According to Review Trackers research, people searching Yelp for local businesses spend 2.5 times more time on a Yelp listing with photos."[15]

Ideally, a business should include pictures with people in them. For example, a staff picture is much more powerful than a picture of the company's logo or the business' retail location. Seeing images of people helps the target audience to connect on a more human level to the business. This is especially important, as the majority of brands on Yelp are B2C.

#8 Recommended Reviews & #13 Hidden Reviews:

On this business page, there are recommended reviews and hidden reviews. Obviously, the more reviews a business has, particularly positive ones, the better it is likely to be perceived. If an individual clicks on the hidden reviews, he or she will often see a mix of positive and negative ones. So, why is Yelp hiding these, especially when the positive ones could help the business?

Interestingly, whether a review is hidden or not has nothing to do with the nature of the business itself. Instead, Yelp's focus is on the reviewer. If he or she is posting fake reviews (indicated by the fact that multiple reviews under different names are coming from the same computer) or is biased (the reviewer is related to the business owner), then that reviewer's content will be hidden.[16]

However, a reviewer's content can also be hidden if he or she has not built up credibility through an established history of reviews on Yelp. Therefore, if a reviewer is new and posts his or her first review, Yelp won't show it. Or, if someone has only posted one or two reviews over a year, they won't be shown either. As the reviewer posts more, his or her previous content will start appearing. This process is built into Yelp's often misunderstood algorithm.

#12 Search Terms (Key to SEO):

The information in this section indicates that these terms should appear in the business' description, if they are not there already, with the proviso that they must represent the company's Unique Selling Proposition (USP). In other words, if a brand wants to rank higher in Yelp search results, it needs to optimize its page using the right terminology. On the flip side, business owners and marketers should be aware that reviews containing these keywords will also help to rank a company in Yelp search results, making it more visible.

Note 1: Yelp needs an algorithm such as this because it must stay relevant, useful, and credible. If people stop viewing Yelp as a trustworthy source, no one will continue to utilize it and it will ultimately fail. With this in mind, Yelp has a vested interest in being perceived as an honest, reliable source of feedback.

Note 2: This sample page contains all the necessary information Yelp suggests the owner fill out. It also contains images. A more complete page appears better and ranks higher.

ACTIVITY: CRITIQUE A BUSINESS PAGE

PART ONE

Recall all of the elements we have just discussed and refer to the sample page to complete the following activity. Also, refer back to the section on Yelp in Course 1, *Digital Marketing Fundamentals*, if possible.

1. Select a company that you are familiar with *and* that has claimed its business page on Yelp.

2. Critique the business page, examining its content and images. What elements are missing? What could be improved?

3. Read through the reviews. Has the business owner responded to them? How has he or she handled negative reviews, if at all?

PART TWO

1. Find a partner. Your classmate will show you the business page that he or she has just critiqued.

2. Read through the page and the reviews.

3. You now need to imagine that you are the owner of the business that is associated with this Yelp page, and your partner is a marketer you have hired to help improve your page.

4. Listen to your partner's recommendations for improvements. Do you agree with them?

5. Switch roles. You are now going to give recommendations to your partner.

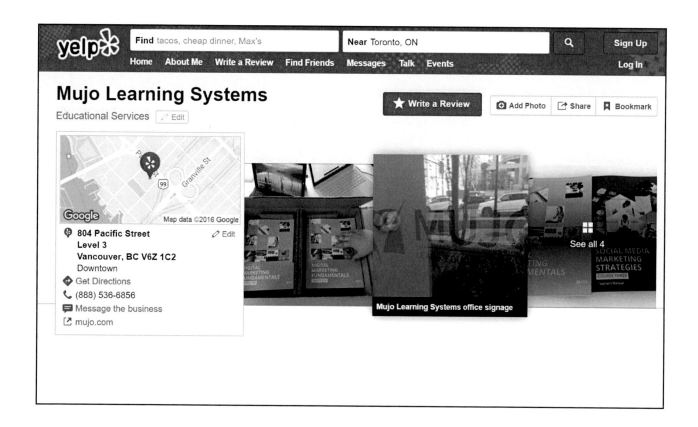

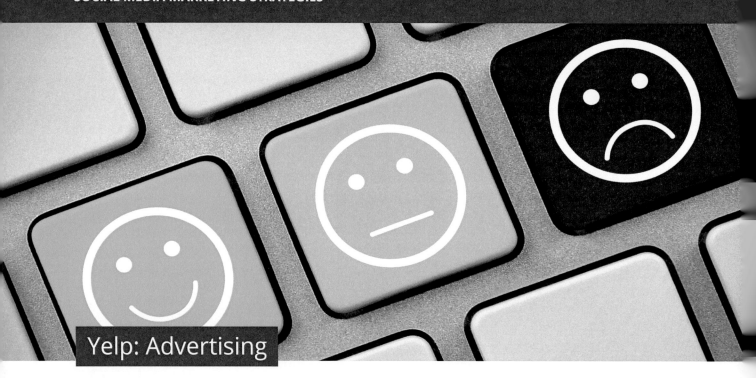

Yelp: Advertising

Discussion Questions

Note for Teachers

Ask students to respond to the following questions. Note their answers on the whiteboard, and ensure that the answers noted are added, if students do not recall them.

In Course 1, **Digital Marketing Fundamentals**, you learned how business owners can best respond to negative reviews. What do you recall from that text?

1. Should responses be public or private? Explain.

2. How should business owners phrase their responses?

*Now, think about how business owners should respond to positive reviews? Should they respond publicly? How should they phrase their responses?

Answers

1. *It is critical that business owners respond to negative reviews publicly, and in an appropriate way to protect the image of their brand. It is important to respond publicly so the reviewer and other people looking at the page can see that the business owner cares about his or her customers.*

2. *Yelp recommends that business owners respond to negative reviews by keeping "it simple and polite. Yelpers appreciate honesty and like to know when businesses are making changes based on their feedback."[3]*

*Show students, "A Simple Guide to Showcasing Your Business Online": http://www.yelp-business.com/rs/yelpinc/images/Yelp_US_Ebook.pdf and refer to the flowchart on pages 11 and 12

***Extension Activity:** Show students the following video from Yelp, "Responding to Reviews" (04:14): https://biz.yelp.ca/support/responding_to_reviews*

It discusses both positive and negative reviews and how to respond to the latter.

👓 CASE STUDY: Botto Bistro: A Big Pizza Pie in Yelp's Eye

Note for Teachers

1. *Ask students to read the Botto Bistro case study.*
2. *Then, ask them to watch "Botto Bistro is Fighting Yelp":* https://www.youtube.com/watch?v=dwI8TL57c0w *(09:09). Note: This video is not on Mujo's YouTube playlist, as it contains an incidence of strong language. It is up to individual to determine whether this video is appropriate for their students.*
3. *Students can respond to questions that follow the case study in pairs or groups.*

Not all businesses are concerned about responding appropriately to negative reviews. In fact, one California pizzeria is actually asking its customers to give it a one-star rating on Yelp. Why? Well, it all began when Botto Bistro lost its amore for this social media channel.

Originally, business owner Davide Cerretini's restaurant was just being reviewed on Yelp like any other. However, he soon felt significant pressure to advertise with the review site as well. He told the publication **Ars Technica** that the restaurant was contacted repeatedly by Yelp in order to get him to advertise, "'30 times a week, sometimes five times a day'".[17] Eventually, Cerretini relented and did begin advertising with the review site. However, after six months of doing so, he decided to stop. According to Cerretini, he experienced a backlash from Yelp. One of the pizzeria's most positive reviews disappeared and the number of negative reviews on the site increased.[18] Rather than accept the situation, Botto Bistro chose a more proactive approach.

In 2014, the pizzeria began asking its customers to write negative, one-star reviews about it on Yelp. Cerretini even offered his customers a 25% discount off their pizza if they did so in 2014 and then upped that amount to 50% off the following year.[19] To help his customers craft their negative reviews, he also put suggested things they could complain about on a blackboard mounted in Botto Bistro (e.g. "We don't change the TV channel. We charge for bread. What can you do? Hate us on Yelp and get 25% off any pizza for your one star review."[20]).

The Results of Botto Bistro's Hate Us on Yelp Campaign

Yelp's Response

- Yelp sent Cerretini a letter stating that he had violated the site's guidelines. To which the business owner countered by asking how he could violate guidelines he had never actually agreed to.[21]

- When asked by HuffPost Live for a comment on this story, Yelp sent a statement that noted in part that, "'There is no amount of money a business can pay Yelp to manipulate reviews, nor does our automated recommendation software punish those who choose not to advertise.'"[22]

The Public's Response

- Botto Bistro did indeed get the one-star reviews it asked for. Many were creative and funny, and Cerretini certainly appreciated their support.[23]

Botto Bistro in 2016

- Botto Bistro still continues to offer its customers a 50% discount off pizza for negative reviews.[24]

- On its Facebook page, Botto Bistro posts anti-Yelp rants and encourages its customers to leave one-star reviews on Yelp.[25]

- As of October 2016, the pizzeria has a two-star Yelp rating, and 289 recommended reviews and 68 hidden reviews.[26]

QUESTIONS

Discuss the following questions with your classmate(s).

1. What do you think about Botto Bistro's claims against Yelp?

2. Do you think the pizzeria's campaign to become the worst-reviewed website on the social media channel is a good idea? Why or why not?

3. In general, do you think a business should ask its customers for reviews, good or bad?

Note for Teachers

Students can look at Botto Bistro's Facebook page, of course. However, it is not currently recommended, as there are some terms used that could be offensive to some readers.

Answers will vary, but it's important to point out to students that Botto Bistro's campaign is not just a way to get back at Yelp. It is a clever marketing ploy that got the restaurant the attention of the public and the media. More people would naturally go to the restaurant because of the buzz surrounding it, and although the company is offering discounts to customers, it is quite probable that its profits have still increased.

In terms of asking for reviews, a business may not want to solicit reviews from specific individuals as they leave the establishment, but they can solicit them in more general ways:

At the physical location: A business can put a "Find Us on Yelp" sticker on its door. It can set up a check-in offer that later prompts the recipient to write a review (TBD).[5]

Online: Put a Yelp badge and link on the company site. Ask for reviews via email, but in the context of giving them something valuable in return, like content in a newsletter.

Note: In general, small businesses, especially those with only one location, will get a limited number of reviews. They can manage and respond to them without too much difficulty. However, corporations with many locations may receive a larger volume. Thus, a much more coordinated effort is required for them to ensure customer feedback is dealt with. Most businesses opt for either centralized or decentralized review management.

Centralized Managment: "Corporate manages Yelp reviews using Yelp's aggregate review dashboard which allows you to sort and respond to reviews across all locations by rating, date, or awaiting reply."[27]

Decentralized Managment: "Reviews are managed at the local level by Regional or Store Managers. Yelp's aggregate review dashboard includes hierarchical access levels so individuals only have access to respond on behalf of the locations they manage."[28]

Yelp: Running a Targeted Campaign

ADVERTISING ON YELP

In the previous section, a California pizzeria launched a campaign to become the worst-reviewed restaurant on Yelp. However, many businesses try to work within Yelp to market their brands. Should all businesses advertise on Yelp? No. There are certainly better platforms for B2B, such as LinkedIn, which was discussed in a previous chapter. In the case of Yelp, the main focus is on B2C. Restaurants tend to be the most prolific promoters, and other B2C businesses like hotels, dentists, and service organizations coming into direct contact with customers have a strong presence as well.

As with other social media channels, an ad campaign on Yelp has to be preceded by a company's clear outlining of its goals. For a new restaurant, for example, the goal could be brand awareness. For a more established restaurant, it could be to attract new customers and retain the loyalty of the ones it already has.

🕐 ACTIVITY: LINKING ADS WITH GOALS

1. Yelp offers businesses different ways to advertise. Take some time to read "Yelp Ads". Your instructor will provide you with the link and show you the accompanying video as well. Examples of Yelp ads:

Note for Teachers

Provide students with the link to "Yelp Ads": https://biz.yelp.ca/support/advertising and ask students to click on the 'Watch Video' link for the associated "Yelp Ads" video (02:18)

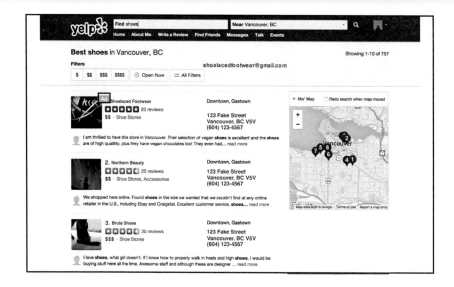

2. Find an ad on Yelp that you believe you can link to a specific goal.

3. Note down what that goal is and explain why you think the ad was effective or ineffective when it came to achieving it (e.g. In other words, if the goal was to attract new customers, do you think the deal being offered was enough of an incentive?).

4. Find a partner and discuss your ads and their objectives

Note: Yelp ad campaigns are PPC-based and clients need to find out what the minimum required budget is. The cost-per-click charge (how much a business owner must pay each time someone clicks on a company ad) for restaurants is less than the one levied on other kinds of businesses, simply because there are more restaurants on Yelp. For example, a CPC charge for a restaurant is $1 – $1.50 whereas for a web design company it may be six to seven times that amount.

THE CHECK-IN OFFER

For businesses that have a physical location(s), a check-in offer may be a great way to market to customers and entice them to become repeat visitors. When a customer checks in to a business, he or she is able to receive a discount or special offer of some kind from that business via a Yelp phone message. This discount would apply on the customer's next visit, thus encouraging him or her to make a return trip. Some companies may also opt to use a check-in offer to reward loyal customers, giving them a free gift after five check-ins, for example.

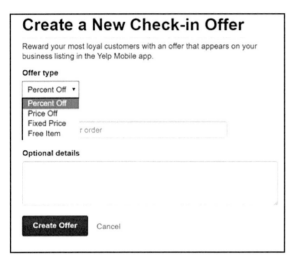

Examples:

- Percent Off: 15% off your next order

- Price Off: $20 off any salon service

- Fixed Price: $25 for our Prix Fixed Menu

- Free Item: 1 free glass of wine with any entrée

Check-in Offers appear on Yelp's Mobile Apps on your business listing, as well as in search results related to your business.

MARKETING ON YELP WITHOUT PAID ADS

Conventional advertising is not the only way to market a business on Yelp. Certainly, any business that is getting a significant number of positive reviews and is employing SEO practices, as discussed in an earlier section, is accomplishing this. In a way, this is where Yelp is an equal opportunity social media channel. Those businesses without big ad budgets can still compete and be successful through online word of mouth. It is also possible to launch contests and other promotional events on Yelp to achieve goals such as increasing brand awareness.

Your instructor will now show you an example of just such a campaign.

Note for Teachers

You may utilize the following example or something similar that demonstrates how contests and event-based promotions can achieve marketing objectives through Yelp:

"Using Yelp to Increase Social and Brand Awareness":

http://www.sociallybuzz.com/used-yelp-to-increase-social-and-brand-awareness/

⏰ ACTIVITY: A FIVE-STAR CONTEST IDEA

1. Select a restaurant that advertises on Yelp.
2. Come up with a goal that you think that restaurant should try to achieve.
3. Describe how you would achieve that goal through a contest-based promotion.
4. Share your idea with a partner.

Yelp: Analytics

ANALYTICS FOR THE YELP BUSINESS PAGE

Note for Teachers
Go through the bar graph visual while explaining the elements of Yelp Analytics.

Businesses that claim their Yelp listing are able to access the social media channel's internal analytics. Those analytics allow a business to learn more about its visibility, user engagement, and lead generation via Yelp.[29]

Visibility: A business owner can see how many views his or her page received during a given period (30 days, one year, or two years).[30] Yelp provides some additional details about the viewing history, including:

- How many of and what percentage of those views came from mobile devices
- How many times a business appeared "in Yelp's organic search results over a rolling 30 day period"[31]

Note: Organic search refers to clicks through from the company's website, as opposed to paid search, which is represented by cost per click.

User Engagement: Through its 'Customer Leads' feature, a business owner can see how people have been interacting with his or her brand on Yelp. "This feature shows you when a Yelp user has recently called your business, mapped directions to your business, or clicked through to your website."[32] The owner will be able to see the day of the week, date, and time on which each individual engaged, through the activity feed.

Lead Generation: "Yelp's 'Revenue Estimate' tool multiplies the customer leads your business receives from Yelp with the average revenue per customer for a business like yours . . . You can modify the revenue estimate anytime to match your business' growth."[33] This feature is key, as it tells a business owner not only how a business is performing, but what its revenue projection is.

YELP ANALYTICS

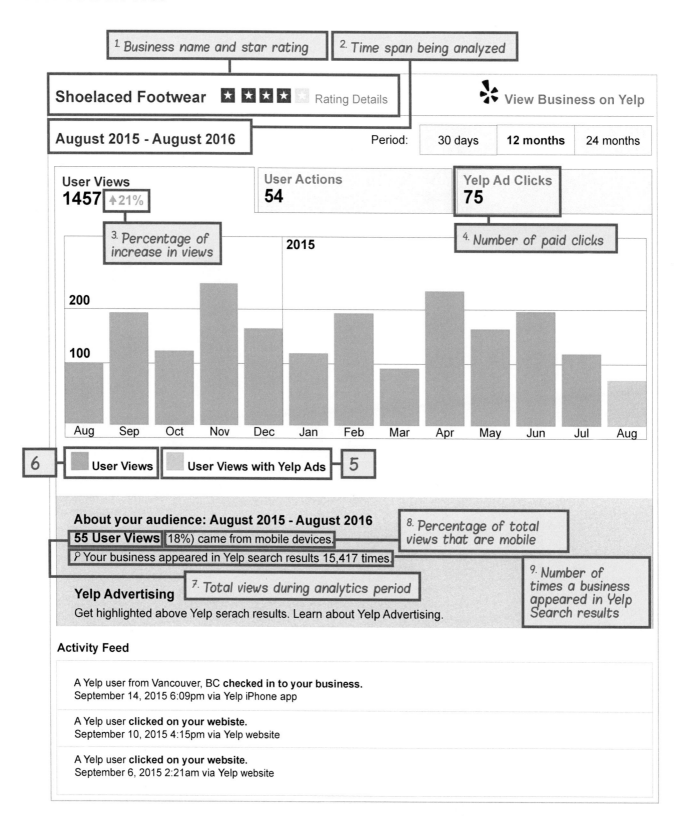

1. Business name and star rating

2. Time span being analyzed

Shoelaced Footwear ★ ★ ★ ★ ☆ Rating Details

View Business on Yelp

August 2015 - August 2016

Period: 30 days | **12 months** | 24 months

User Views
1457 ▲21%

User Actions
54

Yelp Ad Clicks
75

3. Percentage of increase in views

2015

4. Number of paid clicks

200

100

Aug Sep Oct Nov Dec Jan Feb Mar Apr May Jun Jul Aug

6 — User Views | User Views with Yelp Ads — 5

About your audience: August 2015 - August 2016

55 User Views (18%) came from mobile devices.

8. Percentage of total views that are mobile

9 Your business appeared in Yelp search results 15,417 times.

7. Total views during analytics period

9. Number of times a business appeared in Yelp Search results

Yelp Advertising

Get highlighted above Yelp serach results. Learn about Yelp Advertising.

Activity Feed

A Yelp user from Vancouver, BC **checked in to your business.**
September 14, 2015 6:09pm via Yelp iPhone app

A Yelp user **clicked on your webiste.**
September 10, 2015 4:15pm via Yelp website

A Yelp user **clicked on your website.**
September 6, 2015 2:21am via Yelp website

YELP KNOWLEDGE

On June 29th, 2016, Yelp officially launched 'Yelp Knowledge'. This platform enables companies to look at their performance in a more holistic way than they can with current metrics. "By allowing third-party data companies to combine Yelp user data with other sources such as Facebook and Twitter, Yelp hopes to provide a more analytical view of what customers are saying online and how that engagement changes over time."[34]

Yelp Knowledge will also be particularly helpful to businesses with more than one location, and franchises. For example, companies will be able to "see how locations are performing over time and during key periods" and have access to "survey reviews and ratings for specific business locations, clusters, or geographic regions".[35]

On its official blog, Yelp has provided an example of how one company has benefited from Yelp Knowledge. Your instructor will provide you with the link, so you can understand how Yelp thinks this platform can benefit many more business.

Note for Teachers

Provide students with the link to "Yelp Knowledge For Local Analytics Launches with 3 New Partners": https://www.yelpblog.com/2016/06/yelp-knowledge-local-analytics-launches-3-new-partners

🕐 ACTIVITY: AN ANALYTICS UTOPIA

In this course, you have examined various analytics tools available on six different social media platforms. Take a moment now to review the features of all of them. If you could create the ideal internal analytics tool for a social media platform, which features would be must-haves?

Be prepared to explain why a business owner or marketer would need each feature. What information would it yield? How could that information enable the business owner or marketer to make better, data-driven decisions?

Share your ideas with a classmate(s).

Answers will vary.

CHAPTER REVIEW

1. What kind of images should a business owner include on his or her Yelp page?

2. What is one reason why Yelp might not show a particular review?

3. Are each of the following statements true or false? Circle 'T' or 'F'.

    a. Business owners should generally respond to negative Yelp reviews publicly.   (T / F)

    b. Botto Bistro was initially eager to advertise on Yelp. (T / F)

    c. Yelp suspended Botto Bistro's account in 2014 because of its one-star campaign. (T / F)

    d. Yelp tends to be a better platform for B2C marketing than B2B. (T / F)

    e. Ad campaigns on Yelp are PPC-based. (T /F)

Chapter Review (Optional)

The following questions can be utilized in a variety of ways (e.g. Students can complete them for homework, in class with a partner, orally in a whole-class format, etc.).

1. • Images of people (e.g. staff, customers, etc.)
   • This is important because people connect more with a company when they can relate to it on a more personal level.

2. The review is fake. The review is biased. The reviewer hasn't built up credibility or does not have an established history with Yelp.

3. True or False?

   a. True

   b. False

   c. False

   d. True

   e. True

FOOTNOTES: CHAPTER 7

1   Walzer, Philip. "Everybody's a critic, but on Yelp, their opinions carry weight." **Arizona Daily Sun**. 03 Sept. 2015. Web. 04 Sept. 2015. http://azdailysun.com/business/national-and-international/everybody-s-a-critic-but-on-yelp-their-opinions-carry/article_b0b819fd-24f5-5d9d-9abe-2e21d30178da.html.

2   Ibid.

3   Yelp Inc. "Responding to Reviews." Yelp. 2004-2015. Web. 16 Sept. 2015. https://biz.yelp.ca/support/responding_to_reviews.

4   Yelp Inc. "A Simple Guide to Showcasing Your Business Online." Yelp. 2016. Web. 14 Mar. 2017. http://www.yelp-business.com/rs/yelpinc/images/Yelp_US_Ebook.pdf.

5   Ibid.

FOOTNOTES: CHAPTER 7

1   Yelp Inc. "About Us." Yelp. 2014-2015. Web. 31 Aug. 2015. http://www.yelp.com/about.
2   Jackson, Nicholas. "Infographic: The Incredible Six-Year History of Yelp Reviews." **The Atlantic.** 20 Jul. 2011. Web. 31 Aug. 2015. http://www.theatlantic.com/technology/archive/2011/07/infographic-the-incredible-six-year-history-of-yelp-reviews/242072/.
3   Dixler, Hillary. "Yelp Turns 10: From Startup to Online Review Dominance." Eater. 05 Aug. 2014. Web. 31 Aug. 2015. http://www.eater.com/2014/8/5/6177213/yelp-turns-10-from-startup-to-online-review-dominance.
4   Donaker, Geoff. "Ready for Our Close-Up! Announcing Yelp's First TV and Digital Ads." Yelp, Official Blog. 07 May 2015. Web. 31 Aug. 2015. http://officialblog.yelp.com/page/3/.
5   Swanner, Nate. "New 'Yelp Knowledge' program will help big businesses know how much we love (or hate) them." The Next Web. July 2016. Web. 08 Oct. 2016. http://thenextweb.com/business/2016/06/29/yelp-knowledge-program/#gref.
6   Smith, Craig. "By the Numbers: 52 Amazing Yelp Statistics." DMR. 14 Jul. 2016. Web. 08 Oct. 2016. http://expandedramblings.com/index.php/yelp-statistics/.
7   Yelp Inc. "How do I post an update to one of my reviews?" Yelp. 2004-2015. Web. 04 Sept. 2015. www.yelp-support.com/article/How-do-I-post-an-update-to-one-of-my reviews?I=en_US.
8   Walker, Rachel. "Compliments: They're free. Give them!" Yelp. 01 Mar. 2013. Web. 04 Sept. 2015. officialblog.yelp.com/2013/03/compliments-theyre-free-give-them.html.
9   Yelp Inc. "Write a Review." Yelp. 2004-2015. Web. 04 Sept. 2015. https://www.yelp.ca/writeareview.
10 Ibid.
11 Yelp Inc. "A Simple Guide to Showcasing Your Business Online." Yelp. 2016. Web. 14 Mar. 2017. http://www.yelp-business.com/rs/yelpinc/images/Yelp_US_Ebook.pdf.
12. —. "Creating Content for Your Yelp Page." Yelp. n.d. 14 Mar. 2017. PDF.
13 —. "Does Yelp recommend every review?" Yelp. 2014-2015. Web. 14 Sept. 2015. http://www.yelp-support.com/article/Does-Yelp-recommend-every-review?l=en_US.
14 Rozek, Phil. "Yelp Business Categories List." Local Visibility System. 19 Jul. 2013. Web. 14 Sept. 2015. www.localvisibilitysystem.com/2013/07/19/yelp-business-categories-list/.
15 Disilvestro, Amanda. "Yelp Optimization: How to Claim & Optimize Your Business Listing." Search Engine Watch. 10 May 2013. Web. 14 Sept. 2015. searchenginewatch.com/sew/how-to/2267166/yelp-optimization-how-to-claim-optimize-your-business-listing.
16 Yelp Inc. "A Simple Guide to Showcasing Your Business Online." Yelp. 2016. Web. 14 Mar. 2017. http://www.yelp-business.com/rs/yelpinc/images/Yelp_US_Ebook.pdf.
17 Cyrus, Farivar. "Why this tiny Italian restaurant gives a discount for bad Yelp reviews." **Ars Technica**. 21 Sept. 2014. Web. 17 Sept. 2015. arstechnica.com/business/2014/09/why-this-tiny-italian-restaurant-gives-a-discount-for-bad-yelp-reviews/.
18 Cullers, Rebecca. "This Restaurant Wants to Be the Worst Rated on Yelp, and the Reviews are Indeed Hilarious." **Adweek**. 22 Sept. 2014. Web. 17 Sept. 2015. www.adweek.com/adfreak/restaurant-wants-be-worst-rated-yelp-and-reviews-are-indeed-hilarious-160299.
19 Pinkham, C.A. "CA Restaurant Hates Yelp More Than You or I Could Hate Anything." Kitchenette. 11 Jan. 2015. Web. 17 Sept. 2015. kitchenette.jezebel.com/california-restaurant-hates-yelp-more-thanyou-or-i-coul-1678822287.
20 Cullers, Rebecca. "This Restaurant Wants to Be the Worst Rated on Yelp, and the Reviews are Indeed Hilarious." **Adweek**. 22 Sept. 2014. Web. 17 Sept. 2015. www.adweek.com/adfreak/restaurant-wants-be-worst-rated-yelp-and-reviews-are-indeed-hilarious-160299.
21 Buxton, Ryan. "The Owner of California's Botto Bistro is Proud to Have Yelp's Worst Rated Restaurant." HuffPost Live. 02 Oct. 2014. Web. 17 Sept. 2015. www.huffingtonpost.com/2014/10/02/botto-bistro-yelp_n_5923910.html.
22 Ibid.
23 Ibid.
24 Botto Bistro. "Yelp's One Star is the New Five Stars." Facebook. 24 Aug. 2016. Web. 10 Oct. 2016. https://www.facebook.com/bottobistro/.
25 Ibid.
26 Yelp Inc. "Botto Italian Bistro." Yelp. 2004-2016. Web. 10 Oct. 2016. https://www.yelp.ca/biz/botto-italian-bistro-richmond-9.
27 —. "Yelp Reviews: Best Practices for National Businesses" Yelp. 2016. Web. 14 Mar. 2017. PDF.
28 Ibid.
29 —. "Business Analytics." Yelp. 2004-2015. Web. 18 Sept. 2015. https://biz.yelp.ca/support/analytics.
30 Ibid.
31 Holloway, Darnell Justin. "Yelp Metrics: New and Improved." Yelp. 27 Mar. 2012. Web. 18 Sept. 2015. officialblog.yelp.com/2012/03/yelp-metrics-new-and-improved.html.
32 Ibid.
33 Yelp Inc. "Business Analytics." Yelp. 2004-2015. Web. 18 Sept. 2015. https://biz.yelp.ca/support/analytics.
34 Kirkpatrick, David. "Yelp launches 'Knowledge' program to provide deeper analytics and insights." Industry Dive. 29 Jun. 2016. Web. 21 Sept. 2016. http://www.marketingdive.com/news/yelp-launches-knowledge-program-to-provide-deeper-analytics-and-insights/421845/.
35 Yelp Inc. "Yelp Knowledge." Yelp. 29 Jun. 2016. Web. 21 Sept. 2016. https://www.yelp.com/knowledge.

 # 8 **PINTEREST**
MARKETING STRATEGIES

Pinterest: History	Pinterest: Personal	Pinterest: Business	Pinterest: Advertising	Pinterest: Targeted Campaign	Pinterest: Analytics
212	213	217	222	224	227

MUJO
LEAD · EDUCATE · INSPIRE

Pinterest: History

In 2010, Pinterest was launched online. This very visual social media platform has made 'pinning' a daily ritual for many of its users, a phenomenon that perhaps only its founders (Ben Silbermann, Evan Sharp, and Paul Sciarra) could have forseen.

LAUNCHES

MARCH 2016
How-To Pins

JUNE 2015
Buyable Pins

AUGUST 2014
Pinterest News Tab

OCTOBER 2013
Related Pins

MARCH 2013
Pinterest Web Analytics

NOVEMBER 2012
Secret Boards

OCTOBER 2012
Blocking Feature

AUGUST 2011
Video Pins

MAY 2011
iPhone App

JUNE 2010
Group Pinboards

MARCH 2010
Pinterest Launched

MILESTONES

MARCH 2016
110 Million Active Monthly Users

SEPTEMBER 2015
100 Million Active Monthly Users

APRIL 2014
750 Million Pinterest Boards Created

FEBRUARY 2013
48 Million-Plus Active Monthly Users

APRIL 2012
17 Million Active Monthly Users

2011
Time lists Pinterest as one of the top 50 websites of the year

AUGUST 2010
5000 Users

1, 2, 3, 4, 5, 6

Pinterest: Personal

 Discussion Questions

1. Do you use Pinterest? If so, what do you use it for? If not, why haven't you utilized this social media channel?

2. How is Pinterest similar to and different from Instagram?

3. How could Pinterest be used for business? What kind of businesses do you think would find Pinterest a particularly effective marketing medium?

Answers

1. *Answers will vary.*

2. *Answers will vary, but sample answers can include:*
    * *Similar: Both platforms allow account holders to upload, like, and share pictures and videos.*
    * *Similar: Both channels are not invitation-based (i.e. An account holder can follow whoever he or she wants and can be followed without needing to get or give permission).*
    * *Different: Pinterest allows the account holder to organize images/videos ('pins') into subject-based boards, whereas Instagram organizes images by date.*
    * *Different: Pinterest does not have a built-in image filtering function, whereas Instagram does.*

3. *Note: At this point, the aim is just to get students to use the knowledge base they have and their own ideas to respond to the question. Explain that this topic will be discussed in detail in the Pinterest: Business section.*

PINTEREST PERSONAL PROFILE PAGE NOTES

Refer to the sample Pinterest page and read through the following notes.

#3: About You:

- The account holder must describe himself or herself in 160 characters or less.

#4: Boards:

- Pinterest boards are where an account holder saves images or videos, referred to as 'pins'. Each board has a title, description, and central topic or idea that gives it a focus.

#5: Pins:

- Images or videos that the account holder saves and assigns to a board or 'likes'.

#6: Like:

- 'Like' functions in a similar way as it does on other platforms (i.e. Someone appreciates an image or video that another individual has posted and wants to demonstrate that). On Pinterest, 'liking' is sometimes also used "as a way to quickly collect pins before later repinning them to an appropriate pinboard".[7]

#10: Make a Widget:

- Allows the account holder to include a button like the one that follows on his or her website or app:

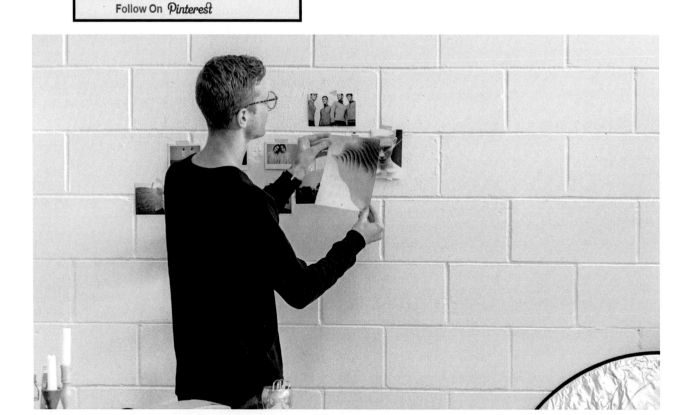

PINTEREST PERSONAL PROFILE

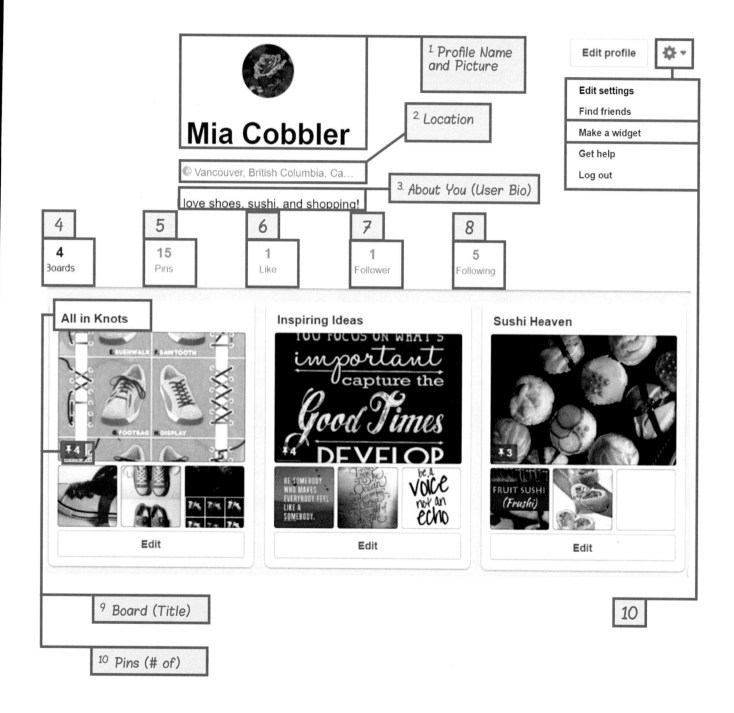

Note for Teachers

For the example "KLM Royal Dutch Airlines", show students the link to its Pinterest page: https://www.pinterest.com/KLM/

HOW CONSUMERS INTERACT WITH BRANDS ON PINTEREST

Well-known retailers, restaurants, airlines, and other brands have a presence on Pinterest. People may save or 'like' pins the corporation has shared, follow its boards or entire page, and/or send individual pins to others. Some boards are devoted entirely to images or videos that directly connect with the theme identified. Other boards link to content or images that allow the consumer to interact with the brand in a more in-depth fashion or just in a different way.

For example: KLM Royal Dutch Airlines

This Dutch airline flies to locations around the world. Its Pinterest page certainly reflects that, with boards devoted to some of its most popular destinations: Amsterdam, Dubai, Hong Kong, New York City, etc. People interested in traveling with this Netherlands-based carrier can find inspiration in the images of the popular landmarks and experiences tourists can have in these cities.

However, KLM's Pinterest page also features a board devoted to its blogs. Along with seeing each blog post's feature image, users also get access to the link which will give them a more in-depth understanding of what it's like to fly with this airline. This type of cross-platform promotion is evident in its other boards:

- **Instagram:** featuring selected photos from KLM's Instagram account

- **KLM #travelquiz:** focusing on a weekly Twitter photo guessing game; users can go to the KLM Twitter page to give their answers and later see if they were right

- **iFly Magazine:** presenting covers of each issue of its in-flight magazine and linking to its Pinterest page devoted entirely to the magazine itself[8]

In the previous example, it is clear how an individual can interact with a major brand depending on what that brand chooses to include on its Pinterest page. Yet, by simply following a brand's page or board, or liking or saving a brand's pin, a consumer is having a powerful interaction with the brand and with other users who witness that interaction through their news feed.

By interacting in a positive and public way with a brand on Pinterest, an account holder becomes like an endorser of that brand. If other pinners see a particular brand getting a lot of positive attention, they are more likely to check out its page, and perhaps ultimately make a purchase. It is through this 'word-of-mouth' function that Pinterest becomes more like an inferential kind of Yelp-like platform.

Some 'pinners' are more direct in their brand endorsements. They may create a board called something like "Stuff I Love" and 'pin' images of various products to this board. They may find pictures of these products already pinned by other users, through brand pages, or could choose to upload them themselves. Through this kind of interaction, Pinterest truly becomes a review-based platform that can be influential. For instance, one Pinterest user sees that some of his or her friends have 'pinned' a particular product image or followed a brand's board or page. This positive 'review' may serve as a compelling enough reason for that user to give the product or brand a try. Even celebrity pinner Paris Hilton has a board called "That's Hot". Her followers may be more inclined to buy the shoes she has pinned to that board because they want to emmulate her. Thus, her unpaid celebrity 'endorsement' on Pinterest becomes very powerful.[9]

Pinterest: Business

A Pinterest business page is very similar to a personal page. This becomes obvious when comparing the following business profile with the personal profile featured earlier in this chapter. However, the way a business utilizes pins differs greatly from the way a personal user does. Rather than pinning things of personal interest, a business selects and creates pins that will help to promote its products and/or services.

In the Think Profits' example that follows, there are several boards devoted to the segments of the market that the digital marketing agency targets: 'Hotels & Travel', 'Retail & Services', and 'Education'. The pins included in each board offer informative value to existing and potential clients, as they link to the company's industry-focused blog posts. The other boards help to showcase the company's positive workplace culture. This use of Pinterest makes sense for the type of services Think Profits provides.

A more product-based business might devote its Pinterest boards to the various kinds of items it sells. For example, Tom Lee Music Canada's Pinterest page has multiple boards devoted to the musical instruments it has on offer (e.g. 'Pianos and Piano Art', 'Guitars, Amps and Accessories', 'Drums and Percussion', etc.), though not every pin is an image of an item it has for sale. Instead, its pins sometimes act more as inspiration. For instance, on its board, 'Pianos and Piano Art', there is a pin which features an image and accompanying description of a Steinway piano at the famous La Scala opera house in Milan, Italy. Tom Lee sells Steinway pianos. Thus, while the consumer may not get the exact type of piano in the pin or even visit the opera house in Milan, he or she can buy the same brand of piano close to home.[10]

Note for Teachers
Show students the link to Tom Lee Music Canada's Pinterest page: https://www.pinterest.com/tomleemusic/

PINTEREST BUSINESS PROFILE

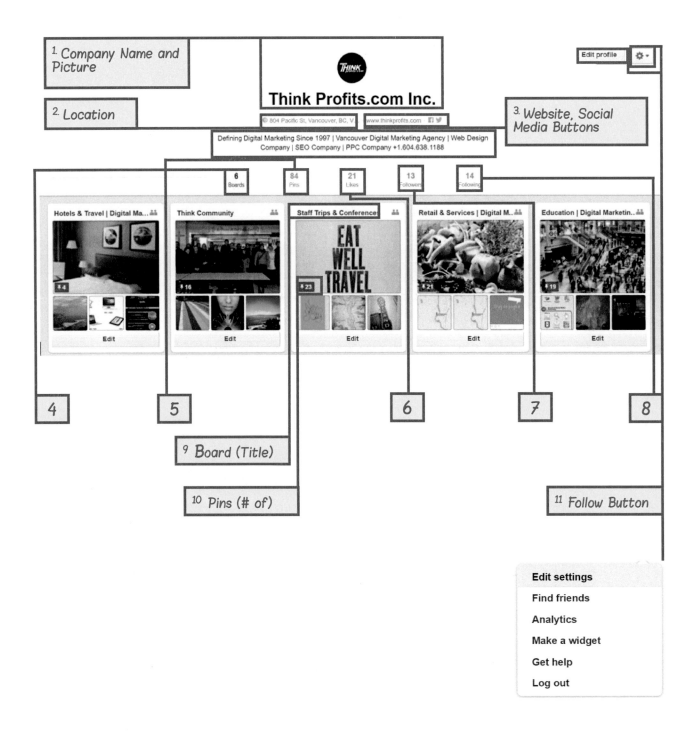

Note: The only item that requires additional information is 'analytics'. Please see the analytics section of this chapter for further details.

PROMOTED PINS

Pinterest launched promoted pins first for American-based businesses and then ones in the United Kingdom in 2016. According to the social media channel, "promoted Pins are just like regular Pins, only you pay to have them seen by more people. They're native ad units that perform just as well, if not better, than organic Pins, helping people discover and save ideas."[11] Promoted pins are designed to help a company increase its engagement, or website traffic. When deciding to promote a pin, a company must choose its campaign objective, name, budget, length of campaign, and the pin itself.

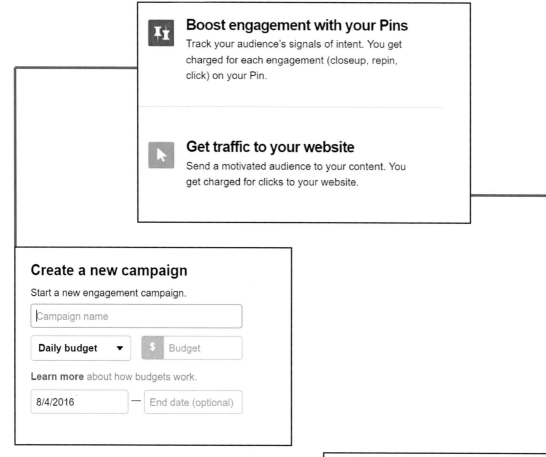

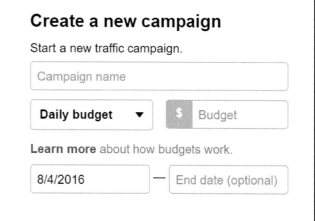

PROMOTED PINS CONTINUED

A business also needs to decide what kind of audience it wants to target.

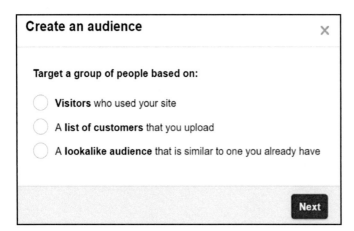

Then, keywords should be added. That way, the promoted pin will appear in search results and home and category feeds. Beyond this, the company can select: locations, languages, devices, genders, and its maximum cost per click (CPC) bid.[12]

⏰ ACTIVITY: BUYABLE PINS AND RICH PINS

Like promoted pins, buyable pins and rich pins offer businesses a way to market their products and/or services via Pinterest. Conduct some online research and respond to the following questions about these two types of pins.

Be prepared to share your responses with your instructor and classmates.

1. What are buyable pins? What are rich pins? How do they differ?
2. How could a business benefit from using place pins? Give at least three examples.
3. Which eCommerce platforms has Pinterest partnered with to make buyable pins possible?
4. Buyable pins aren't available in Canada yet. However, for the sake of this activity, select a Canadian coffee shop, either a chain or small business . Describe what image that business could pair with one of the coffee shop's beverages or food items. The image would need to be compelling, attractive, and interesting enough that pinners would want to read more about it and ultimately purchase it (i.e. a cup of coffee on its own is not sufficiently enticing). *You may show a sample stock or free image.

Answers

1. *Buyable Pins: allow consumers to buy products they see on Pinterest without leaving the Pinterest site by clicking on a blue 'buy' button[1]*

   Rich Pins: provide extra information about a pin on the pin (six types: app, movie, recipe, article, product, and place)[2]

   How they differ: "Rich Pins allow content creators to add additional information to their Pins. ... Buyable Pins expand on that functionality by allowing Pinterest users to shop and securely checkout, right within Pinterest's mobile app and desktop experience."[3]

2. *Answers will vary, but first and foremost, place pins will help potential consumers to find the business' location(s). They can help a business to engage in more specific and targeted marketing (e.g. create a board of tips for clients based on their locations). They help to humanize a business (e.g. a business can turn the focus on its employees by creating a board showing all their hometowns and favorite places to visit there).[4] More ideas are listed in "6 Ways to Promote Your Business With Pinterest Places": http://www.socialmediaexaminer.com/pinterest-place-pins/*

3. *BigCommerce, Demandware, IBM Commerce, Magento, and Shopify[5]*

4. *Answers will vary.*

Extension Activity:

Ask students to read the article, "Pinterest Puts Its Own Spin on Video Ads With These Cinematic Pins": http://www.adweek.com/news/technology/pinterest-puts-its-own-spin-video-ads-these-cinematic-pins-164854

Then, ask them to think about how they could use cinematic pins to promote a particular restaurant food item (see Wendy's example). Students can share their ideas with the class.

Pinterest: Advertising

PINTEREST WIN

👓 CASE STUDY: Jetsetter's Cure for Wanderlust

About Jetsetter

Jetsetter is travel site that was launched in 2009. Its focus is to provide insider deals on luxury hotels, resorts, activities, and more worldwide. Its other function is to inspire people. By viewing beautiful pictures of exotic destinations and accommodations, Jetsetter's aim is to get people motivated to take that trip of a lifetime. [13][14]

Becoming Part of the Jetset

From April 22 – May 6, 2012, Jetsetter challenged its users to make "'the ultimate destination pinboard'".[15] They became 'Jetsetter curators' and were asked to focus their boards on one of the following travel styles: 'adventure', 'cosmopolitan', 'escape', and 'style'.[16] "For their boards to be eligible to win they were required to hashtag #JetsetterCurator and have Jetsetter Curator in their board name."[17]

Note for Teachers
At this point, show students an example of the kind of Pinterest boards Jetsetter wanted its 'curators' to make:
Cosmopolitan example: https://www.pinterest.com/jetsetterphoto/jetsetter-curator-cosmopolitan/

The best board in each category was chosen by the Jetsetter editorial staff and a high-profile judging panel. Each category winner "won a three-night stay at a Jetsetter destination pertaining to that category — the escape winner won a trip to Turks and Caicos, cosmopolitan to Miami, style to Los Angeles and adventure to Belize. The most followed Jetsetter Curator board won its owner $1,000 in Jetsetter credit, a reward that incentivized pinners to share their boards and pins with friends." [18]

Jetsetter's Winning Numbers

The winners of this Pinterest contest were not the only ones that came out on top. In fact, it could be argued that Jetsetter itself was the biggest winner, at least by digital marketing standards. The numbers that emerged during the Pinterest campaign tell the Jetsetter success story:

How the Jetsetter Website Benefited

- Referral traffic from Pinterest to Jetsetter.com: up 100%

- Jetsetter.com page views: up 150%

- Jetsetter.com **bounce rate:** down 10 to 15%

How Jetsetter's Pinterest Benefited

- 1100 pinners entered the contest: 50,000 images pinned (increasing Jetsetter's reach)

- Jetsetter's Pinterest followers: 3300 new followers[19]

QUESTIONS

Discuss the following questions with a classsmate.

1. What do you think Jetsetter's initial goals were for 'the ultimate destination pinboard' campaign?

2. Did Jetsetter achieve its goals? Explain.

3. How else could Jetsetter have used Pinterest effectively as a way to achieve those same goals? Spend time online looking at other successful Pinterest-based campaigns first. Then, describe a different campaign that Jetsetter could have launched. Present this campaign to another pair of students and get their feedback. Make any modifications necessary to your description and then present it to the rest of the class and your instructor.

Answers

1. *According to Jetsetter's social media manager, Jonathan Goldmann, "The overall goal of our Jetsetter Curator contest was branding, quality content generation and engagement with members."[6]*

2. *Answers will vary, but yes it did. Jetsetter got some significant brand exposure through the contest. It also got a sense of what kind of images and destinations the public were interested in (market research), and the statistical data demonstrates that engagement increased.*

3. *Answers will vary.*

Pinterest: Running a Targeted Campaign

PIN OPTIMIZATION

Pinterest is more like a search engine than it is like Facebook. Before a business attempts to launch a Pinterest campaign, it must acknowledge this basic truth. When a person opens Pinterest, he or she is looking for interesting images. Thus, to find pins, he or she needs to type in search terms. Pins will only appear in search results if Pinterest can find those terms. It is here that a second truth has to be acknowledged: pin content matters (e.g. pin titles, descriptions, and image file names).

It is possible to make SEO-friendly Pinterest content, much in the same way as it is to make an SEO-friendly landing page. A business owner's first step should be to use the Google AdWords Keyword Planner. Then, once he or she has found keywords that relate to a pin and his or her company, the business owner needs to apply them to the pin-related content. It is key that pin descriptions, for example, sound natural and make contextual sense while still incorporating those keywords.[20]

Note: Another element that can be borrowed from landing pages, is to add a 'call to action', or in the case of Pinterest, a 'call to pin'. While not as direct as a traditional call to action (i.e. Not 'buy now'), "a call-to-pin will significantly increase the engagement of your pins. In fact, you'll get 80% more engagement with a CTP. In your pin's description, add a little something like: 'Repin to your own inspiration board.'"[21]

🕐 ACTIVITY: CREATING AN SEO-FRIENDLY PIN

Select a pin from a B2C's Pinterest board. Optimize the pins using the process described in the previous section, and what you have learned about Google AdWords in Course 1, *Digital Marketing Fundamentals*. Share your SEO-friendly pin content with your instructor and classmates.

PIN IMAGE

Once the content surrounding a pin is optimized, it's key that the quality of the image itself is examined. It would seem obvious, but still bears mentioning, that pins that look good get more attention than those that don't. What constitutes a good-looking pin? Several criteria must be met:

- The image must be high-quality/high-resolution.

- It should be clear and present the desired message in a simple and straightforward manner.[22]

Also, it's important to note that lighter pictures are repinned more than darker ones, and that images without faces tend to be repinned more often than those containing faces.[23]

Other elements to consider are the pin size and orientation. "All pins have the same width, with an unlimited length. A good size to shoot for is 736×1102 pixels for a typical pin. It's not too big, and not too small."[24] In general, vertical pins are preferable because many people use Pinterest on their mobile phones and Pinterest organizes feeds into columns.[25]

PRIME PINNING TIME

When is the ideal time for a business to post its pins? To a certain extent, this depends on who the target audience is, and it is best for a business to conduct the necessary testing to find out when that audience would be engaged. That being said, there are some general ideas about when the best posting time on Pinterest is, "according to SocialFresh, on average, the best times to post are 2PM – 4PM EST and 8PM – 1AM EST; and research by HubSpot says Saturday morning is THE best time to post."[26]

⏰ ACTIVITY: TYING IT ALL TOGETHER

Before a company selects a particular item to post, ensuring its content and image are going to generate engagement, it has to come up with a larger campaign with a larger goal. Pinterest and pins will often be part of helping the company to achieve that campaign goal.

1. Pretend that a service-based, B2C establishment's goal is to establish itself as an industry expert. That business could be a florist, tutoring agency, car rental service, etc. You are free to select the type of business.
2. Describe three kinds of images/content this business could post that would be likely to attract the attention of the target audience.
3. Now, think of a different goal that same business would like to achieve. What could you pin that could help the business achieve that goal?
4. Share your responses with your instructor and classmates.

Note for Teachers

Answers will vary, but the following example should provide some direction as to what is expected in response to #2:

Business selected: Florist

Type of post: infographic

Explanation: An infographic pin could fit in very well on a variety of how-to boards. It could demonstrate how to care for cut flowers, for example.

Type of post: finished product image

Explanation: The florist should show what he or she is capable of doing. A series of pins could act as a gallery of work, but also note in the description what flowers are in season when and what kind of decorations/setting would pair well with each floral centerpiece.

Type of post: cultural images

Explanation: Pictures of floral traditions from around the world (e.g. ikebana from Japan) would inform the unaware consumer, while appealing to specific cultural segments of the audience. It would also demonstrate that the florist knew how to create arrangements for a variety of cultural groups.

Pinterest: Analytics

ANALYTICS FOR THE PINTEREST BUSINESS PAGE: PROFILE

Companies that create a Pinterest business page can utilize the social media channel's internal analytics to see how well its pins, boards, and ads are performing. This begins with 'profile' anaytics. In terms of pins, the first metric Pinterest analytics presents is '**impressions**', which means "the number of times a Pin showed up in the Home Feed, search results and category feeds".[27] The following graph serves as an example of the number of impressions for pins in a specified time period:

Pinterest analytics also measures the impressions that a business page's boards get over a 30-day period. The example demonstrates this, displaying the boards from the highest to lowest number of impressions (included are the number of clicks, saves, likes, and the number of pins within each board):

Boards with top Pin impressions from the last 30 days	Impressions	Clicks	Saves	Likes	# of Pins
Gardening Blogs by The Midnig…	13	0	0	0	4
Digital Marketing Blogs by The Midnig…	13	0	0	0	5
Accessibility Blogs by The Midnig…	9	0	0	0	3

The next metric Pinterest analytics focuses on is the '**repin**'. Here, Pinterest analytics tells the account holder how his or her pins spread and were shared across Pinterest, including: average daily saves, average daily people saving, and pins and boards saved most in the last 30 days.[28] Pinterest also advises account holders to, "pin eye-catching images with useful descriptions and Rich Pins so people will want to save them for later."[29] The third metric is '**clicks**', which refers to the traffic that goes to an account holder's site via Pinterest.[30] If not enough traffic is reaching the account holder's site through Pinterest, it is suggested that he or she ensure that pins "link to mobile-friendly pages so people can take action when they get there."[31] Finally, the account holder reaches '**all-time**'. This encompasses, 'most saves: your most shared pins',[32] as well as the following:

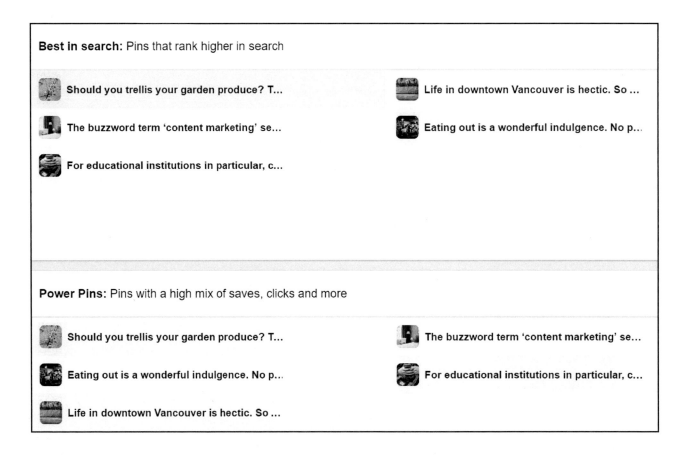

ANALYTICS FOR THE PINTEREST BUSINESS PAGE: AUDIENCE

Learning more about followers, repinners, and any other individuals who demonstrate an interest in a Pinterest business page can be very important for the company itself. It can enable that company to create pins that will continue to engage those users and new users that it may not be reaching. This is why Pinterest provides demographic information to its business account holders. This information includes:

- Country

- Metro (city)

- Language

- Gender

Beyond this basic information, Pinterest gives businesses additional insights into these individuals. The 'interests' section of the audience analytics contains the following:

- "What Your Audience is Into" (what else the audience likes)

- "Boards With Lots of Your Pins" (how the audience is categorizing your pins)

- "Businesses Your Audience Engages" (what other businesses your audience engages with)

ANALYTICS FOR THE PINTEREST BUSINESS PAGE: WEBSITE

The purpose of website analytics is to provide metrics (impressions, repins, clicks, and all-time) for all pins that link back to a company's website. For example, Pinterest provides analytical data about the top pins from the last 30 days to help a business decide:

- What kinds of pins and boards it should add to its profile

- What it should feature on its website

- What types of products it could create[33]

Pinterest also gives a company information about the top boards from the last 30 days. This data is key because it gives the business an understanding of:

- How pinners are organizing its content

- More information about those pinners

- How those pinners are thinking about company products[34]

'Original pins', or unique pins that users get from a company website, have metrics applied to them as well, in order to help a business to understand "how much unique content is being added to Pinterest from [its] site, as well as the latest trends in Pinning from [the company] site."[35]

🕐 ACTIVITY: ANALYZE THIS

Note for Teachers

Ask students to respond to the questions, individually or with a partner. Discuss their responses in a whole-class format.

1. It's said that a pinner goes on a four-stage journey:
   - Just Looking,
   - Maybe I Could,
   - Narrowing It Down, and
   - I Know What I Want

In the first two stages, the pinner is aspirational, and will want to see pins of that nature.

In the last two stages, the pinner is more focused on finding the right products, so pins need to be product-based.[36]
   - Pretend you are the owner of a wedding planning business. Give an example of the kind of pins (aspirational and product-based) that you would include to attract the pinner at every stage of his or her journey. You need to find four relevant images and describe why you selected each one for a particular stage.

2. Pretend you actually posted the images you selected in question one on Pinterest. Based on what you have learned in the analytics section, what would it mean if:
   - Pin #1 had a high number of impressions?
   - Pin #2 had a high number of repins?
   - Pins #3 and 4 had a high number of clicks?

Answers

1. *Answers will vary.*
2. *Pin #1: A high number of impressions means that this particular pin is showing up in search results frequently, which means it is well-connected to what the business' audience is looking for.*

Pin #2: A high number of repins indicates that many users found the pin compelling and saved and shared it.

Pins #3 and 4: A high number of clicks demonstrates that many people have a higher level of interest in the product-based pin, and are more likely to convert on the website.

CHAPTER REVIEW

1. What two kinds of campaign objectives can a company choose from for its promoted pins?

2. What are the six kinds of rich pins that Pinterest offers?

3. Why should a company ensure its pin descriptions are SEO-friendly?

4. When is the best time for a company post its pins?

5. What is the purpose of website analytics?

Chapter Review (Optional)

The following questions can be utilized in a variety of ways (e.g. Students can complete them for homework, in class with a partner, orally in a whole-class format, etc.).

1. *It can choose either to boost engagement or get website traffic.*
2. *The six kinds of rich pins are: app, movie, recipe, place, article, and product.*
3. *Pinterest is more like a search engine than a social network like Facebook. Thus, if a company wants its images to be found, it needs to add keywords so they appear in users' search results and home pages.*
4. *It depends on its target market, but generally the best time is Saturday morning.*
5. *The purpose is to provide metrics for all pins that link back to a company's website.*

FOOTNOTES: CHAPTER 8

1   Pinterest, Inc. "Buyable Pins." Pinterest. 2016. Web. 05 Aug. 2016. https://business.pinterest.com/en/buyable-pins.
2   —. "Rich Pins." Pinterest. 2016. Web. 05 Aug. 2016. https://business.pinterest.com/en/rich-pins.
3   Simas, Jordan. "Everything You Need to Know About Pinterest's New Buyable Pins." Shopify. 05 Jun. 2015. Web. 05 Aug. 2016. https://www.shopify.ca/blog/33341508-everything-you-need-to-know-about-pinterest-s-new-buyable-pins.
4   Francis, Anna. "6 Ways to Promote Your Business With Pinterest Places." Social Media Examiner. 11 Mar. 2014. Web. 05 Aug. 2016. http://www.socialmediaexaminer.com/pinterest-place-pins/.
5   Pinterest, Inc. "Buyable Pins." Pinterest. 2016. Web. 05 Aug. 2016. https://business.pinterest.com/en/buyable-pins.
6   Drill, Lauren. "How Pinterest Boosted Jetsetter's Traffic by 150%." Mashable. 23 May 2012. Web. 22 Jul. 2016. http://mashable.com/2012/05/23/jetsetter-pinterest/#aDvTokXTWPq4.

FOOTNOTES: CHAPTER 8

1   Pinterest, Inc. "Press." Pinterest. 2016. Web. 08 Jul. 2016. https://about.pinterest.com/en/press/press.
2   Pinterest, Inc. Pinterest Blog. Pinterest. 2016. Web. 08 Jul. 2016. https://blog.pinterest.com/en.
3   Teoh, Ivonne. "Pinterest Users Statistics 2016." LinkedIn. 05 Mar. 2016. Web. 08 Jul. 2016. https://www.linkedin.com/pulse/pinterest-2016-statistics-110million-monthly-users-ivonne-teoh.
4   Lawler, Ryan. "Pinterest Hits 30 Billion Total Pins, Up 50% In 6 Months." TechCrunch. 24 Apr. 2016. Web. 08 Jul. 2016. https://techcrunch.com/2014/04/24/pinterest-30b-pins/.
5   Carlson, Nicholas. "Pinterest CEO: Here's How We Became the Web's Next Big Thing." Business Insider. 24 Apr. 2012. Web. 08 Jul. 2016. http://www.businessinsider.com/pinterest-founding-story-2012-4.
6   Brookegandhi. "The History of Pinterest." Timetoast. 2013. Web 08 Jul. 2016. http://www.timetoast.com/timelines/the-history-of-pinterest?beta=1.
7   Sciarra, Paul. "What is the point of liking a pin on Pinterest?" Quora. 10 Oct. 2011. Web. 22 Jul. 2016. https://www.quora.com/What-is-the-point-of-liking-a-pin-on-Pinterest.
8   Pinterest, Inc. KLM Royal Dutch Airlines. Pinterest. n.d. Web. 22 Jul. 2016. https://www.pinterest.com/KLM/.
9   —. Paris Hilton. "That's Hot." Pinterest. n.d. Web. 22 Jul. 2016. https://www.pinterest.com/ParisHilton/that-s-hot/.
10 —. Tom Lee Music Canada. Pinterest. n.d. Web. 03 Aug. 2016. https://www.pinterest.com tomleemusic/.
11 —. "Promoted Pins." Pinterest. 2016. Web. 03 Aug. 2016. https://business.pinterest.com/en/promoted-pins.
12 —. "Ads." Pinterest. 2016. Web. 04 Aug. 2016. https://ads.pinterest.com/promoted_pin/create/?step=setup_details.
13 Drill, Lauren."How Pinterest Boosted Jetsetter's Traffic by 150%." Mashable. 23 May 2012. Web. 22 Jul. 2016. http://mashable.com/2012/05/23/jetsetter-pinterest/#aDvTokXTWPq4.
14 "Jetsetter Review" Reviews.com. 18 Nov. 2015. Web. 09 Aug. 2016. http://www.reviews.com/travel-sites/jetsetter/.
15 Drill, Lauren."How Pinterest Boosted Jetsetter's Traffic by 150%." Mashable. 23 May 2012. Web. 22 Jul. 2016. http://mashable.com/2012/05/23/jetsetter-pinterest/#aDvTokXTWPq4.
16 Waldron, Zoe. "Case Study: Jetsetter – Leading the Travel Category on Pinterest." HelloSociety. 13 Aug. 2014. Web. 09 Aug. 2016. https://hellosociety.com/blog/case-study-jetsetter-leading-the-travel-category-on-pinterest/.
17 Ibid.
18 Drill, Lauren."How Pinterest Boosted Jetsetter's Traffic by 150%." Mashable. 23 May 2012. Web. 22 Jul. 2016. http://mashable.com/2012/05/23/jetsetter-pinterest/#aDvTokXTWPq4.
19 Ibid.
20 Daley, Rachel. "The Ultimate Pinterest Marketing Guide: How to Improve Your Reach and Promote Your Brand." Kissmetrics Blog. 2015. Web. 08 Aug. 2016. https://blog.kissmetrics.com/ultimate-pinterest-marketing-guide/.
21 Ibid.
22 Ibid.
23 Ibid
24 Ibid
25 Milbrath, Sam. "How to Use Pinterest for Business: The Definitive Guide." Hootsuite. 20 May 2016. Web. 10 Aug. 2016. https://blog.hootsuite.com/how-to-use-pinterest-for-business/.
26 Daley, Rachel. "The Ultimate Pinterest Marketing Guide: How to Improve Your Reach and Promote Your Brand." Kissmetrics Blog. 2015. Web. 08 Aug. 2016. https://blog.kissmetrics.com/ultimate-pinterest-marketing-guide/.
27 Pinterest, Inc. "A Guide to Pinterest Analytics." Pinterest. n.d. Web. 09 Aug. 2016. http://pinterest.app.box.com/s/4u9wx06yk91r463upuar.
28 Pinterest, Inc. "Your Pinterest Profile: Repins." Pinterest. n.d. Web. 09 Aug. 2016. https://analytics.pinterest.com/profile/?tab=repins&app=all.
29 Ibid.
30 Pinterest, Inc. "Your Pinterest Profile: Clicks." Pinterest. n.d. Web. 09 Aug. 2016. https://analytics.pinterest.com/profile/?tab=clicks&app=all.
31 Ibid.
32 Pinterest, Inc. "Your Pinterest Profile: All-time." Pinterest. n.d. Web. 09 Aug. 2016. https://analytics.pinterest.com/profile/?tab=all_time&app=all.
33 Pinterest, Inc. "A Guide to Pinterest Analytics." Pinterest. n.d. Web. 9 August 2016. https://pinterest.app.box.com/s/4u9wx06yk91r463upuar.
34 Ibid.
35 Ibid.
36 Ibid.

POSTSCRIPT

Social Media Marketing Analysis

234

Social Media Fatigue and Fickleness

236

Social Media Marketing Analysis

Note for Teachers

Discuss the 'Core and Specialty Social Media Channels' chart and accompanying information with the students. Then, ask them to turn their attention to the 'Social Media Chart'. Based on what they learned throughout the course, they should be able to summarize in one sentence what the most important thing each social media network can offer in terms of marketing potential. Suggested answers are provided.

Answers will vary.

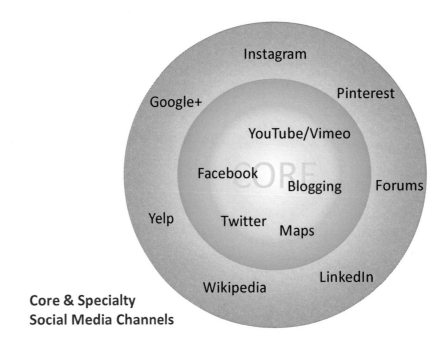

Core & Specialty Social Media Channels

When deciding which social media channels to use for a business, consider using these core channels first. These are the channels that have the broadest appeal. Secondarily, consider using specialty channels that appeal to a particular audience like Pinterest.

⏰ ACTIVITY: UNIQUE SOCIAL MEDIA CONTRIBUTIONS

In this course, you have examined seven social media channels in detail. Based on what you have learned, note what each one is able to do for a business as part of a larger marketing campaign.

Suggested Answers

Facebook: Facebook crosses most demographic lines, and as a marketer of consumer-oriented goods or services, provides the company with the broadest reach.

Twitter: Twitter allows the marketer to create or participate in 'conversations' pertaining to a topic related to the brand (active and frequent participation is crucial for success).

Instagram: Instagram is a more visual medium used for sharing brand activity that allows for the uploading of images or video that is often used to promote news, new products, or offer a behind-the-scenes look at an organization.

LinkedIn: Similar to Facebook, but without the embarassing pictures of last week's party, LinkedIn allows the marketer both to target a professional audience and create a conversational blog or topic that enhances the brand.

YouTube: YouTube is an inexpensive platform for video publishing that allows account holders to create a virtual 'TV channel' or embed videos in their own websites for streaming.

Yelp: When searching for businesses, Yelp often appears high in the results. When potential customers click on Yelp and they are presented with reviews, there is an opportunity to promote the brand and move more viewers to the company site.

Pinterest: Like Instagram, Pinterest is a more visual social media channel. It acts likes a search engine for images and videos. Pinterest can create more brand engagement and direct traffic to a company website.

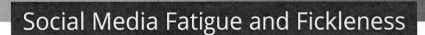

Social Media Fatigue and Fickleness

Throughout Course 3, you have examined a number of social media channels, and have discovered that there are many more out there. Personally and professionally, people have to choose which platforms are deserving of their time and money. Inevitably, the constant stream of posts and updates filling your life, combined with others pulling you towards new platforms results in a social media fatigue and fickleness.

Updating profiles, liking and unliking, following and unfollowing, all of this and more goes into maintaining a meaningful presence on various social networks. Trying to market a brand as effectively as possible on each platform can be overwhelming. It requires that the business owner or marketer knows how to utilize all the important functions and advertising options that a channel makes available, not to mention staying abreast of any changes a channel may implement.

New technology is giving birth to new social media platforms at an astounding rate causing established platforms to struggle and sometimes fade away. Remember MySpace? Friendster? Facebook has made them the stuff of Throwback Thursday.

So, is it possible to reduce social media fatigue, and keep social media account holders loyal? What do you think?

Discuss your ideas with a classmate(s).

Note for Teachers

Answers will vary, however, social media fatigue is an inevitability. The degree to which individuals are affected by it, and the number of social media channels they can maintain at any one time, will be somewhat dependent on whether they are digital natives or digital immigrants: "digital natives (the generation of people born during or after the rise of digital technologies) and the digital immigrants (people born before the advent of digital technology)".[1] For someone who has grown up with social media and can't remember a time before it, staying up to date with various platforms will just be a part of his or her existence, and perhaps reduce his or her loyalty as new platforms are quickly introduced and often embraced. However, for someone who has to adapt to such a reality, it may be harder to justify the time and money that will be required to maintain a presence or advertising on various platforms. In the short term, there are things individuals can do to ease social media fatigue. Refer to "The Diagnosis and Treatment of Social Media Fatigue": http://www.socialmediatoday.com/content/diagnosis-and-treatment-social-media-fatigue

In terms of fickleness, there have been a number of examples in social media history where people have fallen in and out of love with various channels. This is likely to continue. In the case of Facebook, people stayed loyal to it in preference to Friendster or MySpace for several reasons:

- Like email, a critical mass of users makes it likely that those you know are already on Facebook.
- Account holders were able to create pages for their businesses or brands.
- Fans followed their stars/celebrities.
- Facebook ensured that its platform was available in multiple languages.
- Facebook has its own search engine.
- Media hype carried forward successfully.

Students can also refer to users' comments on this question. Provide them with the link to "Why did Facebook succeed where MySpace and Friendster did not?: https://www.quora.com/Why-did-Facebook-succeed-where-MySpace-and-Friendster-did-not

New and emerging social media channels can take a lesson out of Mark Zuckerberg's book.

APPENDIX

Social Media in Brief

 ## Facebook

Purpose: To enable the account holder to connect with people that he or she already knows.

Use: To allow the account holder to keep in touch with others, share what's occurring in his or her life, and convey information about personal interests.

Key Features:
- Permission-based
- Events (create or join)
- News Feed

 ## Twitter

Purpose: To ensure the account holder can connect with people of interest (e.g. celebrities, politicians, etc.), brands, and organizations.

Use: To keep the account holder abreast about breaking news and events happening in realtime. Twitter also acts as a microblog-style platform.

Key Features:
- 140-characters (brevity of message)
- Hashtags (allowing for content categorization)

 ## Instagram

Purpose: To serve as a visual representation of real-time life experiences.

Use: To allow the account holder to share photos, and to a lesser extent, video clips. He or she can also follow people of interest, brands, and organizations.

Key Features:
- Distilled information (through images and their captions, and video clips)
- Photo filters

 ## LinkedIn

Purpose: To enable the account holder to build a professional profile, conduct a job search, and network with other industry professionals.

Use: To ensure that the account holder can keep up-to-date with corporate content, topics of professional interest, and career opportunities.

Key Features:
- Groups
- Uploading resumes, projects, a portfolio, etc.
- Blogging Platform (posting original content)

YouTube

Purpose: To entertain the account holder, serving as online television.

Use: To enable the account holder to view, upload, like or dislike, and comment on videos.

Key Features:
- Channels
- Follow and subscribe to content creators
- Recommendations

Yelp

Purpose: To inform the account holder about the quality of restaurants, retail outlets, etc.

Use: To allow the account holder to write reviews, rate businesses, read reviews, and comment on reviews.

Key Features:
- Star rating system
- Filter reviews via the reviewer's standing on Yelp (i.e. Reviews will only appear if the reviewer has reviewed a significant number of businesses.)

Pinterest

Purpose: To act as a visual, inspirational medium (i.e. Not reflective of who the user is now, but who he or she would like to be).

Use: To make it possible for the account holder to pin and share images and videos.

Key Features:
- Boards
- Repinning, saving, liking, and sharing pins

Social Media Strategy Project Example

PHOTO © SHELLY SALEHI

PART ONE

Farzad's Barber Shop

Farzad's Barber Shop is a service-oriented business located in the Yaletown district of Vancouver, British Columbia. Since February 2006, Farzad Salehi has been giving haircuts and hot shaves to a male-only clientele. Farzad's wife, Shelley Salehi, manages the business and the social media marketing on various channels, including Facebook, Twitter, and YouTube. The shop employs only one other barber, and is truly a small business operation. However, it is very successful and generally receives positive reviews from clients.[1]

TRANSCRIPT OF VIDEO INTERVIEW[1]:

Interview with Farzad Salehi (co-owner) and Shelley Salehi (co-owner/manager) of Farzad's Barber Shop

Interview conducted by Adam Wilkins (June 19, 2015)

Adam Wilkins (AW): Ok, so here we are at Farzad's Barber Shop. I'm getting my hair cut at the moment, and here are the two people that own Farzad's. I'll get you guys to introduce yourselves.

Shelly Salehi (SS): I'm Shelly Salehi.

Farzad Salehi (FS): And, I'm Farzad.

SS: And, we are the owners of Farzad's Barber Shop.

FS: I cut and she promotes.

AW: So, the purpose of this interview is to kind of talk about digital marketing. So, tell me about the social media uses that help promote Farzad's Barber Shop.

SS: Facebook is probably the top platform that I use for the Barber Shop, the Facebook page. And, I also use Twitter, Instagram, Google+, Pinterest, but Facebook would be the main one. And, I also have my Facebook page connected to my Twitter account, which makes my life a bit easier because whatever I post to the Facebook page will automatically update the Twitter feed. 'Cause I just don't have time to be sitting, 'tweeting' all day long.

AW: So, while we're on the subject of time, how much time does it take you as a small business, there's the two of you here, how much time do you spend on social media?

SS: It's a lot I'd say...

FS: All day.

SS: I'm plugged into it all day long when I'm here at the shop. Basically, checking any updates, if there's anything I need to respond to, if people message me, on the Facebook page which they sometimes do. Or, message me through Yelp. Yelp is another platform obviously that every business really needs to be on.

FS: Or, if you're researching to find something interesting to post on Facebook.

SS: Yeah, so pretty much it's all day long for me from the time I get to the shop about ten o'clock in the morning until we leave at 6:30.

FS: Seven.

SS: And again, that's not that every second I'm on there doing something, but it's always there and I'm always checking on it, and I try to do minimum at least one update per day. Sometimes, if there's something particularly interesting that catches my eye, like an interesting article to share or something that happens at the shop that's really exciting, there might be more than one post. There might be two or three posts in a day. That would be maximum.

FS: Or even the time of the day you post it is very important. What time it reaches more people. What time is less people online. Right now, people are working, they're not online.

SS: You've also got people in different time zones too. Because we've got an audience of, as well as our own clients, we're connected with other barbers and people from all over the world. So at different times they may see your post, whereas somebody here won't. If you want it to be effective, you do have to be on it. It's not enough to just create a page for your business, invite people to 'like' it, and then just sit on it and expect people to keep following you. Myself, if I want to follow a page, I want to see something that will keep me engaged every day that I check back...

FS: In the meantime, tell them to come visit me.

SS: Right, exactly, it's less about trying to get more business for us because we are busy, thankfully, but it's more about just keeping people engaged who are already following us. And, just trying to keep it interesting so that we don't sort of fade away from view because people are bombarded with so many things in their newsfeeds that it's easy to get lost. So, I think that's why it's important for any business if you're going to do it to be on top of it. It doesn't mean you have to be hours and hours every day. At least be checking and trying to post something, and definitely respond to people. It's one thing I really try to do. Any comments, any messages, I try to get to them within a couple of hours. Or, at the most, if I'm not at my computer, at least by the next day that would be the maximum length of time. People see that and they appreciate that.

FS: The check-in is really good. You don't need to check in to restaurants. When you arrive in a restaurant it's not about bragging where you're eating. You promoting that restaurant. Your friends see where you are, Indian restaurant, and when they see that they might click on their Facebook page to see where you are, and they like it, and then they end up trying the food. So, I also every morning come to the shop. As soon as I get to the shop, every morning my time is very correct, the same time every morning I check in to the Barber Shop. So, one day I got a phone call as soon as I checked in, and I was two hours early before my website says the shop is open. I said to the client, I said, "How do you know I am here?" [The client said] "Well, I saw you check in on Facebook." So, that's why, that's $35 business right there. So, that's how you get the jobs.

SS: Yep, being present...

FS: And discipline.

SS: They see you're there. People that get to know us. They know, for example, Farzad rides motorcycles. They know we like to do road trips. And being a small business, you can bring in a little bit of that your sort of personal life into it without getting too personal, obviously. So, even when we go on holiday, like we'll be on holiday for the next two weeks, I'm not going to just drop all the social media and just let it sit for two weeks. There's no way I would do that. So, I'll post photos from the road, and I've had people tell me that they love that.

FS: They can't wait to see...

SS: They look forward to seeing our road trip photos and where we've been and where we're going. Again, it's always being on it and making sure that you just don't drop the ball because people will lose interest very quickly.

FS: There is something more interesting out there.

AW: Do you see a tangible link between your efforts on social media, and business that comes through the front door?

SS: Yes, I do in the volume of new clients that we still get.

FW: We lose a lot of clients, then it replaces very easy.

SS: People coming in, phoning, they always say they found us online. You guys were the most visible; you had the best reviews, so they're definitely seeing us there, online. They comment often that you've got great photos. So, yeah, I would say in that way definitely for bringing new people, attracting new people, it does help.

PART TWO

Pinterest is a highly visual social media platform. Farzad's Barber Shop has a presence on this channel, but it hasn't been actively promoted recently. I believe that by revitalizing the Pinterest page, the business could amplify its social media marketing presence. This highly visual platform pairs very well with the hair styling service industry. It is a great place to post pictures and short videos of positive transformations through hair grooming. The best way to relaunch Farzad's Pinterest page is through a contest. It is described as follows:

Farzad's Barber Shop Pinterest Contest

We are relaunching our Pinterest page! To celebrate our relaunch and the fast-approaching end of Movember, we are announcing our first ever Pinterest contest:

Follow us on Pinterest. Pin pictures of your own amazing Movember mustaches and beards and send them to us. We'll add them to our album, 'Farzad's Movember Contest'. The most epic hair growth, 'liked' by our followers will win! The gentleman sporting the winning facial fuzz will receive a free hot shave and haircut by Farzad and the amazing transformation will appear on our Pinterest page.

This campaign will be successful because it will be announced via the client's already well-promoted social media channels, which have a devoted and significant following. It will also showcase Farzad's ability as a barber and raise his profile on multiple social media channels. People will be motivated to participate because they will want to win the prize and/or vote for the winner. The campaign should also receive a certain amount of traction because of the Movember event.

Sample Pinterest submissions and a winning transformation:

PART THREE: Feedback from Farzad's Barber Shop

I would like to thank the students on their work reviewing our social media efforts and for their suggestion that we run a Pinterest competition as a way of approaching a new social media audience. We are not actively using Pinterest, but as the students pointed out, we are missing the opportunity to use images on Pinterest to drive people to our website.

We will consider running the competition in the coming months and will certainly let you know how it turns out.

Regards,

Shelley Salehi

Farzad's Barber Shop

126-1208 Homer St.

Vancouver, B.C.

V5B 2Y5

http://farzadsbarbershop.com

MIDTERM EXAM   /30

Name: _____

SECTION ONE: MULTIPLE CHOICE   /10

Circle the correct answer to each multiple-choice question. All questions are worth one mark.

1. Which of the following social media networks is known to appeal to the female demographic?

   a. Twitter
   b. Pinterest
   c. Google +
   d. LinkedIn

2. Which of the following is an example of a "brand metric"?

   a. impressions
   b. comments
   c. likes
   d. none of the above

3. A person can tell that a Twitter post is an ad because of its:

   a. hashtags
   b. URLs
   c. boxed presentation
   d. all of the above

4. Instagram is owned by:

   a. Facebook
   b. Twitter
   c. Google
   d. Pinterest

5. Marketers can utilize which of the following to create an accurate buyer persona?

   a. questionnaires
   b. analytics
   c. social media listening
   d. all of the above

6. Which of the following is **not** true about Instagram?

    a. It has been a source of breaking news.
    b. Unsolicited ads appear.
    c. It allows Instagrammers to share photos.
    d. It offers Instagrammers suggestions or recommendations

7. What is the main goal of the following ad?

    A toy store owner posts the same image on Facebook, Twitter, and Instagram. It is a picture of a local woman making puppets in her home. These puppets are sold in the owner's toy store. Before the owner posted the image, he knew many of his customers believed the puppets were made in China.

    a. To increase brand awareness
    b. To shift perception
    c. To generate likes
    d. None of the above

8. How long can an Instagram video be?

    a. 30 seconds or less
    b. 15 seconds or less
    c. 45 seconds or less
    d. 1 minute or less

9. If a brand puts an Instagram button on its Facebook page, the business is engaging in:

    a. Persona-driven marketing
    b. Cross-marketing
    c. A loop giveaway
    d. None of the above

10. Which of the following is most important when it comes to increasing brand awareness on Instagram?

    a. Weekly impressions
    b. Monthly reach
    c. Number of followers
    d. Number of positive comments

SECTION TWO: FILL IN THE BLANKS   /10

Complete each statement with the correct word(s). Write in the space(s) provided.

1. A carousel ad allows a marketer to put up to _____ images in one post. (1 mark)

2. Account insights and ad insights allow Instagram advertisers to track _____ and metrics. (2 marks)

3. The three kinds of Facebook advertising mentioned in the text are: _____ , _____ , and _____ . (3 marks)

4. _____ and _____ hashtags can be useful to business owners and marketers. (2 marks)

5. Regrams, shares, likes, and comments help a marketer to measure_____ on an Instagram post. (1 mark)

6. _____ is the kind of goal a startup company would want to achieve on Twitter. (1 mark)

SECTION THREE: SHORT ANSWER   /10

Respond to the following questions in the space provided. You may write in point form.

1. What does the following quotation mean, and teach people about social media?

    (2 marks)

    "Aim to have content on the web be 'professional' not 'confessional'"[2]

    —E. Chandlee Bryan

    _____

    _____

    _____

2. Why do Facebook account holders often follow and 'like' small, local businesses' pages? (1 mark)

    _____

    _____

    _____

    _____

3. What are three reasons why an Instagram ad might be underperforming?   (3 marks)

    a. _____

    b. _____

    c. _____

4. What does Instagram's ad staging help marketers to do?   (1 mark)

    _____

5. How do keywords function differently on Twitter advertising versus SEO-based advertising?

    (3 marks)

    _____

    _____

    _____

    _____

YOUTUBE ANALYTICS RESOURCE PACKAGE

Resource #1: YouTube Analytics Basics

Link: https://support.google.com/youtube/answer/1714323?hl=en

Note: Please view the "Guide to YouTube Analytics" video included on this page.

Resource #2: About YouTube Analytics

Link: https://creatoracademy.withgoogle.com/page/lesson/using-analytics?hl=en

Note: Watch the video on this page first. Then, work your way through the content and activities. Sign in where directed by your instructor using your Gmail account.

CARDS REPORT/ANALYTICS RESOURCE PACKAGE

Resource #1: Cards Report

Link: https://support.google.com/youtube/answer/6165415?hl=en

---

Resource #2: YouTube Cards Analytics - How To Analyze The Effectiveness Of Cards On YouTube

Link: https://www.youtube.com/watch?v=yRd64HYrsQE

FOOTNOTES: APPENDIX

1   DeGraff, Jeff. "Digital Natives vs. Digital Immigrants." **The Huffington Post**. 16 Jun. 2014. Web. 18 Sept. 2015. http://www.huffingtonpost.com/jeff-degraff/digital-natives-vs-digita_b_5499606.html.
2   Salehi, Farzad and Shelley Salehi. Personal Interview. 19 Jun. 2015.

FOOTNOTES: APPENDIX

1   "About Us." Farzad's Barber Shop. n.d. Web. 23 Jul. 2015. http://www.farzadsbarbershop.com/About_Us.html.
2   Bryan, Chandlee E. "Creating & Maintaining an Online Persona." Best Fit Forward. 2010. Web. 29 Jun. 2015. http://graduate.dartmouth.edu/docs/Creating_an_online_persona_Linked_In_Twitter_Blogging.pdf.

GLOSSARY

Note 1: All definitions, unless indicated by footnotes, come directly from Mujo Learning Systems' *Digital Marketing Fundamentals* and *Social Media Marketing Strategies* textbooks.

Note 2: Starred terms indicate a general definition only. Consult each chapter for platform-specific descriptions.

The Google AdWords Glossary is also a good reference to consult to find platform-independent definitions of various digital marketing terminology:

https://support.google.com/adwords/topic/3121777?hl=en&ref_topic=3119071

----

*Analytics: automatic feedback mechanisms that allow monitoring of online marketing efforts

Audience or Target Market: the type of people a business is attempting to attract and where they are located

Brand: the personality of a product, service, or company as perceived by key constituencies

Brand Metrics: enable a company to measure impressions, reach, clicks, and frequency

Bounce Rate: the proportion of web traffic that leaves a site quickly, after only one click

Business-to-Business (B2B): "A transaction that occurs between two companies, as opposed to a transaction involving a consumer. The term may also describe a company that provides goods and services for another company"[1]

Business-to-Consumer (B2C): a company to person transaction

Budget: "amount of money available for spending that is based on a plan for how it will be spent"[2]

Call To Action (CTA): telling or commanding others to do something (using the imperative)

Click: when someone actually clicks on the ad

Conversion: "point at which a recipient of a marketing message performs a desired action"[3] (e.g. buys something, becomes a client, heeds a call to action, etc.)

Cost per Click (CPC): how much a business owner must pay each time someone clicks on a company ad

*Cost per Conversion: measures how much it costs in advertising to convert one person

Digital Marketing: "the marketing of products or services using digital channels to reach consumers; the key objective is to promote brands through various forms of digital media"[4]

Email Marketing: a digitized subset of direct mail; the direct marketing of a message (e.g. special offers, promotional messages, newsletters, etc.) to a group of people using email

*Engagement: gives the audience (target market) a sense of involvement in the marketing process

*Frequency: how often an account holder posts or the number of times an individual sees something related to a specific brand

*Impression: the number of times a particular ad appears on a page

Interruption Marketing: type of advertising that forces the audience to encounter a brand and its message

Logo: a mark which generally consists of letters, a pronounceable word, or words in type, sometimes combined with an image, used to identify a company, brand, project, or group

Organic Search: clicks through from a company website

Pay Per Click (PPC): the buying of advertising space from search engines like Google

Paid Search: represented by **Cost per Click**

Public Service Announcement (PSA): ad designed to educate the public about important issues; often commissioned by the government, activist groups, and charitable organizations

Questionnaire: a survey that asks for consumer responses

*Reach: how many people will be part of the viewing audience for a particular marketing campaign across either online or offline channels

Relevance: refers to something being pertinent at a particular moment in time (e.g. an ad); must work within the context in which audience members will encounter it

Search Engine Optimization (SEO): tagging a company's website with keywords, so that search engines can identify them and present them as relevant search results to users

Social Media Listening: reading through what people are saying online and taking note of what they are doing on the company's social media channels

Social-Specific Metrics: helps a business owner to gauge post engagement (e.g. likes and comments)

Target Consumer Persona (Target Market Profile): identifying the ideal potential customer a business wants to attract with its marketing efforts

Target Market: see **Audience**

Visibility: the number of views a page receives during a given period (30 days, one year, etc.)

FOOTNOTES: GLOSSARY

1   WebFinance, Inc. "B2B". InvestorWords. 2015. Web. 09 Mar. 2015. http://www.investorwords.com/364/B2B.html.
2   Merriam-Webster Incorporated. "Budget." Merriam-Webster. 2015. Web. 10 Apr. 2015. http://www.merriam-webster.com/dictionary/budget.
3   Kirpatrick, David. "Marketing 101: What is conversion?" MarketingSherpa Blog. 15 Mar. 2012. Web. 27 Mar. 2015. http://sherpablog.marketingsherpa.com/marketing/conversion-defined/.
4   The Financial Times Ltd. "Definition of digital marketing." *The Financial Times*. 2015. Web. 06 Feb. 2015. http://lexicon.ft.com/Term?term=digital-marketing.

VIDEO BIBLIOGRAPHY

All of the following videos are available on the Mujo Learning Systems Inc. channel under the "Social Media Marketing Strategies" playlist: https://www.youtube.com/playlist?list=PLFxihBCgPmRpfJvSk4Cxp4jftvai7IC-w

"Social Media Dos and Donts" (02:09)

"How to Set Up Your LinkedIn Company Page" (02:08)

"A Quick Walkthrough of LinkedIn Company Page Analytics" (03:12)

"Youtube for Viewers and Uploaders" (02:41)

"Psy - Gangnam Style" (04:12)

"Components of YouTube for Business" (02:38)

"Introducing Google My Business" (01:25)

"Google My Business" (05:12)

"Hyundai: Pipe Job" (01:01)

"Effects of Smoking on the Human Body" (00:33)

"Dumb Ways to Die" (03:02)

"Dumb Ways to Die - Dumb Ways to Die Parody" (03:06)

"Dumb Ways to Die (Minecraft Edition)" (03:12)

"Dumb Ways to Die 2 - Leg Training" (00:31)

"Dumb Ways to Die 2 - Spin Training" (00:31)

*The videos that follow are not part of the YouTube playlist, as they are embedded on other sites:

"Success Stories (Case Studies) | Facebook for Business" playlist: (50 videos)*: https://www.youtube.com/playlist?list=PLE6673621EA00DF45

"Why Does Yelp Recommend Reviews?": http://www.yelp-support.com/article/Does-Yelp-recommend-every-review?l=en_US (01:53)*

"Responding to Reviews": https://biz.yelp.ca/support/responding_to_reviews (04:14)*

"Yelp Ads": https://biz.yelp.ca/support/advertising (02:18)*

**The following video contains strong language, so it is not part of Mujo's playlist. It is up to individual instructors to determine whether this video is appropriate for students:

"Botto Bistro is Fighting Yelp": https://www.youtube.com/watch?v=dwI8TL57cOw (09:09)**

Note: To access the following videos, please view Mujo Learning Systems' Vimeo channel:
"Facebook Insights for Analytics" (05:35)
"How to Track Facebook Ads in Google Analytics" (04:17)
"Farzad's Barber Shop" (07:32)
https://vimeo.com/user56677158

LINKS BIBLIOGRAPHY

Note: *Some links are for extension activities and may be omitted. Some links are for the instructor's use and do not need to be given to students, refer to each specific activity.*

Chapter One

"How to Choose the Best Social Media Site for Your Business": http://www.inc.com/michelle-manafy/how-to-choose-the-best-social-media-sites-to-market-your-business.html

Chapter Two

Klout: Klout.com

Google News Alert: https://www.google.com/alerts

"Getting Started with Pages": https://www.facebook.com/business/learn/facebook-page-basics

"6 Publishing Tools From Facebook for Marketers": http://www.socialmediaexaminer.com/6-publishing-tools-from-facebook-for-marketers/

"Shop Section on Pages": https://www.facebook.com/business/help/846547442125798

"A Beginner's Guide to Facebook Insights": https://blog.kissmetrics.com/guide-to-facebook-insights/

Spool of Thread: https://www.facebook.com/SpoolofThread?ref=profile

"Facebook Promoted Posts: A Step-By-Step Guide": http://mashable.com/2012/05/31/facebook-promoted-posts-tips/#gallery/facebooks-promoted-posts-for-brand-pages/521294c95198406611000eed

"A New Look for Ads in the Right-Hand Column": https://www.facebook.com/business/news/A-New-Look-for-Ads-in-the-Right-Hand-Column

"How to Choose the Right Type of Facebook Contest": http://www.socialmediaexaminer.com/how-to-choose-the-right-type-of-facebook-contest/

"This Man's $600,000 Facebook Disaster Is A Warning For All Small Businesses": http://www.businessinsider.com/mans-600000-facebook-ad-disaster-2014-2#ixzz3em3X5YNd

"Smucker's Jelly Company Hides Behind a Traditional Image While Saying This About GMOs": http://althealthworks.com/1714/the-smuckers-jelly-company-traditional-brand-comes-out-in-support-of-gmos-will-boycotts-result/

"C & A Fashion Magazine Ad With Like Buttons By DM9DDB": http://www.theinspiration.com/2014/09/c-fashion-magazin-add-like-buttons-dm9ddb/

"Guidelines and Specs for Creating Ads": https://www.facebook.com/business/help/www/458369380926902

"How Much Should You Budget for Facebook Ads?": http://www.jonloomer.com/2014/07/08/facebook-ads-budget-2/

Chapter Three

"Getting Started Guide": https://dev.twitter.com/cards/getting-started

"Keyword Targeting": https://business.twitter.com/help/keyword-targeting

"Twitter Ads": https://ads.twitter.com/login

"Twitter brands can now target ads based on the emoji you use": http://thenextweb.com/twitter/2016/06/15/twitter-brands-can-now-target-ads-based-emoji-use/#gref

"Trendsmap": http://trendsmap.com

"RiteTag": https://ritetag.com

"Twitter Account Analytics": https://analytics.twitter.com/

"Twitter Card Analytics": https://business.twitter.com/en/help/campaign-measurement-and-analytics/twitter-card-analytics-dashboard.html

Chapter Four

"Instagram, Help Center": https://help.instagram.com

"Instagram Stories: How 18 Brands And Influencers Are Using It (And You Can Too!)":
https://blog.bufferapp.com/instagram-stories-who-to-follow

"Content Strategy Tips": https://business.instagram.com/getting-started/

"Advertising on Instagram": https://business.instagram.com/advertising/

"3 Outstanding Use Cases for Branded Hashtags on Instagram": sproutsocial.com/insights/3-outstanding-use-cases-branded-hashtags-instagram

"Adding Video to Carousel Ads": http://blog.business.instagram.com/post/144613122511/video-carousel-ads

"Instagram's analytics will offer audience demographics, post impressions, reach & more": https://techcrunch.com/2016/05/16/instagrams-analytics-will-offer-audience-demographics-post-impressions-reach-more/

"The Best Times to Post on Facebook, Instagram, and Twitter": www.businessinsider.com/best-times-to-post-on-facebook-instagram-twitter-2015-7

"Here's the Best Time to Post a Photo on Instagram": www.huffingtonpost.com/2015/02/25/get-instagram-likes_n_6751614.html

"This Social Network Engages Audiences Better Than the Rest": https://www.entrepreneur.com/article/279827

Chapter Five

"5 Tips for Picking the Right LinkedIn Profile Picture": https://business.linkedin.com/talent-solutions/blog/2014/12/5-tips-for-picking-the-right-linkedin-profile-picture

Think Profits' LinkedIn page and Showcase pages: http://www.linkedin.com/company/think-profits-com-inc

"LinkedIn Company Pages": https://business.linkedin.com/marketing-solutions/company-pages/best-practices

Chapter Five cont...

13 Creative Ways to Use LinkedIn for Lead Generation": smallbiztrends.com/2014/02/ways-use-linkedin-for-lead-generation.html

"Market to Who Matters": https://business.linkedin.com/marketing-solutions

"This is the Real Reason Microsoft Bought LinkedIn" (Yes, LinkedIn was worth it): http://www.forbes.com/sites/grantfeller/2016/06/14/this-is-the-real-reason-microsoft-bought-linkedin/#6d1f0cca4acd

"LinkedUp (No, LinkedIn was not worth it): http://www.economist.com/news/business-and-finance/21700605-it-one-most-expensive-tech-deals-history-it-may-not-be-smartest-making-sense

Chapter Six

"Why Gangnam Style Became So Popular – The Reasons Behind Its' Horse-Riding Success!": http://blog.socialmaximizer.com/why-gangnam-style-became-so-popular/

"YouTube Advertising Formats": https://support.google.com/youtube/answer/2467968?hl=en

"Add Cards to Videos": https://support.google.com/youtube/answer/6140491?hl=en

Chapter Seven

"Does Yelp Recommend Every Review?": http://www.yelp-support.com/article/Does-Yelp-recommend-every-review?l=en_US

"A Simple Guide to Showcasing Your Business Online": http://www.yelp-business.com/rs/yelpinc/images/Yelp_US_Ebook.pdf

"Yelp Ads": https://biz.yelp.ca/support/advertising

"Using Yelp to Increase Social and Brand Awareness": http://www.sociallybuzz.com/used-yelp-to-increase-social-and-brand-awareness/

"Yelp Knowledge For Local Analytics Launches with 3 New Partners": https://www.yelpblog.com/2016/06/yelp-knowledge-local-analytics-launches-3-new-partners

Chapter Eight

KLM Royal Dutch Airlines' Pinterest page: https://www.pinterest.com/KLM/

Tom Lee Music Canada's Pinterest page: https://www.pinterest.com/tomleemusic/

"6 Ways to Promote Your Business With Pinterest Places": http://www.socialmediaexaminer.com/pinterest-place-pins/

"Pinterest Puts Its Own Spin on Video Ads With These Cinematic Pins": http://www.adweek.com/news/technology/pinterest-puts-its-own-spin-video-ads-these-cinematic-pins-164854

Jetsetter Curator – Cosmopolitan: https://www.pinterest.com/jetsetterphoto/jetsetter-curator-cosmopolitan/

Postscript

"The Diagnosis and Treatment of Social Media Fatigue": http://www.socialmediatoday.com/content/diagnosis-and-treatment-social-media-fatigue

"Why did Facebook succeed where MySpace and Friendster did not?: https://www.quora.com/Why-did-Facebook-succeed-where-MySpace-and-Friendster-did-not

BIBLIOGRAPHY

"About Us." n.d. *Farzad's Barber Shop.* Web. 23 July 2015.

Adsoftheworldvideos. "Hyundai: Pipe Job." 8 August 2014. *YouTube.* Online Video Clip. Web. 28 August 2015.

Alba, Davey. "NASA Teams Up with Instagram to Debut Pluto Surface Photo." 14 July 2015. *Wired.* Web.

Alcala, Lori. "The Smucker's Facebook Fail: How to Protect Your Brand." 6 November 2014. *CMSWire.* Web. 29 June 2015.

"Andrew Carnegie Quotes." 2015. *BrainyQuote.* Web. 27 October 2015.

Arruda, William. "5 Easy Ways to Create a Brilliant Background for Your LinkedIn Profile." 9 November 2014. *Forbes.* Web. 24 August 2015.

Bennett, Shea. "What are the Best Times to Post on #Facebook, #Twitter and #Instagram? [INFOGRAPHIC]." 6 January 2015. *Adweek.* Web. 6 July 2015.

Berry, Megan. "5 Tips for Dealing with Complaints on Twitter." 13 August 2010. *Mashable.* Web. 17 July 2015.

Botto Bistro. "Yelp's One Star is the New Five Stars." 24 August 2016. *Facebook*. Web. 10 October 2016.

Box, Toni. "Instagram Advertising: Consumer's Aren't Loving It...Yet." 7 August 2014. *PM Digital.* Web. 22 July 2015.

Brookegandhi. "The History of Pinterest." 2013. *Timetoast*. Web. 8 July 2016.

Bryan, Chandlee E. "Creating & Maintaining an Online Persona." 2010. *Best Fit Forward.* Web. 29 June 2015.

Buck, Stephanie. "10 Things You Can Fit Into Your 63,206-Character Facebook Status." 4 January 2012. *Mashable.* Web. 7 August 2015.

Bunskoek, Krista. "3 Hashtags Strategies: How to Market Your Business & Content." 2015. *Wishpond.* Web. 5 August 2015.

—. "52 Tips: How to Market on Instagram." 2014. *Wishpond.* Web. 19 August 2015.

Butzbach, Alex. "Want Instagram marketing data? Brands can now see impressions, reach and engagement." 27 August 2014. *Brafton.* Web. 20 August 2015.

Buxton, Ryan. "The Owner of California's Botto Bistro is Proud to Have Yelp's Worst-Rated Restaurant." 2 October 2014. *HuffPost Live.* Web. 17 September 2015.

C&A Inc. "Labels." n.d. *C&A.* Web. 3 July 2015.

Callan, Nadine. "What You Need to Know About Instagram Loop Giveaways." 8 June 2015. *Blog Brighter.* Web. 10 August 2015.

Carlson, Nicholas. "Pinterest CEO: Here's How We Became the Web's Next Big Thing." 24 April 2012. *Business Insider*. Web. 8 July 2016.

Casti, Taylor. "The History of Twitter from Egg to IPO." 4 October 2013. *Mashable Infographic.* Web. 9 July 2015.

CBC/Radio-Canada. "Hyundai apologizes for offensive suicide ad." 25 April 2013. *CBC News.* Web. 29 August 2015.

ColdfusTion. "The Surprising History of YouTube!" 4 February 2015. *YouTube.* Online Video Clip. Web. 24 August 2015.

Conner, Cheryl. "New Research: 2014 LinkedIn User Trends (And 10 Top Surprises)." 4 May 2014. *Forbes.* Web. 29 June 2015.

Constine, Josh. "Facebook launches Marketplace, a friendlier Craigslist." 3 October 2016. *TechCrunch*. Web. 4 October 2016.

Cooper, Sam. "TransLink is the most popular transit system in North America, says new study." 15 February 2015. *The Province.* Web. 8 June 2015.

Cullers, Rebecca. "This Restaurant Wants to Be the Worst Rated on Yelp, and the Reviews are Indeed Hilarious." 22 September 2014. *Adweek.* Web. 17 September 2015.

Cunningham-Scharf, Sarah. "Instagram Launches Carousel Ads in Canada." 29 May 2015. *Marketing.* Web. 21 September 2016.

Cyrus, Farivar. "Why this tiny Italian restaurant gives a discount for bad Yelp reviews." 21 September 2014. *Ars Technica.* Web. 17 September 2015.

Daley, Rachel. "The Ultimate Pinterest Marketing Guide: How to Improve Your Reach and Promote Your Brand." 2015. *Kissmetrics Blog*. Web. 8 August 2016.

Daoud, Houssem. "8 Essential Elements of a Social Media Marketing Strategy." 16 July 2014. *Social Media Examiner*. Web. 26 May 2015.

DeGraff, Jeff. "Digital Natives vs. Digital Immigrants." 16 June 2014. *The Huffington Post.* Web. 18 September 2015.

Desreumaux, Geoff. "The Complete History of Instagram." 3 January 2014. *We Are Social Media.* Web. 15 July 2015.

Diaz, Ann-Christine. "How 'Dumb Ways to Die' Won the Internet, Became the No.1 Campaign of the Year." 11 November 2013. *Advertising Age.* Web. 24 June 2015.

Dickey, Megan Rose. "The 22 Key Turning Points in the History of YouTube." 15 February 2013. *Business Insider.* Web. 24 August 2015.

Dirks, Brent. "Instagram opens the advertising floodgates by launching its new API." 4 August 2015. *AppAdvice.* Web. 21 August 2015.

DiSilvestro, Amanda. "Yelp Optimization: How to Claim & Optimize Your Business Listing." 10 May 2013. *Search Engine Watch.* Web. 14 September 2015.

Dixler, Hillary. "Yelp Turns 10: From Startup to Online Review Dominance." 5 August 2014. *Eater.* Web. 31 August 2015.

Donnaker, Geoff. "Ready for Our Close-Up! Announcing Yelp's First TV and Digital Ads." 7 May 2015. *Yelp, Official Blog.* Web. 31 August 2015.

Drill, Lauren."How Pinterest Boosted Jetsetter's Traffic by 150%." 23 May 2012. *Mashable.* Web. 22 July 2016.

DumbWays2Die. "Dumb Ways to Die" *YouTube.* Online Video Clip. 14 November 2012. Web. 14 October 2016.

Duggan, Maeve, Nicole B. Ellison, Cliffe Lampe, Amanda Lenhart, and Mary Madden. *Demographics of Key Social Networking Platforms*. Demographic Research. Washington, D.C.: Pew Research Centre, 2015. Web.

Facebook, Inc. "Company Info." 2015. *Facebook.* Web. 25 May 2015. *Facebook.* Web. 2 July 2015.

—. Facebook for Business. "5 Tips for Using Facebook on Small Business Saturday." 22 November 2013. *Facebook.* Web. 23 September 2016.

—. "Stats." 2016. *Facebook.* Web. 4 October 2016.

Farfan, Barbara. "Funny and Inspirational Quotations About Competition - Pro- and Anti-Competition." 2015. *About. com.* Web. 3 June 2015.

Francis, Anna. "6 Ways to Promote Your Business With Pinterest Places." 11 March 2014. *Social Media Examiner*. Web. 5 August 2016.

Frier, Sarah. "Snapchat Passes Twitter in Daily Usage." 2 June 2016. *Bloomberg*. Web. 5 Oct. 2016.

Fruit of the Loom, Inc. "Fresh Gigs." 13 August 2015. *Fruit of the Loom.* Web. 13 August 2015.

—. "The Fruit Story." 2015. *Fruit of the Loom.* Web. 14 August 2015.

Garst, Kim. "Instagram Ads Are Now Open to Everyone!" 16 August 2015. *Boom Social Media Marketing LLC.* Web. 19 August 2015.

Gonzalez, Leah. "Fruit of the Loom and LinkedIn Team Up for Ad Campaign." 7 October 2013. *PSFK.* Web. 13 August 2015.

Google. "Add Cards to Videos." 2016. *YouTube.* Web. 11 October 2016.

—. "Card Types." 2015. *YouTube.* Web. 11 September 2015.

—. "YouTube Community goes beyond video." 13 September 2016. *YouTube.* Web. 8 October 2016.

Griner, David. "DiGiorno Is Really, Really Sorry About Its Tweet Accidentally Making Light of Domestic Violence." 9 September 2014. *Adweek*. Web. 13 July 2015.

Gross, Max. "5 marketing campaigns that had real world impact." 16 February 2015. *Marketing Eye Atlanta.* Web. 30 June 2015.

Hartmann, Margaret. "Bill Cosby Asks Internet to 'Meme' Him; Twitter Responds With Rape Allegations." 10 November 2014. *Vulture: Devouring Culture.* Web. 10 July 2015.

Hawes, Alex. "5 Intriguing Twitter Marketing Case Studies." 15 July 2013. *Our Social Times.* Web. 13 July 2015.

Heaney, Katie. "Spare Us Your Customer Service Complaint Tweets." 3 April 2013. *BuzzFeed.* Web. 17 July 2015.

Herman, Jenn. "What are Your Limits on Instagram?" 16 June 2014. *Jenn's Trends.* Web. 7 August 2015.

Hernandez, Brian Anthony. "Twitter Rewind: Big Highlights from 2012 to 2006." 21 March 2012. *Mashable Infographic.* Web. 9 July 2015.

Hines, Kristi. "How to Create a Social Media Strategy By Spying Your Competitors." 10 December 2013. *Social Media Examiner.* Web. 6 June 2015.

Holloway, Darnell Justin. "Yelp Metrics: New and Improved." 27 March 2012. *Yelp.* Web. 18 September 2015.

Holmes, Ryan. "Why an Instagram Tweak Spells the Beginning of a Multibillion-Dollar Industry." 19 August 2015. *Re/Code.* Web. 19 August 2015.

Hooker, Lauren. "What I Learned from Gaining 3,000 Followers in One Day." 17 February 2015. *Elle & Co.* Web. 12 August 2015.

Hyundai Motor Corporation. "History." 2015. *Hyundai.* Web. 28 August 2015.

Indigo. "Red Notice: A True Story." 2015. *Indigo.* Web. 20 July 2015.

Indigo Chapters (@chaptersindigo). "A tale that makes the dirty dealings of House of Cards look like Snow White." 20 July 2015. *Twitter.* Web.

—. "Red Notice is a compelling real-life thriller about an American financier #HeathersPicks indg.ca/74pX." 20 July 2015. *Twitter.* Web.

Instagram, Inc. "Adding Video to Carousel Ads." May 2016. *Instagram.* Web. 23 September 2016.

—."A New Way for Brands to Tell Stories on Instagram." April 2015. *Instagram.* Web. 19 August 2015.

—. "Announcing a New Suite of Business Tools for Brands on Instagram." 2014. *Instagram.* Web. 18 August 2015.

—. "Content Strategy Tips." 2015. *Instagram.* Web. 10 August 2015.

—. "Creating an Account & Username." 2015. *Instagram.* Web. 6 August 2015.

—. "Exploring Photos and Videos." 2015. *Instagram.* Web. 7 August 2015.

—. "FAQ." 2015. *Instagram.* Web. 13 August 2015.

—. "Instagram Help Centre." 2016. *Instagram.* Web. 23 September 2016.

—. "Instagram Today: 500 Million Windows to the World." 21 June 2016. *Instagram.* Web. 8 October 2016.

—. "Introducing Instagram Stories." 2 August 2016. *Instagram.* Web. 8 October 2016.

Jackson, Nicolas. "Infographic: The Incredible Six-Year History of Yelp Reviews." 20 July 2011. *The Atlantic*. Web. 31 August 2015.

Jefferson, Whitney. "24 Utterly Annoying Celebrity Complaints on Twitter." 12 June 2013. *BuzzFeed.* Web. 17 July 2015.

"Jetsetter Review" 18 November 2015. *Reviews.com.* Web. 9 August 2016.

Jimmy Kimmel Live. "Celebrities Read Mean Tweets #1." 22 March 2012. *YouTube.* Online Video Clip. Web. 10 July 2015.

—. "Celebrities Read Mean Tweets #2." 25 July 2012. *YouTube.* Online Video Clip. Web. 16 July 2015.

Joss, Elizabeth. "A Beginner's Guide to Facebook Insights." 2015. *Kissmetrics*. Web. 2 July 2015.

Kalra, Achir. "Instagram Bolsters Ad Analytics Offerings - Are More Advertisements to Follow?" 21 August 2014. *Forbes.* Web. 20 August 2015.

Karimi, Shireen. "GMO Inside: With a Social Media Policy Like Smuckers, a Comment Has to Be Good...Or It's Gone." 3 November 2014. *GMO Inside*. Web. 21 December 2015.

Kirkpatrick, David. "Yelp launches 'Knowledge' program to provide deeper analytics and insights." 29 June 2016. *Industry Dive*. Web. 21 Sept. 2016.

—. "Marketing 101: What is conversion?" 15 March 2012. *MarketingSherpa Blog.* Web. 27 March 2015.

Laird, Sam. "High Tech, High Fashion: Clothes Hangers Show Real-Time Facebook Likes [VIDEO]." *Mashable.* 7 May 2012. Web.

Lattin, Pace. "McDonalds Fails with Instagram Campaign." 18 May 2015. *Performance Marketing Insider.* Web. 22 July 2015.

Lawler, Ryan. "Pinterest Hits 30 Billion Total Pins, Up 50% In 6 Months." 24 April 2016. *TechCrunch.* Web. 8 July 2016.

Lee, Kevan. "Marketing Personas: The Complete Beginner's Guide." 27 March 2014. *Buffersocial.* Web. 3 June 2015.

LinkedIn Corporation. "15 tips for compelling Company Updates." 2015. *LinkedIn.* Web. 28 August 2015.

—. "A Brief History of LinkedIn." 2015. *LinkedIn.* Web. 16 July 2015.

—. "Analytics Tab for Company Pages." 18 August 2015. *LinkedIn.* Web. 3 September 2015.

—. "Best LinkedIn Company Pages of 2014." 2015. *LinkedIn.* Web. 28 August 2015.

—. "Company Pages Best Practices." 2017. *LinkedIn.* Web. 2 June 2017.

—. "LinkedIn Company Pages and Followers." 2015. *LinkedIn.* Web. 28 August 2015.

—. "LinkedIn Publishing Playbook." 2015. *LinkedIn.* Web. 28 August 2015.

—. "Showcase Pages." 2017. *LinkedIn.* Web. 2 June 2017.

—. "The Sophisticated Marketer's Product Showcase Series: LinkedIn Sponsored Updates." 6 August 2015. *LinkedIn.* Web. 2 September 2015.

LinkedIn Marketing Solutions. "How to Set Up Your LinkedIn Company Page." 15 April 2014. *YouTube.* Online Video Clip. Web. 27 August 2015.

Loomer, Jon. "How Much Should You Budget for Facebook Ads?" 08 July 2014. *JonLoomer.com.* Web. 2 September 2015.

Lui, Kevin. "Twitter's Revamped Character Limit is Finally Here." 19 September 2016. *Time*. Web. 6 October 2016.

Malatesta, Irene. "How to Fail at Instagram: McDonald's." 12 August 2014. *Irene Kaoru Malatesta*. Web. 22 July 2015.

Martin, Russ. "Instagram Rolls Out Ads in Canada." 10 November 2014. *Marketing*. Web. 23 September 2015.

McGovern, Michele. "3 great ways to handle customer complaints on Twitter." 16 January 2015. *Customer Experience Insight*. Web. 17 July 2015.

Merriam-Webster Incorporated. "Budget." 2015. *Merriam-Webster*. Web. 10 April 2015.

Milbrath, Sam. "How to Use Pinterest for Business: The Definitive Guide." 20 May 2016. *Hootsuite*. Web. 10 August 2016.

Moore, Shawn and Adam Wilkins. *Digital Marketing Fundamentals*. Vancouver: Mujo Learning Systems Inc., 2016. Print.

Nanton, Nick and JW Dicks. "4 Big Ideas on How to Manage Your Online Persona." 7 March 2014. *Fast Company.* 7 March 2014. Web. 6 July 2015.

Newman, Andrew Adam. "Fruit of the Loom Sees Workers in Their Underwear." 7 October 2013. *The New York Times.* Web. 14 August 2015.

News Staff. "TransLink's Twitter team gives transit a human touch." 27 February 2015. *News 1130.* Web. 8 June 2015.

Newton, Casey. "Twitter launches Moments, its dead-simple tab for browsing the best tweets." 6 October 2015. *The Verge*. Web. 5 October 2016.

O'Neill, Megan. "An Infographic timeline of YouTube's First 8 Years." 6 February 2013. *Adweek.* Web. 24 August 2015.

O'Reilly, Lara. "Instagram just made a major move that will turn it into a huge advertising business." 4 August 2015. *Business Insider.* Web. 19 August 2015.

Parker, Rob. "Copywriting for Facebook Ads." 23 May 2013. *Voz Media.* Web. 6 July 2015.

Parrack, Dave. "7 Reasons Why You Should Be Using Twitter." 3 April 2013. *MakeUseOf.* Web. 17 July 2015.

Paunescu, Delia. "Bill Cosby's massive social media fail." 10 November 2014. *New York Post.* Web. 10 July 2015.

Pelletreau, Claire. "How to Write Facebook Ad Copy that Gets Clicks." 7 August 2014. *Claire Pelletreau.* Web. 6 July 2015.

Perez, Sarah. "YouTube Launches YouTube Newswire, A Channel Featuring Verified Eyewitness Videos." 18 June 2015. *TechCrunch.* Web. 24 August 2015.

Pindoriya, Vishal. "How to Effectively Use Hashtags for Maximum Engagement." 30 July 2014. *Sendible.* Web. 19 August 2015.

Pinkham, C.A. "CA Restaurant Hates Yelp More Than You or I Could Hate Anything." 11 January 2015. *Kitchenette.* Web. 17 September 2015.

Pinterest, Inc. "Ads." 2016. *Pinterest*. Web. 4 August 2016.

—."A Guide to Pinterest Analytics." n.d. *Pinterest*. Web. 9 August 2016.

—."Buyable Pins." 2016. *Pinterest*. Web. 5 August 2016.

—.KLM Royal Dutch Airlines. n.d. *Pinterest*. Web. 22 July 2016.

—.Paris Hilton. "That's Hot." n.d. *Pinterest*. Web. 22 July 2016.

—.Pinterest Blog. 2016. *Pinterest*. Web. 8 July 2016.

—."Press." 2016. *Pinterest*. Web. 8 July 2016.

—."Promoted Pins." 2016. *Pinterest*. Web. 3 August 2016.

—."Rich Pins." 2016. *Pinterest*. Web. 5 August 2016.

—.Starbucks. "Starbucks Cup Art." n.d. *Pinterest.* Web. 15 July 2015.

—.Tom Lee Music Canada. n.d. *Pinterest*. Web. 3 August 2016.

—."Your Pinterest Profile: All-Time." n.d. *Pinterest*. Web. 9 August 2016.

—."Your Pinterest Profile: Clicks." n.d. *Pinterest*. Web. 9 August 2016.

—."Your Pinterest Profile: Repins." n.d. *Pinterest*. Web. 9 August 2016.

Priestley, Theo. "LinkedIn is Not Facebook, But It Clearly Wants To Be And It's Turning Away Users." 25 July 2015. *Forbes.* Web. 20 July 2016.

Prodromou, Ted. "9 Ways to Advertise on LinkedIn." 28 April 2015. *Entrepreneur.* Web. 26 August 2015.

PromoSimple, Inc. "What to Do After a Giveaway Ends to Increase Your Credibility." 2015. *PromoSimple.* Web. 12 August 2015.

Rakos, Mikaela. "The History of Instagram." 12 May 2014. *Dashburst.* Web. 15 July 2015.

Rawden, Jessica. "Jimmy Kimmel Live Continues to Improve in Ratings." 2013. *Cinema Blend.* Web. 10 July 2015.

Rediff.com. "20 milestones in the history of YouTube." 19 February 2013. *Rediff.com.* Web. 24 August 2015.

RiteTag. "About RiteTag." 2015. *RiteTag.* Web. 6 August 2015.

Roslansky, Ryan. "Introducing LinkedIn Learning, A Better Way to Develop Skills and Talent." 22 September 2016. *LinkedIn*. Web. 8 October 2016.

Rozek, Phil. "Yelp Business Categories List." 19 July 2013. *Local Visibility System.* Web. 14 September 2015.

Salehi, Farzad and Shelley Salehi. *Farzad's Barber Shop.* Adam Wilkins. 19 June 2015. Video.

Sawers, Paul. "10 more Facebook campaigns to inspire your business." 11 September 2013. *The Next Web.* Web. 3 July 2015.

Sciarra, Paul. "What is the point of liking a pin on Pinterest?" 10 October 2011. *Quora.* Web. 22 July 2016.

sight, eye. "Hannibal Buress Called Bill Cosby a Rapist During a Stand Up." n.d. *YouTube.* Online Video Clip. Web. 10 July 2015.

Simas, Jordan. "Everything You Need to Know About Pinterest's New Buyable Pins." 5 June 2015. *Shopify*. Web. 5 August 2016.

Sloane, Garett. "Instagram Unleashes a Fully Operational Ad Business." 2 June 2015. *Adweek.* Web. 18 August 2015.

Smith, Craig. "By the Numbers 125+ Amazing LinkedIn Statistics." 21 July 2015. *DMR.* Web. 29 July 2015.

—. "By the Numbers: 133 Amazing LinkedIn Statistics." 16 August 2016. *DMR.* Web. 8 October 2016.

—. "By the Numbers: 150+ Amazing Twitter Statistics." 5 June 2015. *DMR.* Web. 9 July 2015.

—. "By the Numbers: 52 Amazing Yelp Statistics." 14 July 2016. *DMR.* Web. 8 October 2016.

Smith, Matt. "The YouTube Guide: From Watching to Production." 8 February 2012. *MakeUseOf.* Web. 29 August 2015.

Smucker Foods of Canada Corp. "About Smucker's." n.d. *Smucker's.* Web. 2 July 2015.

"Social Media Fail: McDonald's (again)." 21 August 2014. *Social Media Knowledge.* Web. 22 July 2015.

"Social Media Fail: Smucker's." 26 March 2015. *Social Media Knowledge.* Web. 2 July 2015.

Starbucks Corporation. "Starbucks Newsroom." 2015. *Starbucks.* Web. 24 June 2015.

Statistics Brain. "YouTube Company Statistics." 1 September 2016. *Statistics Brain.* Web. 8 October 2016.

Steimle, Josh. "Should I have a Facebook Page for Business or Just Use My Personal Profile." 6 August 2013. *Forbes*. Web. 2 July 2015.

Stricker, Gabriel. "The 2014 #YearOnTwitter." 10 December 2014. *Twitter.* Web. 9 July 2015.

Swanner, Nate. "New 'Yelp Knowledge' program will help big businesses know how much we love (or hate) them." July 2016. *The Next Web.* Web. 8 October 2016.

Teoh, Ivonne. "Pinterest Users Statistics 2016." *Linkedin*. 5 March 2016. Web. 8 July 2016.

The Financial Times Ltd. "Definition of Digital Marketing." 2015. *The Financial Times.* Web. 6 February 2015.

Twitter, Inc. "About Moments." 2016. *Twitter.* Web. 28 September 2016.

—. "Analytics." 2015. *Twitter.* Web. 31 July 2015.

—. "Audience Insights." 2016. *Twitter.* Web. 28 August 2016.

—. "Card Content." 2015. *Twitter.* Web. 29 July 2015.

—. "Followers." 2015. *Twitter.* Web. 29 July 2015.

—. "Learn Twitter." 2015. *Twitter.* Web. 20 July 2015.

—. "Tweet activity dashboard." 2016. *Twitter.* Web. 28 August 2015.

—. "Twitter Cards." 2015. *Twitter.* Web. 22 July 2015.

—. "Types of Campaigns." 2015. *Twitter.* Web. 29 July 2015.

VerticalResponse. "A Quick Walkthrough of LinkedIn Company Page Analytics." 17 August 2015. *YouTube.* Online Video Clip. Web. 3 September 2015.

Viper Gaming Central. "Youtube Tips: An Overview of Cards on YouTube." 20 October 2015. *YouTube.* Online Video Clip. Web. 9 November 2015.

Waldron, Zoe. "Case Study: Jetsetter – Leading the Travel Category on Pinterest." 13 August 2014. *HelloSociety*. Web. 9 August 2016.

Walker, Rachel. "Compliments: They're free. Give them!" 1 March 2013. *Yelp.* Web. 4 September 2015.

Walzer, Philip. "Everybody's a critic, but on Yelp, their opinions carry weight." 3 September 2015. *Arizona Daily Sun*. Web. 4 September 2015.

"Warren Buffet Quotes." 2015. *BrainyQuote.* Web. 29 June 2015.

WebFinance, Inc. "B2B". 2015. *InvestorWords*. Web. 9 March 2015.

—. "Lead Generation." 2015. *Businessdictionary.com.* Web. 2 September 2015.

Wisuri, Rachel. "How to Boost Your YouTube Visibility." 4 June 2015. *Social Media Examiner.* Web. 9 September 2015.

Woodyard, Chris and Fred Meier. "Hyundai Yanks Suicide Ad." 25 April 2013. *USA Today*. Web. 29 August 2015.

Yelp Inc. "About Us." 2014-2015. *Yelp.* Web. 31 August 2015.

—. "A Simple Guide to Showcasing Your Business Online." 2016. *Yelp.* Web. 14 March 2017.

—. "Botto Italian Bistro." 2004-2016. *Yelp.* Web. 10 October 2016.

—. "Business Analytics." 2004-2015. *Yelp.* Web. 18 September 2015.

—. "Creating Content for Your Yelp Page." n.d. *Yelp.* 14 March 2017. PDF.

—. "Does Yelp recommend every review?" 2014-2015. *Yelp.* Web. 14 September 2015.

—. "How do I post an update to one of my reviews?" 2004-2015. *Yelp.* Web. 4 September 2015.

—. "Responding to Reviews." 2004-2015. *Yelp.* Web. 16 September 2015.

—. "Write a Review." 2004-2015. *Yelp.* Web. 4 September 2015.

—. "Yelp Knowledge." 20 June 2016. *Yelp.* Web. 21 Sept. 2016.

—. "Yelp Reviews: Best Practices for National Businesses." 2016. *Yelp.* 14 March 2017. PDF.

Yeung, Ken. "LinkedIn is 10 years old today: Here's the story of how it changed the way we work." 27 June 2015. *The Next Web.* Web. 27 July 2015.

YouTube Spotlight. "The A-Z of YouTube: Celebrating 10 Years." 28 May 2015. *YouTube.* Web. 24 August 2015.

Zeevi, Daniel. "The Ultimate History of Facebook [INFOGRAPHIC]." 21 February 2013. *Social Media Today.* Web. 25 May 2015.

ACKNOWLEDGMENTS

This book and this series of books would not have been possible without a team of committed people behind the scenes rolling up their sleeves. My personal thanks and gratitude go out to my business partner Adam Wilkins for being the founding partner and seeing my vision, then taking that vision and putting it on steroids and making it happen. To Rebecca Saloustros for her research, studious work ethic, and countless hours putting the content together and assembling the books. To Nathan Kondra for his 15-plus years of technical knowledge, and to Timothy Serrano for his project management, passion, and relentless attention to detail on digital marketing strategies and our processes. Their insights help to make our publications the great resources that they are.

Made in the USA
San Bernardino, CA
05 August 2018